Business and Politics

A Comparative Introduction

THIRD EDITION

Graham K. Wilson

CHATHAM HOUSE PUBLISHERS

SEVEN BRIDGES PRESS, LLC

NEW YORK • LONDON

Published in the United States by

Chatham House Publishers of Seven Bridges Press, LLC
135 Fifth Avenue
New York, NY 10010-7101

Library of Congress Cataloging-in-Publication Data

Wilson, Graham K.
        Business and politics : a comparative introduction /
    Graham K. Wilson. — 3rd ed.
            p. cm.
        Includes bibliographical references and index.
        ISBN 1–8891–1988–1 (pbk.)
        1. Industrial policy. 2. Business and politics. I. Title.
    HD3611 .W55 2003
        338.9–dc21   2002015548

Manufactured in Great Britain
10   9   8   7   6   5   4   3   2   1

Contents

Preface to the Third Edition

I delayed writing the third edition of this book considerably and to a significant degree deliberately. It was clear to any reasonably attentive newspaper reader during the 1990s that the relationship between business and government was changing unusually rapidly. The extensive discussion of globalization, the sometimes violent protests against the alleged misdeeds of international organizations such as the World Trade Organization and the visible surge in international trade in the late twentieth century all drew attention to the considerable changes that seemed to be taking place. Not everyone agreed that radical change was in fact occurring; some academics see their role in life as being to pour cold water on exciting ideas and inevitably voices were soon raised suggesting that not very much had changed, that trends towards globalization had been exaggerated and that, in any case, we had seen all these developments before in the early twentieth century. Nonetheless, arguments that globalization was transforming the relationship between business and government seemed sufficiently compelling to lead me to suppose that it was wise to let the rapid changes play themselves out before writing a third edition.

Globalization raised a particular problem for the structure of this book. The basic organizing idea underpinning the two preceding editions has been that there were important differences between countries in the patterns of business–government relations. Some countries could be taken as models of different modes of business–government relations and were also worth studying in their own right. Thus Japan could be studied not only to learn more about an intriguing country and, at that time, successful economy, but to understand how governments could foster economic growth. Sweden could be studied profitably not only by those interested in Scandinavia but by people who wished to understand how neocorporatist partnerships between government, unions and business could maintain competitiveness and prosperity. The idea that individual countries could be used to exemplify particular models of business–government relations was not original. Andrew Shonfield's magisterial work *Modern Capitalism*[1] deserves to be recognized and acclaimed as the progenitor of this approach. It assumed, however, that the contrasting relationships between business and government in different countries are deep-seated and relatively stable. The relationship between business and government was shaped by enduring influences including political culture, political and business institutions, the influence of contending interests and a country's situation in the global economy. Because these influences on business–government relations were unlikely to change much, the relationship in each country was likely to endure.

The strongest arguments for the importance of globalization suggested however that these national differences would be swept away. The pressures that arose from the need to compete in integrated global markets would oblige countries to abandon policies and practices that impeded economic efficiency. In spite of the past successes of neocorporatist nations, such as Sweden, or economies, such as Japan's or South Korea's, in which government had played a leadership role, it was generally assumed that the American model of business–government relations was most consistent with the demands of globalization: government 'interfered' little in the workings of the 'free market', taxes and the welfare state were kept at a sufficiently low level that they did not distort incentives and government eschewed any attempt to shape economic development. There are of course enormous problems with this view of the United States conceptually and empirically. As we shall discuss later, economic markets are not spontaneously occurring phenomena but are shaped and determined by governments. This is, of course, true even of the worldwide markets that globalization represents. Global markets were achieved by the action of governments, such as the Uruguay Round of the General Agreement on Tariffs and Trade (GATT) in which they acted to eliminate most tariffs on many goods and reduce discrimination against imports. The United States is also in fact (as I have argued extensively elsewhere)[2] far from being the land of free markets and minimal government as claimed by both its admirers and critics. Government intervenes extensively through regulations and the tax code to influence business behaviour. Important social policies such as racial integration, equality for women and opportunities for the handicapped are promoted effectively, if indirectly, by requiring all who wish to do business with government to adopt policies to promote these goals. Nonetheless, there was a widespread belief that globalization would compel other countries to become more like the United States, meaning that they would have to cut back on their welfare states, regulations and taxation in a 'race to the bottom' to attract investment. Again, it seemed wise to allow time in order to see whether or not this trend really would happen.

The chapters that follow continue the approach used in the first two editions in selecting countries that are not only intrinsically interesting but illustrate different forms of business–government relations. In contrast to the first two editions, however, I consider how these forms of business–government relations were challenged by globalization and explore its consequences. Whereas in earlier editions, I had given primacy (though not exclusive coverage) to the impact of domestic influences (culture, institutions and so on) on business–government relations, in this edition I give much greater prominence to the impact of global forces on national patterns of business–government relations and consider explicitly whether or not globalization has made some of the once apparently secure modes of business–government relationships unviable. It would be giving away the game too early to reveal my conclusions here and I hope that these remarks will merely encourage readers to continue.

I have incurred many debts in preparing this edition. My project assistants, particularly Dan Maxwell and Amy Forster Rothbart, have been invaluable. The students of the La Follette School and the Department of Political Science have been a kindly audience as I have tried to develop the ideas that follow. My publisher, Steven Kennedy, has been patient and understanding as administrative responsibilities have slowed my work. Most of all, however, I am indebted to my wife, Virginia Sapiro, and our son, Adam Wilson. Much of the book that follows is about things that sometimes surprisingly change; their love and support does not. This book is dedicated to them.

Preface to the Second Edition

The 1980s proved to be a fascinating decade for students of business and politics. The importance of the topic was illustrated by the prominence of economic issues in election campaigns and by the growing visibility of political activity by corporations through techniques such as political action committees in the United States. The quantity and quality of writing on relations between business and government continued to grow dramatically; those who tried to 'bring the state back in' made particularly important contributions. The trends towards neocorporatism and other forms of more organized capitalism had seemed clear in the 1970s; the more neocorporatist or state-led economies seemed to perform better on a variety of dimensions. In the 1980s, however, neoconservative politicians such as President Reagan and Mrs Thatcher achieved a degree of political and economic success that dismayed and surprised most social scientists. The resurgence of faith in market mechanisms and enthusiasm for 'shrinking the state' has been the most striking feature of economic policy thinking in the 1980s, not only sweeping the USA and Britain but influencing countries such as France with apparently very different traditions.

I hope I have learned much since the first edition of this book appeared. I have certainly enjoyed much of the literature on business–government relations that has appeared in the 1980s. I have also benefited from discussions with colleagues here at Wisconsin, including several graduate students who have widened my intellectual horizons. I am more grateful than ever to Virginia Sapiro for love, support and my son, Adam. This edition is dedicated to both of them.

GRAHAM K. WILSON

Preface to the First Edition

One of the few useful by-products of the economic difficulties which have afflicted the world in the 1970s and 1980s is a revival of interest in political economy. The central place of discussion of the performance of economies in political debate has encouraged many to ask again some of the basic questions about the relationship between government and the economy. Does government dominate business, or does business dominate government? Is the relationship between business and government effectively structured so that such widely shared goals as economic growth and full employment are likely to be attained, or not? How do business and government interact?

Although the relationship between business and government now forms part of almost all university courses on individual political systems, the topic is rarely studied *comparatively*. Courses on the comparative study of legislatures, executives and political parties are far more common than courses which compare the relationship between government and business, in spite of the importance and popularity of the topic. It is my belief, which I hope the following book will substantiate, that there is at least as much variation in the business–government relationship as there is in the character of political parties. Failure to appreciate the variation in this relationship from country to country may result in practical disadvantages for those who wish to make their careers in business; it also enfeebles debate within individual countries about the nature of their own political economy. Failure to appreciate the unique aspects of one's own system leads in political economy – as in the study of political institutions and practices – to an unnecessarily shallow understanding of it; a comparative approach is the only remedy.

Any attempt to cover as broad a range of countries as concisely as I have attempted in this book is to run a high risk of writing a book which the experts on individual countries will find in their own area to be shallow and incomplete. I hope that they will accept my apologies for trespassing outside my own usual specialisms. I have taught courses on business and politics for several years now in both Britain and the USA, and have been aware of the lack of a short book which would provide students with some picture of the range of relationships between business and government found in the capitalist, industrialized democracies. I have attempted to fill that gap with this book, and hope that the range of countries covered will compensate for my failure to provide more extensive detail on each. As those used to planning long car journeys will know, there are advantages to both detailed and more comprehensive maps. I hope the Bibliography of this book will provide some assistance to students who wish to obtain more detailed 'maps' of the topics covered in outline here.

Inevitably, portions of such a general work as this rest on my reading of secondary sources. I am deeply indebted to the Nuffield Foundation, however, for their generous support in conducting research on aspects of the relationship between business and government which has informed many sections of this book. I am also profoundly grateful for the intellectual companionship of Virginia Sapiro during the writing of this book.

GRAHAM K. WILSON

List of Abbreviations

CBI	Confederation of British Industry (UK)
CEA	Council of Economic Advisers (USA)
CEO	chief executive officer (UK, USA)
DEFRA	Department for Environment, Food and Rural Affairs (UK)
DTI	Department of Trade and Industry (UK)
ECB	European Central Bank
EPB	Economic Planning Board (South Korea)
ERM	exchange rate mechanism (EU)
EU	European Union
FDI	foreign direct investment
Fed	Federal Reserve Bank
GATT	General Agreement on Tariffs and Trade
GDP	gross domestic product
ICC	International Chamber of Commerce
ILO	International Labor Organization
IMF	International Monetary Fund
LDP	Liberal Democratic Party (Japan)
MAFF	Ministry of Agriculture, Fisheries and Food (UK)
MITI	Ministry of International Trade and Industry (Japan)
NAFTA	North American Free Trade Agreement
NEDC	National Economic Development Council
NGO	non-governmental organization
OECD	Organization for Economic Cooperation and Development
OMB	Office of Management and Budget (USA)
PAC	political action committee (USA)
TUC	Trades Union Congress (UK)
USSR	Union of Soviet Socialist Republics
WHO	World Health Organization
WTO	World Trade Organization
WWF	World Wildlife Fund

1

Introduction

A Varied Relationship

The relationship between business and government lies at the heart of contemporary political debate. Business executives, particularly in the United States, applaud calls to 'get the government off our backs'. Critics of business among the general public demand to know why government agencies have failed to protect them adequately if there are allegations that unsafe tyres have been sold, unsafe meat reaches homes and restaurants (as during the BSE crisis in Britain) or that a monopoly has been created that exploits consumers. Businesses and employees often demand to know why foreign competitors appear to receive greater assistance from their governments in winning and keeping markets than they do from their own. For many businesses, however, government is primarily a major customer purchasing roads, school buildings and pharmaceuticals as well as warships, aircraft and other military supplies.

Those brief examples show the business–government relationship in very different lights. In the first, government is seen as a police officer controlling business – its regulator and in all probability its adversary. In the second, government is expected to be the friend of business, protecting it from foreign competition and supplying advice on markets, technical assistance and possibly cheap loans (particularly to help with export sales). In the third case, government is a customer, but a customer of a special type, one that can be persuaded to buy a product not only through a combination of the usual commercial skills but also through political pressures. The fact of the matter is that the relationship between business and government has many different forms, which are worth distinguishing.

1

First, government establishes the *legal framework* within which commercial activity is conducted. Although we talk easily of 'free markets', markets in fact rely not only on agreements between individuals or corporations but on an underlying framework of laws and regulations that give such agreements credibility. The ability to go to court to obtain restitution if payment is not made for goods supplied, for compensation if a product is defective and for repayment of a loan on which the debtor has defaulted are all very basic aspects of a market system. In general, though with some interesting exceptions such as the post-Soviet states, business people assume that governmental power is available through the courts to enforce legally-binding agreements.

Yet even this basic legal structure for a market economy is not without its interesting political aspects.[1] Rules of the game, in markets as in many other aspects of life, are likely to favour some groups and interests over others rather than being neutral. For example, the facility with which contracts can be enforced varies. Bankruptcy laws differ considerably in terms of the ease or difficulty with which debtors can be forced to compensate creditors. It is easier – and less onerous in its consequences – to escape debts by declaring bankruptcy in the United States than in Britain. The ability of consumers to go to court and sue businesses varies greatly from one country to another. American consumers are better able to sue corporations than are British consumers; American lawyers operate on a contingency fee basis, receiving their pay from damages that they win for their clients rather than in fees that are paid irrespective of the result. Labour laws have varied over the years as well as between countries in terms of union formation and acceptance and in terms of the rights they confer on employees. British governments in recent years (both Conservative and Labour) have boasted that it is easier for employers to 'hire and fire' in Britain than in continental European countries such as France. The fine details of laws tilt the balance between businesses and banks, employers and their workers, citizens and corporations. Take, for example, the question of who has first claim on the assets of a bankrupt company. In some states and nations, the firm's former workers have first claim on these assets to cover wages they are owed. In other jurisdictions, the first claim goes to lenders such as banks who had made loans for which the assets were security. There is, in short, no such thing as 'the market' that exists as an abstraction. Rather, there are a variety of markets whose laws, rules and regulations tilt the balance of advantage between interests.[2]

Second, government *imposes limits on market relationships*. No society leaves everything to the market, although considerable differences exist between countries in the degree to which markets are constrained. Sometimes governments limit markets by taking over functions directly; the creation of the National Health Service in Britain in the 1940s, for example, reduced to insignificance the market for healthcare in the UK at that time. The creation of welfare states changes labour markets to the advantage of workers. In the case of some more generous welfare states, such as Sweden, they are changed to the extent that one authority has termed the 'decommodification' of labour by limiting the degree to which employment is determined by market forces.[3] Unemployed workers are not forced to take any available work whatever the wage offered because they have substantial benefit to rely on instead. In the United States, government has acted most commonly through an extensive array of regulations to assert the supremacy of certain non-market values over commercial considerations. The Environmental Protection Agency (EPA), for example, acting under authority granted by Congress, insists that businesses limit or avoid pollution even when it is costly for them to do so. The Occupational Safety and Health Agency (OSHA) insists on measures to protect the health and safety of workers that a profit-maximizing business would not have taken.[4] Businesses that seek contracts from the government are required to adopt a wide array of measures to assist racial minorities, women and the disabled to gain employment or subcontracts. American state administrations, such as Wisconsins, provide potential contractors with a large book that sets out social policies with which they must comply.

The political demand that government should pull back and 'let the market work' is therefore greatly at variance with practice in any advanced industrialized democracy. Market forces are limited and constrained by laws and regulations justified by claims that other goals and values are so important that they over-ride market forces. Governments also combine the carrot of tax concessions with the stick of regulation in attempts to manipulate the behaviour of businesses. Tax breaks are given to investments which protect the environment, provide employment for disabled workers or build on environmentally-contaminated 'brown field' sites.

In spite of the complaints of business executives, it may well be in the long-term interests of business that government successfully over-rides their every wish. It was common in the nineteenth and twentieth centuries to suggest that capitalism, like feudalism before it, was a passing mode of social organization. Capitalism has, in fact, proved to be much more durable than its critics expected. Perhaps one explanation for this durability is that its worst consequences have been overcome, or at least substantially alleviated, by government action. The welfare state has provided a safety net for workers and their families that in most advanced industrialized countries avoids the crushing poverty that Marx thought would be the workers' lot. It became evident after the fall of communism in the USSR and eastern Europe that capitalist countries protected the environment better than socialist regimes, whose environmental records were in general appalling. Business leaders nearly always opposed the introduction of welfare states and stricter environmental regulation. Yet it can be argued that it is such policies that have made capitalism secure by avoiding problems that would have undermined its legitimacy. It is often said of President Franklin Roosevelt that, though opposed by business leaders, his New Deal policies saved American capitalism. Much the same is probably true of reformers in other countries.

Third, government is itself a major *customer*, although not as large a customer as might be supposed from the proportion of gross domestic product (GDP) it controls. Governments in advanced industrialized countries control between one-third of GDP and three-fifths. However, most government expenditure goes on transfer payments, shifting money from tax payers to the recipients of benefits such as retirement pensions (known as Social Security in the USA), assistance for the old and disabled and so on. Nonetheless, governments do buy a wide range of products including new jails, schools, hospitals, roads, military aircraft and paper. In some cases, it is more or less the monopolist purchaser. Naturally, therefore, producers of, for example, military equipment are highly focused on government and politics. Readers of highly detailed periodicals focused on politicians and civil servants in the United States, such as *Congressional Quarterly Weekly Report* or the *National Journal*, will be familiar with full-page advertisements promoting the virtues of a particular fighter plane or bomber. Not even in the United States are ordinary citizens allowed to purchase these products themselves to complement their firearms; the advertisements seek instead to create a favourable political climate for selling the product to government.

Fourth, businesses rely on government to *protect and defend their interests overseas*. In extreme cases, this may involve government assistance in ensuring that their property is not expropriated without compensation, that their business is not nationalized and that, in the case of banks, loans are repaid. On a more mundane level, businesses also depend on governments to promote their interests in trade negotiations. American banks and insurance companies, for example, are currently very eager to obtain access to markets in countries in which they have been unable to operate freely. United States airlines would like to be able to fly as many flights as they wish into London's Heathrow airport; British airlines would like to be able to form partnerships with US-owned airlines and to fly passengers originating in the USA to countries such as Australia. In all these instances, corporations are dependent on governments to assert their interests. It is arguable that, in an era of increasing globalization, corporations need the assistance of their home government more, not less, in order to obtain favourable trading arrangements and protection of their property – including intellectual property – overseas. Corporations themselves cannot remake the international trading system, no matter how much they think they would gain by a change.

Fifth, business is dependent on government to *maintain sound economic conditions*, generally defined as acceptable levels of inflation and unemployment. From the Second World War until the 1970s, most governments pursued these goals through 'Keynesian' economic policies. Named after the great British economist, John Maynard Keynes, who developed this approach in the 1930s to deal with the Great Depression, Keynesian economics asserted that governments could achieve stable economic growth without inflation or high unemployment by stabilizing aggregate demand. When unemployment threatened, governments should spend more and tax less, producing a deficit to inflate demand; when inflation threatened, governments should tax more and spend less, generating a surplus and depressing aggregate demand. Until the economic and even governance crises of the 1970s that began with the sharp increase in oil prices and the collapse of the Bretton Woods international monetary system discussed below, confidence grew that Keynesian economics had eliminated the threat of depression. In the decades since the late 1970s, Keynesian approaches have been displaced by monetarist policies. Monetarist approaches to economic management place the emphasis, as the name suggests, on the quantity of money in circulation in the economy and its 'price', namely the prevailing interest rate. In practice, monetarism has focused on interest rates as the quantity of money in circulation proved too difficult to manage. Central banks, such as the Federal Reserve Board, the Bank of England and the European Central Bank (ECB), attempt to restrain inflation and secure steady growth by manipulating the rate of growth of the money supply and the prevailing interest rate. While some monetarists argue that the only sound monetary policy is one that increases the money supply at a rate that matches the underlying rate of increase of productivity in the economy, most central banks, like the Keynesian policy-makers before them, attempt to steer the economy. The American central bank, the Federal Reserve Board, for example, cut interest rates frantically at the start of the twenty-first century in a desperate effort to ward off recession. The Japanese central bank brought interest rates close to zero as it attempted to halt Japan's economic decline early this century. An important difference between Keynesian and monetarist economic management, however, is that nearly all central banks are highly independent from political control; the shift to monetary approaches has, therefore, diminished democratic political control of economic policy in important respects. In consequence, economic policy may be more likely to emphasize minimizing inflation rather than achieving full employment. Both goals are important to business, however, in terms of securing a favourable business environment.

Sixth, and finally, business is an important supplier of *resources* to government. To take an obvious example, businesses pay taxes equivalent to about 10 per cent of total income and profits in the United States and 12 per cent in Britain. Businesses pay around 13 per cent of social security contributions in the United States, 10 per cent in Britain and between 20 and 25 per cent in France, Italy and Sweden.[5] Tax policy creates many opportunities for interaction between business and government. No organization likes to pay more tax, and business corporations are no exceptions. Business leaders in many countries have campaigned successfully to secure lower levels of corporation tax. Tax codes, like all laws and regulations, tend to favour some interests over others. Numerous tax allowances exist for corporations as they do for individuals, rewarding activities, such as investment, that governments wish to encourage. These allowances have different impacts on different companies. Tax allowances for investment in new plant and machinery, for example, are much more appealing to capital-intensive corporations than to those that are labour-intensive (needing large numbers of people to operate). Debates over tax reform often pit one corporation against another.[6] Businesses may also undertake certain social functions or responsibilities that would otherwise fall on government. An obvious example is the provision of healthcare for workers and their families by many employers such as Ford, General Motors and USX. Were it not for this 'private sector welfare state', it is reasonable to assume that the pressure on the US government to provide some form of national health insurance (as in every other advanced industrial democracy) would have been overwhelming.

It is important to appreciate the multifaceted relationship between business and government because, as Theodore Lowi[7] pointed out several decades ago, different types of policies can produce, different types of politics. Some issues tend to divide business other issues tend to unite it. Many businesses are likely to unite in opposition to proposals to raise corporation tax, alter labour to advantage unions or tighten environmental regulations; on the other hand, different corporations have conflicting interests on issues such as changing tax allowances, giving out government contracts and foreign trade policy where lowering trade barriers helps some and hurts others. Yet it is also the case that governments differ in terms of how far they attempt to integrate these different forms of interaction with business. In the decades following the Second World War, some governments (notably the Japanese and French) appeared to achieve economic success by following *industrial policies* that attempted to coordinate all government dealings with industries into a coherent, purposive whole. French and Japanese officials tried to integrate different aspects of the business–government relationship, such as tax policy, government contracts, trade policy and research spending, so that they could promote the growth of industries likely to achieve long-term economic growth. Other countries tended to tackle these issues without much attempt at coordinating or integrating them. In the United States, for example, tax policy, education policy, environmental policy and transport policy have tended to proceed on separate tracks without any consideration of their impact on the pursuit of economic goals.

The Structure of the Relationship

The nature of the policy issue at stake between business and government has a major impact on the way in which it will be handled. It is not the only influence, however. Enduring patterns of business–government relations exist so that there is an established way of doing business in each country. There are major differences from one country to another in the patterns of these institutionalized relationships. We may imagine these patterns arrayed along a spectrum ranging from the comparatively loosely organized end, which is termed pluralism, to the highly structured and hierarchic end of the spectrum[8] often called 'organized capitalism'.

In pluralist systems, individual businesses are the dominant actors. Much of the interaction between business and government takes the form of dealings between individual businesses, politicians and administrators. There are, of course, organizations in pluralist systems that represent the collective interests of groups of businesses. *Trade associations* represent the collective interests of businesses in the same industry and *peak organizations* attempt to represent the collective interests of business as a whole. In pluralist systems, however, individual corporations choose to be members of both trade associations and peak organizations because they agree with their policies or feel that they provide value for money. The power of trade and peak associations in pluralist systems is, in consequence, severely constrained by the possibility that, if they upset even a minority of their members by taking a stance with which those members disagree, those firms are likely to leave, thus weakening the organization by reducing its income and the credibility of its claim to speak for the particular industry or business as a whole. The relationship between the individual corporation and the trade association or peak organization is a customer–client relationship. Corporations remain members only so long as they are convinced that they receive value for money from their subscriptions in the form of commercially useful information and services or in political representation. The peak organization or trade association has little or no authority to make commitments that are binding on members. Indeed, in pluralist systems there is often competition between organizations claiming to be the more effective trade association or peak organization. Competing organizations claim to offer better services or to represent their members' interests more determinedly and effectively than their rivals.[9]

In more structured and 'organized' patterns of business–government relations, the significance of individual corporations is reduced and that of the trade association or peak organization increased. All corporations are expected (in a few countries, even legally required) to belong to the relevant trade associations which are in turn affiliated to one, dominant peak association representing business as a whole. Both the trade association for a particular industry and the business peak association can be said to be *encompassing* in their memberships; they recruit a very high proportion of their potential membership. Individual corporations tempted to resign from these bodies do not have an alternative organization to join and run substantial risks that their interests will not be represented effectively to government. Politicians and administrators focus heavily on trade associations and peak organizations rather than individual corporations when they are seeking advice or information from business. There may even be some feeling that pressure from individual corporations represents illegitimate 'special interest' politics. Business organizations may be expected to accept responsibility for certain types of governance, such as running apprenticeship schemes, national health insurance programmes and even forms of environmental protection.[9] Nineteenth-century German trade associations, for example, operated their own health and safety inspection schemes in which the trade association employed inspectors to visit members' premises, admittedly in part to forestall government regulation. While it would be an exaggeration to picture individual corporations as subservient to trade associations or peak organizations in such countries, the balance of power between them is less favourable to the individual corporation than in pluralist systems.

In consequence, business organizations can make more or less binding commitments on behalf of their members with government.

Just as forms of business representation vary, so do the ways in which government organizes its relationship with business. In the United States, government is highly fragmented. The constitutional structure itself has three separate power-sharing branches, the executive, the legislative and the judicial. Fragmentation is also extensive within these branches. Agencies such as the EPA, OSHA, and the Departments of Commerce and Treasury at any given moment can be following policies that are significantly at variance with each other. The capacity of agencies at the centre of the executive branch, such as the Office of Management and Budget and other groups within the Executive Office of the President (such as the White House staff), to impose a coherent policy on these agencies is limited. Within Congress, the splitting of authority between the separately elected House and Senate is amplified by the committee system and the weakness of American political parties compared to their counterparts in other democracies. While the cohesiveness of governments in other countries is often exaggerated, agencies such as the *Commissariat du Plan* in France and the Ministry of International Trade and Industry (MITI) in Japan have been able to secure a degree of integration of the different government policies affecting industry that could not be achieved in the United States.[10] Not all governments are capable of producing an integrated industrial policy just as not all business interest groups are cohesively and hierarchically organized.

The Shifting Balance of Power

Perhaps the most important and frequently asked question underlying the study of the relationship between business and government concerns their relative power. Is business just another interest group that sometimes wins and sometimes loses in its political battles or does business have a degree of power that other interest groups cannot match? Several positions in this dispute can be distinguished.

The first is that of orthodox pluralists.[11] Orthodox pluralists argue that there is nothing very special about business as an interest group. Indeed, there is no such thing as business as a single interest. Business is fragmented into many different interest groups that often conflict with each other as high-tech and low-tech firms fight over the nature of allowances accorded business in tax legislation, competitive and uncompetitive firms fight over whether to move towards more open trading relations with other countries, and distributors of goods fight with railroads, truckers and airlines over the degree to which government insulates them from competition. Sometimes business steps up its political involvement and mobilization; sometimes business (as in the United States in the 1950s) is surprisingly poorly organized. Orthodox pluralists also insist that we have to take the preferences and interests of people as more or less identical. If workers and consumers say that they are content to live in a capitalist system, perhaps because they believe that such a system gives them a higher standard of living than any alternative, then we must accept that judgement as a reasonable assessment of where their interests lie. We should not, as some Marxists would, declare that they have been hoodwinked into 'false consciousness' by clever capitalists so that they espouse beliefs which are inconsistent with their interests.

The second position is taken by revisionist pluralists.[12] Revisionist pluralists start by agreeing with other pluralists that there is nothing special about business as an interest group in principle. In practice, however, revisionists argue, business is not merely another interest group. From the outset business has an advantage because it does not have to solve the 'logic of collective action' problem identified by Mancur Olson.[13] Consumer groups are faced with the difficulty of establishing why an individual consumer should be bothered with spending the time and money required to join an interest group. Consumers will reap the benefits of campaigns by consumer organizations whether or not they bother to join. An individual's decision on whether or not to join an organization with a membership of hundreds of thousands has little impact on its overall strength. The business corporation already exists. It does not have to solve the problem that presses so heavily on its opponents, who lead consumer and environmental groups, of persuading potential members to join and current members to remain.[14] Until recently, US corporations could offset their lobbying expenses against their tax liabilities and can still pay the operating expenses of the Political Action Committees (PACs) which donate contributions from managers and stockholders to sympathetic or well-placed politicians.

British corporations, like their counterparts in the USA, could until recently make payments from their general funds to political parties more or less unhindered by law. Only since the 'sleaze' controversies of the Conservative government in the mid-1990s have more stringent limits and reporting requirements been adopted. Revisionist pluralists argue that, not surprisingly, business is far from being just another interest group but in fact possesses resources – and therefore enjoys power – far beyond other groups. Business dominates the interest-group system by employing more lobbyists, donating more money to politicians and so on than any other interest. After all, the costs of running a PAC are a miniscule proportion of the total budget of a corporation.[15] Revisionist pluralists, while sharing the reluctance of orthodox pluralists to claim to know other people's interests better than they do themselves, accept that business possesses some ability to manipulate how issues are framed. A variety of techniques ranging from advertizing to funding think-tanks sympathetic to business are used to develop an image of corporations as servants of the public interest, not as selfish profit-maximizers, grappling hard and reasonably successfully with practical problems such as ensuring adequate fuel supplies, developing better pharmaceuticals and so on. Revisionist pluralists note that, after American business felt that it had suffered major political reverses in the late 1960s and early 1970s, corporations undertook a major programme to improve popular perceptions of them. Few, if any, other interests could have waged a similar campaign.

The third position in the controversy is taken by those who adopt a structuralist view of the power of business. Their approach is exemplified by Lindblom who in his influential book, *Politics and Markets*,[16] argued that business enjoyed what he termed a 'privileged position' compared with other interests. Lindblom starts by accepting revisionist pluralist arguments that business, in practice, has greater political resources than other interest groups and that it has an unusual capacity to influence popular opinion towards it. The crucial aspect of Lindblom's argument is that business is not merely an interest group but is also entrusted with the vital task of investing for economic growth, prosperity and employment. A government – be it at the city, county, state or national level – that taxes or regulates business interests more than elsewhere, even in pursuit of a good cause such as a cleaner environment, risks business moving away to another location where it is treated more sympathetically by the government. As politicians are themselves vulnerable to electoral defeat in poor economic times, Lindblom argues that they do not need to be bribed, pressured or coerced into giving business what it wants.

But what does business want? Most structuralist arguments suggest that business wants merely to be left alone. Businesses want to minimize taxes and costly regulations. However, in many cases corporations want much more than to be left alone. High-tech companies need an educated workforce; they also tend to locate near high-quality universities in American states such as California and Massachusetts rather than in low-tax, low-skill and below-average educational attainment states such as Mississippi and Arkansas. When Boeing moved its headquarters from Seattle to Chicago, one of the factors that Chicago stressed was its cultural wealth, including an outstanding art gallery and symphony orchestra; indeed, one of the receptions for Boeing executives was held at the Art Institute against a background of some of its most famous canvasses. Many corporations want an agreeable environment to which they can attract skilled workers and promising executives. At least some corporations are happy to locate in places with high taxes and regulations as long as they are provided with benefits (such as a quality workforce and high quality research) that they require. Nor can all industries pick up and move easily. A corporation engaged in gold or diamond mining or in pumping oil has a limited number of places in which it can operate because the commodities it extracts are located in a limited number of places. A diamond mining company dissatisfied with its treatment in South Africa cannot relocate its mine to Iowa, for example. Much of the service sector has to locate near to its customers; a Beverly Hills hairdressing salon, to take an extreme case, would not retain many customers if it relocated to Vietnam! Moreover, there are often advantages to clustering with other companies in the same industry in order to share many of the costs of business, such as training, or to cope with a sudden surge of orders that one firm lacks the capacity to handle. Financial institutions still congregate in very high-cost areas, such as the City of London or Manhattan, even though office rents and similar expenses would be much lower in, for example, Swansea (Wales) and Dubuque, Iowa. The structuralist argument, in short, turns out to be much more complicated than might be supposed.

Both pluralist and revisionist pluralist perspectives on the power of business are open to the possibility that the power of business is more of a variable than a constant. Conventional pluralists argue that there is no certainty as to whether or not business wins or loses. It is merely one of many contending interests. Business may well lose when faced with a powerful coalition of motivated opponents such as unions and environmentalists. The success of these groups in blocking a further round of trade negotiations in the late 1990s is perhaps a case in point. Even revisionist pluralists, generally confident of the power of business, believe that there are moments when business lets down its guard, fails to mobilize adequately and is caught by a surge of criticism. David Vogel suggests that such a phenomenon occurred in the United States in the late 1960s when public interest groups and unions rode a wave of suspicion of business (along with other major institutions in the United States) and secured numerous, costly laws that were much disliked by business, including Clean Air, Clean Water and Occupational Safety and Health legislation.[17]

At first sight, those who stress the importance of the structural power of business might be expected to see business as constantly powerful; the dependence of governments on business never ceases. However, there are important elements in the structural relationship between business and politics that do vary. For example, companies can relocate further away from their markets in major cities if there is a good transport system, generally provided by government. The ease with which a company can relocate to a different country is determined in part by whether or not there are government controls on the movement of capital, as was the case for most countries until the 1980s, or whether capital can move without restriction, as has generally been the case since the 1990s. Similarly, a textile company that wishes to move its operations to a low-wage, low-tax and low-regulation environment may be able to do so much more readily when there is free trade than when import tariffs and restrictions are in place. The structural power of business is not, then, set at a fixed level but varies according to the laws and policies of governments. It is particularly important to keep this in mind today because we have passed through an era in which many changes in public policy, such as the near elimination of tariffs on industrial goods and abolition of capital controls, have increased the power of business. It is far easier for business to relocate today than thirty years ago and, correspondingly, more plausible for businesses to threaten to move if confronted with unwelcome public policies.

Internationalization and Globalization

Globalization has many aspects, some of which are not purely economic; the spread of the McDonald's hamburger chain around the world, for example, is seen by many as a cultural phenomenon as much as an economic one. Similarly, the grip of Hollywood on the world cinema market is condemned by critics overseas as undermining their nations' cultures. In general, however, globalization refers to economic forces that have apparently grown in intensity in the last few decades and are manifested in phenomena such as the growth in world trade as a proportion of all economic activity, a vast increase in the trading of currencies and large increases in the flow of capital across borders. Tables 1–4 in the Appendix give data on the important changes that have occurred. Global foreign direct investment (FDI) increased from $198,382 million in 1990 to $619,258 million in 1998. The average daily turnover in foreign exchange dealing globally increased from US$590 billion in 1989 to US$1490 billion in 1998. In addition, there was an average daily turnover in 1998 of US$362 billion in foreign exchange and interest rate derivatives that had not existed in 1989. It is important to note that much of the increase in trade is between developed countries. Trade between the EU and USA has almost doubled in value in recent years from $201.4 billion in 1993 to $379 billion in 2001.[18] In contrast, the strength of organized labour has diminished, possibly as a consequence of globalization.

Globalization represents an important change but, as many writers have noted, the forces driving it have been with us for some time.[19] After all, the Labour government in Britain collapsed in 1931 in the face of demands for policy changes from foreign bankers. Even the 'U turn' in policy executed in 1982 by the French Socialist government in the face of a foreign-exchange crisis preceded most of the changes associated with globalization. It is also the case that there has not been a steady, unilinear trend towards globalization. The degree to which the world economy is globalized has varied over time. Vast amounts of capital moved around the world in the nineteenth century as Britain took the lead in financing developments such as railroads, not only within its empire but in Latin American countries such as Argentina and Uruguay as well as in the United States. At the start of the twentieth century, for example, the trade dependence of the United States was as high as at present. Most advanced industrialized economies were more self-contained from the Great Depression until the 1970s than they were prior to the First World War. We may argue that this forty-year era, in which trade was less important and national economies were more self-contained, was the unusual era which needs explaining.

Even if there are interesting historical parallels, it is still worth asking why the recent upsurge in globalization has occurred. Part of the answer is no doubt that modern technology makes it easier and cheaper to move goods and capital than ever before. The development of 'ro-ro' (roll on, roll off) ships made it possible to transport cars from Japan to the United States and Europe far more cheaply and with less risk of them being damaged than in the days when cargo had to be lowered into the holds of ships. Electronic communications make it possible to switch billions of currency units into different currencies almost instantaneously. Data such as credit card bills or airline reservations can be processed thousands of miles away from customers. India has enjoyed a boom in telephone call centres, handling reservations for airline customers in Britain or the United States; the workers are trained in small talk about topics such as the weather in the customer's home town in order to seem as though they are close by. But globalization is not some sort of phenomenon that occurs by force of nature. Globalization results from the decisions of governments at least as much as from technological changes such as the growth of email and the internet. Governments have fostered international trade by reducing tariffs drastically; the average industrial tariff was 44 per cent in the aftermath of the Second World War and is less than 4 per cent today, a level that makes tariffs inconsequential as an influence on trade. Similarly, it took decisions by governments to facilitate the flow of capital; in recent decades, nearly all governments have abandoned controls over the flow of capital thus allowing investors to move their money around the world much more freely than in the decades following the Second World War.

There is great controversy, however, about the consequences of globalization. One school represented by writers such as William Greider[20] argues that globalization has changed the balance of power between business and the state, unions and public interest groups decisively in favour of business. It has done so by increasing the structural power of businesses. The ease with which corporations can shift money, goods and production around the world has never been greater. The current world economic order is at least as liberal (in terms of the free movement of goods and capital) as in any other period. Today, in addition, technology facilitates trade and transfers: faxes, email, the internet and cheap international phone calls facilitate the movement of capital; containerized shipping, bulk carriers and air transport facilitate the movement of goods. It is now conventional wisdom that governments lack the resources to manipulate exchange rates because the amounts being traded daily are so much greater than the foreign-currency reserves available to governments. Attempts to 'buck the market', such as the Major government's attempts to defend the pound in 1992, merely enrich speculators such as George Soros who made billions of dollars speculating against the pound on that day. Even small-scale enterprises can be part of the globalized economy. A prosaic example illustrates the point. A fish restaurant in the middle of the United States, far from an ocean, bids by fax for fish caught off the coasts of New Zealand or Latin America while the fish are in mid-air bound for Chicago's O'Hare airport from where they will be rushed to the chef. On a somewhat more important scale, automobile manufacturers can switch the production of new models of cars relatively easily between different countries: Ford and GM, for example, have plants in Britain, Germany, France, Spain and Belgium and naturally consider which country will give the highest tax concessions, lowest taxes, least cumbersome regulations and most disciplined workforce in making decisions on car production. The automobiles produced in any one of these countries within the EU can be shipped without restriction or tariffs to any other member country; under WTO rules, the automobiles can also be shipped worldwide with only minimal duty being levied.

It is because of the great strengthening of the structural power of business that globalization, in the view of some writers, necessarily weakens governments, unions and public interest groups.

There has long been competition among American states to provide the most favourable environment for business and the most lavish incentives for new investment. This competition has been intensifying so that, in the case of a BMW plant in Alabama, the state provided subsidies of over $100,000 per job created. Now such competition may happen internationally. Opponents of globalization feel that this will result in a 'race to the bottom' in which governments cut taxes on business and soften regulations that protect workers, consumers and the environment in order to compete for investment. Globalization does not afford other interest groups the same opportunity as business to threaten to leave if it is not given the treatment it wants from government. Consumers and workers, for example, face considerable difficulty in moving to another country, and individuals' threats to emigrate are scarcely likely to worry governments sufficiently to compel a change in policy. Even unionized workers may well find their ability to exercise leverage through collective action, such as the threat of strikes, decreased by the reduction in their collective bargaining power caused by competition from overseas. Their own governments may also reduce the power of unions or the strength of regulations protecting employment rights in order to attract or retain investment that might go elsewhere in the world.

The ultimate outcome of globalization might be, therefore, convergence around a single, market-dominated approach to life. Faced with the choice between an inexorable decline in living standards as investment and employment shifts to countries providing the most favourable business environment or making their own country equally business-friendly, governments will choose the latter. What is sometimes in continental Europe referred to as 'the Anglo-Saxon model' of lower taxes, weaker regulations and 'flexible labour markets' within which employers can readily hire and fire will spread around the world.

This bleak vision of the impact of globalization has been challenged by critics such as Garrett[21] on a number of grounds.

First, the dependence of business on government continues and in some respects may have increased. As we noted earlier, businesses rely on governments to promote their interests in negotiations with international organizations such as the WTO. Businesses also depend even more on governments to provide the funding for research and the creation of a skilled workforce, through education and training, on which their future competitiveness depends. Competitiveness in an era of rapid technological change requires more than low wages. It requires a skilled workforce, vibrant universities and a good infrastructure of public works such as roads.

Second, as David Vogel has noted,[22] there seems to be more evidence of what he calls 'trading up' than of a race to the bottom. Vogel argues that some rich and powerful nations, such as the United States and Germany, have consumer or environmental protection movements so powerful that they cannot be defeated even in the quest for competitiveness. Once the governments of these countries have realized this fact, they then set to work to oblige other countries to raise their standards – and hence their costs – of regulation to the level prevailing domestically. For example, the US has pressed Latin American and Asian countries to adopt measures to protect dolphins and sea turtles from tuna and shrimp fishing. Only by raising the costs of regulation for other countries can they prevent their domestic producers from being disadvantaged in world trade. Because the countries with strong environmental movements tend to be rich and powerful, they are generally able to obtain the agreement of international organizations to adopt stricter international standards. Of course a conservative American administration may act abroad as at home, to block regulations, as when Bush II revoked the Clinton Administration's signature on the Kyoto Treaty.

Third, globalization has helped critics of business, perhaps one of the least expected consequences of globalization. Organizations that campaign for better protection for the environment, workers' rights or human rights more generally have been very adept at using the technological resources of globalization to challenge multinational corporations. The internet has proved to be a useful tool for mobilizing international protest against business. It was a major resource for the protesters who assembled in Seattle to oppose a meeting of the World Trade Organization in 1999, in the spring of 2000 to oppose the World Bank and IMF in Washington DC and in Turin in 2001 to protest against the annual G8 meeting of heads of government from major industrialized nations. Often these protests are highly multinational in character. Advocates of sustainable agriculture in British Columbia, for example, were able to instigate a campaign in Germany that threatened to boycott German magazines printed on paper supplied by the German paper company Handel unless its pulp suppliers in British Columbia adopted sustainable forestry principles. Representatives of First Canadians were flown in to take part in protests and the cause was adopted by German Greens.

Another successful international protest followed the decision by Shell to sink a North Sea oil-storage platform, the Brent Spar, in deep water in the North Atlantic. This story is a wonderful illustration of how globalization brings political difficulties as well as opportunities for business. Shell had convinced the British government, which had authority over the sector of the North Sea in which Brent Spar was located, that sinking the platform was the wisest course of action. Protesters demanded that the Brent Spar be brought ashore and broken up.[23] The British Prime Minister, John Major, defended Shell's policy against criticisms from other heads of government in the EU at a meeting of the European Council. After Major left the meeting, he was informed that Shell had backed down and agreed to break up the platform – not because of pressure in Britain, the nominal site of legal authority on the subject, but because of protests in Germany and the Netherlands. Like an American lawyer 'venue shopping' to find the most sympathetic jurisdiction in which to bring a legal action, globalization has enabled groups such as environmentalists to challenge multinational companies, not necessarily where the legal power to regulate the company lies and where the protesters may be weak, but in a country in which the protesters' strength is greatest and the company's activities are more vulnerable to pressure.

A final example of a global social movement is the campaign in the United States against products with university logos manufactured in sweat shops. The governments with authority to control working conditions in, for example, Vietnam are happy to tolerate the poor working environment because the sweatshops generate economic growth. These conditions were not acceptable, however, to the young Americans who wear clothing with university logos. Retail companies do not usually make the products themselves but buy them from suppliers owned and operating in third world countries. Nevertheless, the big brand-name companies such as Nike were obliged to adopt and to attempt to enforce codes of conduct for their suppliers in order to respond to pressure from American students.

The three examples of successful protests against business described above have a common element. Protesters were able to put pressure on business where the protesters' strength was greatest and correspondingly the vulnerability of the corporation was largest. Thus in a sense, the fact that corporations have extensive assets and operations in numerous countries around the world increases their political vulnerability.

A fourth reason why the bleakest view of globalization may be incorrect is that different countries may find different ways to confront its challenges. In some cases, the answer may come not through trying to adopt American-style flexible labour markets but through negotiating flexible relationships with strong unions. It has been argued that the Netherlands, for example, has achieved both a flexible labour market and more adaptable modes of environmental regulation, not by using conflict and confrontation to destroy the power of unions and interest groups, but through working with them. Agreements with unions arranged by the government allowed Dutch employers to change patterns of employment and to use more temporary workers. Agreements with business organizations allowed corporations to pursue an agreed goal (such as reducing air pollution) in the manner that they found most convenient rather than in the manner the government thought best. The challenges of globalization were tackled not by market-based approaches but by negotiation among government, unions and business organizations. The Dutch claim that this approach achieved the benefits of Thatcherism in terms of more flexible labour markets and greater economic efficiency without the political and social costs. Of course, in a bargain all sides expect some pay-off. It has been argued, therefore, that the main difference between, for example, the United States and the Netherlands, is not that a worker whose job has been made uneconomic by globalization will be fired in the USA and kept on in the Netherlands, but that the Dutch employer will have to offer incentives (including retraining programmes) to persuade the worker to leave. These differences have important consequences, particularly for the distribution of income. In countries such as the Netherlands the distribution of the costs and benefits of globalization is determined by the outcome of bargaining between 'social partners' not merely by market forces. In consequence, globalization has been associated with a sharp increase in inequality in the USA but not in the Netherlands. However, both the American and Dutch approaches address the problems that globalization poses.[24]

Efficiency

Much of the discussion in this chapter so far has focused on the classic issue of the distribution of power between business, government (or the state) and potential adversaries such as unions and public interest groups. In practice, however, concern about the efficiency of the business–government relationship is at least as common among policy-makers as concern about the distribution of power. Is the relationship between business and government organized in a way that maximizes the economic performance of the country?

The traditional mode of thinking in the business communities of the United States and Britain about the business–government relationship that best promotes economic growth is the line much favoured in golf clubs that 'the government ought to leave us [business people] alone'. There may well be a trade-off between economic growth and equity so that government intervention promotes equity, but if growth is the goal, government intervention should be minimized. Individual entrepreneurs are likely to be quicker and more skilful in identifying opportunities for growth and development than government officials. Indeed, governments are likely to intervene in ways that diminish economic efficiency. Interest groups will seek policies such as tariffs or regulations that restrict competition, enabling the interest group to raise its income beyond the level that the market would set in a free market. Economists term the extra income groups obtain by manipulating markets, 'rents'. Government officials may expand programmes unnecessarily in order to increase their status and incomes by maximizing the number of subordinates answerable to them. Politicians may use government programmes and policies to reward supporters with their own re-election in mind. Government, in this traditional view in the United States, necessarily reduces economic efficiency.

The traditional view has come under a number of sustained attacks in recent years. First, economic historians have noted that even in countries such as the United States that pride themselves on building prosperity through free markets, government has played a massive role in building the economy. In the nineteenth century American manufacturing developed behind high-tariff walls that were intended to keep out cheaper imports from Britain and, later,

Germany. Economic growth was stimulated by government-funded programmes, such as the Erie Canal, or by government incentives, such as the vast land grants made to the railroads in exchange for completing a transcontinental railroad. In the modern era, familiar products of the private sector, such as the enormously successful Boeing 747 airliner and the internet, were offshoots of the vast military spending of the Department of Defense. The 747 was developed as an offshoot of the development of a large-scale military transport. The internet was developed initially as a means of maintaining communications in the event of a nuclear attack. Even leaving aside the fact that market processes have to be embedded in a system of laws, regulations and enforcement processes for contracts, the role of the state has been obvious and crucial even in a country that prides itself on restricting the role of government.

A second critique started from the fact that growth rates for several decades after the Second World War were clearly better in countries in which government played a more obvious and important role in promoting growth than in countries in which government played a more passive role. The classic example was of course the Japanese economic miracle, the doubling and then doubling again of gross national product that raised Japan to the rank of second largest economy in the world. This growth was clearly not achieved by allowing market forces to operate untrammelled. On the contrary, the Ministry of International Trade and Industry (MITI) worked in close partnership with business to achieve an accelerated progression up a ladder of production that took Japan from making cheap toys and textiles through a stage of manufacturing steel, ships and so on to making electronic goods, computers and automobiles with a high value-added. Similarly, during the '*trente glorieuses*' (thirty glorious years), France advanced from being an economic laggard to being one of Europe's most prosperous nations under the leadership of the *Commissariat du Plan*, a government agency that, in partnership with major corporations in a process known as indicative planning, tried to steer economic development into production that would achieve the greatest prosperity. How could state-led capitalist systems perform better than more purely market systems? The answer, according to proponents of such systems, is that government officials can take a longer view than a single corporation. Government officials are less prone to the pressures (often said to be particularly strong in the USA and UK) to make high profits in the short term and pay out dividends to shareholders, even if long-term investment and growth is sacrificed to do so. Government officials may be able to take a wider perspective and see that an entire industry (such as coal mining) is in terminal decline while another (electronics) has high promise. The state – and particularly its highly trained, disinterested bureaucracy – may be able to see that developments have future promise even though they are not consistent with short-term market forces.

In countries such as Austria and Sweden, a *neocorporatist* approach was adopted in which government made economic policy in partnership with business peak organizations and unions in order to achieve low inflation and high growth. Writing in the early 1980s, Schmitter argued that neocorporatist countries outperformed less neocorporatist countries on a wide variety of measures.[25] There were several reasons why this might be the case. Unions in neocorporatist countries cooperated in holding down wages, so their governments did not worry about inflationary pressures or a decline in competitiveness resulting from strong economic growth and full employment; these pressures had been a crucial constraint on Britain. Also, both business peak organizations and the union organization are widely encompassing (that is, recruit a high proportion of potential members) and are better able to focus on what is good for business and workers (and therefore probably the economy as a whole) than are the more fragmented organizations found in the USA and Britain.

In short, both the state-led and neocorporatist economies seemed to demonstrate the superiority of organized forms of capitalism over more purely market systems. By the early 1980s as the United States and Britain resisted such highly developed forms of government intervention and wallowed in depression, scholars debated whether they too could adopt a more interventionist, Japanese-style approach to economic policy with government following an active industrial policy.

The last decade of the twentieth century witnessed a sharp reversal in the comparative standing of political economic systems. Rapid growth and low unemployment in the United States attracted favourable, even envious, attention in Europe, which in general experienced low growth and high unemployment in the same era. European leaders agonized over the causes of the unfavourable contrast, searching for the causes of 'eurosclerosis'. The Japanese fall from favour was even more dramatic. The Japanese growth rate fell to almost zero, and the triple crises of economic stagnation, demographic decline and very high levels of public debt raised considerable doubts about the country's future. The combination of the poor performance of the Japanese economy and a major economic crisis in Asia in the late 1990s revived arguments that government involvement in the economy is inherently inefficient. In attacks on 'crony capitalism', critics argued that the collapse of many Asian banks showed the inevitable consequence of a system in which the discipline of market forces was weak and the political connections of bankers allowed them to escape serious supervision by government. The interlocking elites of politics, bureaucracy and business so characteristic of Asian systems – and once thought to be so beneficial for economic growth – were now seen as a major reason for financial collapse. The neocorporatist countries seemed equally unsuited to a globalized world economy. High levels of welfare-state expenditures and protection for employees from dismissal ran counter to the early assumptions (discussed above) that globalization demanded a transition to a low-tax regime, a minimal welfare state and weak regulatory policies. Discussion focused not, as in the 1980s, on whether the United States could be more like Japan (or possibly one of the European success stories) but on whether Japan and Europe could become more like the United States.

The reality is, of course, that countries are very rarely, if ever, free to choose a political economy. Political economies rest on a complex underpinning of institutions, cultures and economic interest groups. Any attempt to adopt a Japanese industrial policy in the United States would almost certainly have failed; the policy would (for reasons we shall explore later) have turned into a source of 'pork' for politicians to dispense in quest of re-election. Why this did not happen entirely and immediately in Japan is an interesting story to which we shall also return in Chapter 4. Nonetheless, even if Japan cannot become like the United States today – just as the United States could not have become like Japan twenty years ago – such discussions have three values. First, they alert us to the fact that there are several contending models of capitalism in the world today. French, British, German, American and Japanese forms of capitalism have functioned noticeably differently from each other;

it is probably inevitable that people will discuss which has worked best, even if other countries are not free to adopt the model. The second reason why discussion of the relative merits of 'rival capitalism' is important is that, even if countries are not free to adopt the most successful model in its entirety, they are free to try to move in that direction. Which model of capitalism is regarded as the more successful thus influences what types of proposals for reform dominate the agenda in other countries. In the early years of the twenty-first century, the success of the United States prompted debates on how other economies could become more 'flexible' even if it was unlikely that they could ever match the United States entirely. The third and final value in discussing different forms of capitalist political economy – the quest for knowledge – is, in a sense, the justification of this book. It is intended not only for those who need to do business with other countries but also for those who are simply anxious to learn about how those countries function. The countries included – USA, France, Japan, South Korea, Germany and the UK – are clearly neither a large nor a representative sample of the world as a whole. They are all advanced industrialized democracies, and they have all been seen as exemplifying different and contrasting models of capitalism. Given that the world has been perceived by some as shifting into an era in which business has outgrown the nation-state, the book includes a discussion of the relationship between business and multinational organizations, such as the WTO, the EU and the World Bank. It concludes with a discussion of whether or not the relationship between business and government has changed significantly under the impact of globalization.

2

Business and Politics in the United States

Background

The United States has long had a reputation as the most capitalist of the advanced industrialized countries. Several factors seem to support this description. The United States is the only advanced industrialized country in which a social democratic party has failed to develop a significant following. In contrast to all the other advanced industrialized democracies, no successful political party in the United States has ever questioned the desirability of capitalism. Similarly, unions are conspicuously weak, organizing only about 14 per cent of the workforce in general and merely 9 per cent of the private-sector workforce. The proportion of national income spent by government is unusually low (see Tables) compared with other advanced industrialized democracies. In consequence, American government provides its citizens with fewer services than citizens of other countries take for granted. The welfare state is small; most notoriously, there is no system of national health insurance in the United States, again distinguishing it from all other advanced industrialized democracies. In consequence some 43 million Americans (about one in six of the population) have no regular access to healthcare except through hospital emergency rooms. Nationalized (government-owned) industries are almost non-existent in the United States leaving little to privatize in the late twentieth century when other countries, notably Britain, pursued that policy vigorously.[1] Free enterprise and capitalism have always been popular in the United States. Many Americans see capitalism and democracy as almost

27

indistinguishable, which perhaps explains the odd fact that a large majority (69 per cent) told opinion poll researchers that they were prepared to make sacrifices to preserve the 'free enterprise system'.[2] While it is hard to be sure why respondents were so enthusiastic about an economic system, one possible explanation is that many Americans identify capitalism with democracy; it is not merely tolerated as an efficient economic system but enjoys active support as a system that is morally superior to its alternatives. The combination of popular support for capitalism, opposition to a more extensive role for government and lower government spending than in other advanced democracies is known as American exceptionalism.[3]

A sophisticated literature has developed over the years to explain American exceptionalism.[4] The great early-twentieth-century German sociologist, Werner Sombart,[5] argued that the weakness of socialist sentiment and class consciousness was due to the great prosperity and high social standing that American workers enjoyed compared with their European counterparts. Others emphasized factors such as the great racial, ethnic and regional differences that set American workers apart from each other and inhibited the development of class solidarity and, hence, unions or a social democratic party. Workers defined their identity in terms of their race, region, ethnicity or religion rather than in terms of their class. Most have stressed the unique historical development of the United States as the key to understanding its development. The USA was born as a new nation and society right at the moment (the late eighteenth century) when capitalism was becoming the dominant form of economic organization in the western world. It did not experience feudalism, and therefore did not inherit any of the anti-capitalist traditions of either the right or the left that were important in European politics until the end of the twentieth century. Forms of conservatism associated with traditional landed aristocracies that were suspicious of business could not flourish in the United States because there was no social base to sustain them. Socialism, theorists such as Louis Hartz[6] contended, had emerged where workers had been forced to fight simultaneously for citizenship rights, such as the vote, and for improvements in their living conditions. The United States, in contrast, full citizenship rights were extended to white males almost as soon as the nation was formed.

More recent scholarship, for example, Smith's,[7] has argued that theorists such as Hartz have overstated the strength of commitment to democracy and liberty in the 'liberal tradition' in the United States. Native Americans, women and African Americans scarcely experienced the respect for rights that Hartz seemed to celebrate; a high proportion of the original thirteen colonies practised slavery – which is hardly compatible with the principles of market economics. More relevant to this book, these historians have pointed to the conspicuous role that US governments played in economic development in ways that were also not compatible with free-market principles. Government intervention to promote economic development included subsidizing the building of infrastructure, such as canals and railroads, in the nineteenth century and nurturing domestic industries by maintaining very high tariffs on imported goods until after the Second World War when American industry was internationally dominant. Yet whatever the departures from the 'liberal' principles of democracy, individual rights and free markets, those principles have been at the very core of defining Americanism. Nations do not define what they are themselves through an objective examination of their practices and histories. Nations embrace myths and values that they believe define them and, in the case of the United States which is populated by people from many lands and continents, loyalty to core principles has been none the weaker because of frequent departures in practice from them. American national identity has been bound up with support for liberal principles, including support for capitalist or free-market economics.

Yet there is another side to the picture. Capitalism, or at least market economies, is popular in the United States but individual industries and corporations are not necessarily liked. Many Americans blamed oil corporations, not OPEC, for increases in fuel prices.[8] Historically, political movements such as Populism and Progressivism have argued that, left to themselves, corporations manipulate markets, engage in collusive price setting and exploit the public. Popular culture reflects a readiness to believe that corporate executives conspire against the well-being of their communities, customers and workers. Hollywood has produced successful movies regularly, such as *A Civil Action*, *The Insider* and *Norma Rae*, that portray corporate executives as villains and juries have awarded huge damages against tobacco companies for causing heart disease and lung cancer.[9]

Criticism of business has periodically produced waves of reform legislation. The Progressive era early in the twentieth century, the New Deal era in the 1930s and the reform era (that has no commonly recognized title) that ran from the mid 1960s until the early 1970s have all left behind a large body of law. These laws, together with the more detailed rules known as regulations issued by government agencies under the authority of these laws, constrain business in the United States in important respects. Each of these reform eras had somewhat different concerns, of course. The Progressive era was concerned with monopoly power and the safety of food and drugs. The New Deal era continued these concerns to some degree but added to them a powerful body of law initially concerned with protecting the rights of workers and unions. The reforms of the 1960s and 1970s focused on environmental and consumer protection.

Even waves of reform not aimed directly at business have had important implications for it. As we saw in Chapter 1, American governments (federal, state and local) use their ability to impose requirements on those who do business with them as a major weapon of social policy. Europeans often imagine that American employers can hire and fire at will. As anyone who has ever had any managerial authority in the United States can testify, civil rights laws, laws protecting the physically or mentally disabled (Americans with Disabilities Act), laws prohibiting discrimination against older workers and federal policies on affirmative action and so on make employment decisions a legal minefield. We will return to regulation later in this chapter; it is sufficient here to note that the popular image of the United States as a country in which business can freely pursue its own will unconstrained by law is far from the truth. Indeed, American business executives can argue convincingly that government regulation is a more intrusive and irritating presence in their lives than it is in other countries.[10]

The federal government is also adept at influencing business behaviour through tax allowances. Perhaps no tax code is ever truly neutral in economic terms. As we discussed in Chapter 1, tax codes nearly always reward some activities and penalize others.[11] The American tax code has been particularly loaded with allowances designed to encourage particular forms of economic activity. Suarez has described how large corporations, particularly pharmaceutical corporations, manoeuvred politically to protect lavish tax allowances for corporations investing in Puerto Rico.[12] Because tax allowances favour one type of business over another they generally are the product of political conflict between different industries. Cathie Jo Martin has described how 'high tech' and capital-intensive industries encouraged Congress to enact tax allowances for capital-intensive rather than labour-intensive industries in the 1980s.[13] Even tax allowances for individuals, such as tax relief on mortgage interest payments, have implications for business by encouraging home ownership and therefore building. Economists emphasize that tax allowances should be treated as government expenditure giving rise to the phrase 'tax expenditures': tax allowances amount to government giving up income just as it might otherwise give up expenditures. The large tax expenditures of the federal government, estimated to be $424,400 million in the mid 1980s,[14] like regulation therefore amount to a significant extension of government influence on business that does not show up in conventional estimates of the size of government.

Market-Shaping Activity

In an influential article, David Vogel argued that the relationship between business and government in the United States was distinctive because 'big business' had developed before 'big government'.[15] In most countries, national governmental authority developed long before the modern corporation. This was not the case in the United States. The great economic historian Alfred Chandler pointed out that it was large-scale corporations that pioneered effective large-scale organization in the USA.[16] No contemporary government bureaucracy in nineteenth-century America could compare with the ability of a nineteenth-century railroad to direct large-scale complex activity across the continent from an east-coast headquarters. It is easy, therefore, to be dismissive of the role of government in building the US economy. It is often remarked that the only government official a nineteenth-century American was likely to meet was the postman (though Theda Skocpol has pointed out that the post office in the nineteenth century was an exciting, relatively complicated innovation). Lacking an effective administrative apparatus because, thanks to Andrew Jackson and his followers, there was no professional and permanent bureaucracy to service government, the American state was, as

Skowronek writes, 'a state of courts and parties'.[17] Whereas Amercian bureaucracy was weak by international standards, judges and political parties (especially their political machines) were unusually strong.

It would be an error to overlook the role of government in creating a national economy in the United States. As we saw in the previous chapter, markets do not just happen; they are created and maintained by the government or the state. The United States is no exception. The growth of the early American economy was spurred by the determined action of federal authorities to prevent individual states from impeding trade. If a national economy was to be created and maintained, the natural inclination of the individual states to protect their citizens and industries had to be checked. The most important institution in this role was the United States Supreme Court, which in a number of notable decisions ensured the development of a single American market. This exercise in market creation, by negating the attempts of state governments to impede free trade within the United States, can be compared with the efforts of the European Union in the 1980s to create a Single European Market, a process in which its own 'Supreme Court' (European Court of Justice) was also very important. The elected branches of the federal and state governments also played a constructive role in the creation of the American economy, however. Both the states and federal government tried to encourage the development of integrative transport systems through grants and subsidies; the builders of the transcontinental railroad received massive grants of federally-owned land along the route to stimulate their enthusiasm. The lands given to companies as payment for building the railroad still generate considerable earnings for those corporations today, for example from minerals under their surface.

One of the main roles played by the federal government in nineteenth-century America was to foster domestic industry by impeding foreign competition. In twentieth-century Latin America, this was often referred to as an import substitution strategy. From the Civil War onwards, the United States maintained extremely high tariffs to discourage free trade in manufactured goods. Tariffs were, in fact, central to American politics from the Civil War until the New Deal.[18] A commitment to high tariffs distinguished the Republicans, the dominant party in this era, from the Democrats.

Republican Presidents and Congresses nearly always raised tariffs while Democrats lowered them slightly, at least in part because their base in the South, dependent on exports of tobacco and cotton, received no benefit from tariffs. Tariffs enabled Republicans to assemble an otherwise implausible coalition of industrial workers and employers, along with the farmers of the Midwest, behind their candidates. High tariffs, by preventing foreign competition, enabled infant industries to grow and employers to pay their workers higher wages. Industrial development was also promoted by laws that gave advantages to employers against unions (on occasion supported by the deployment of federal troops against strikers), the ready availability of labour (by allowing large-scale immigration until the 1920s) and Supreme Court rulings that severely limited the right of states to regulate business.

The New Deal marked the beginning of a significant change in the market-constructing role of government. For about fifteen years, from the passing of the Wagner Act until the adoption of the Taft–Hartley Act in 1947, the federal government assisted the growth of unions. The Wagner Act created an agency, the National Labor Relations Board, to conduct secret ballots to see if workers wished to join a union; if workers voted for a union, their employer was required to bargain with it in good faith. Other New Deal era policies, such as the National Recovery Act and wartime contracts with suppliers, also required employers to accept unions. Fostered by the federal government, American unions grew until, at their peak in the early 1950s, they represented about one-third of the workforce, roughly the same proportion as British unions at that time. American unions also benefited from a major change in policy among one of their great historical enemies, the judiciary. From the nineteenth century until the New Deal, the judiciary had nearly always favoured employers against unions. In a famous switch in direction after 1937, the Supreme Court also abandoned its role as protector of *laissez-faire* capitalism and the rights of business, allowing states and the federal Congress much more leeway in regulating business. An upsurge of Republican strength after the Second World War weakened the position of unions. The Taft–Hartley Act of 1947, passed over the veto of President Truman, helped to arrest the growth in unions whose strength declined gently from the 1950s, while British unions' strength increased. The Taft–Hartley Act ended the mild bias of federal law in favour of unions and contained a number of provisions that ultimately contributed to the decline of unions in the United States. Two of the most important were prohibiting unions not directly involved in a dispute from using their industrial power to assist workers who were, and allowing states to prohibit unions from persuading employers to make union membership a condition of employment.

Not until the Reagan Administration (1980–88) did the federal government resume an actively anti-union stance in its policies, however. Thus, for some fifty years, federal policy switched towards greater acceptance of a more organized form of capitalism in which unions and government regulation played a major role. From the 1970s onwards, however, a backlash developed. Both Democrats and Republicans encouraged the abolition of government regulation of prices and quality of service in industries such as air travel. President Reagan appointed strongly anti-union people to the National Labor Relations Board, whose decisions assisted a strong push by business to weaken unions. The gradual decline which had begun in the early 1950s turned into a rout. The last two decades of the twentieth century witnessed a shift back towards a policy of less restricted markets although environmental and consumer protection regulation had sufficient support to withstand de-regulatory fervour.[19] The period in which a strong union movement had constrained American capitalism proved to have been comparatively short.

US Business and the World

The New Deal also witnessed the beginning of an historic shift in trade policy as well as in the domestic role of government. As we have seen, in nineteenth-century America, infant manufacturing industries sheltered behind high tariff walls. American participation in the global economy was based primarily on the export of primary goods, such as wheat and cotton, and importing capital for development. The American *economy* remained relatively self-contained from the Great Depression until the current era of globalization with foreign trade equivalent to an unusually low proportion of GDP compared with other countries (see Appendix, Table 3). Yet American *corporations* have been active overseas for many years. The major American automobile manufacturers, such as Ford and General Motors, had established foreign subsidiaries in Europe before the Second World War; American corporations became such a familiar part of the landscape in Britain that sometimes their names became synonymous with their industry. Vacuum cleaners in Britain were often known as 'hoovers', for example, and the name of the American corporation was even used as a verb as in 'I'll hoover the living room'. Relations between the British government and American firms were sometimes better than between it and domestic producers. British governments found Ford more responsive to their needs than domestic automobile producers. Although we might suppose that this overseas expansion reflected early American strength in the relevant industries which has now passed, there are numerous contemporary examples of the same corporations still establishing overseas plants, for example General Motors building plants in China. The contemporary era is significantly different, however, from that first era of overseas expansion by American corporations. American corporations today are outsourcing production of components or even products overseas, taking advantage of propitious local circumstances, such as cheap labour, to manufacture all or part of their product outside the United States rather than merely using overseas plants to supply foreign markets, as had been the case with the automobile industry. Familiar American names, such as RCA (Radio Company of America), are attached to television sets made in Taiwan or Malaysia. Products carefully associated with American sports heroes (for example, Nike's relationship with basketball superstar Michael Jordan) are manufactured by local contractors in poor nations including China and Vietnam.

The attitudes of American business to trade policy naturally reflect the circumstances and interests of the industries in which they are involved. Boeing, which exports aircraft all over the world, is naturally keen on free trade. Boeing exemplifies the support of high-tech, high-skill American corporations for free trade since the 1930s when General Electric set the pattern. Textile manufacturers, who compete with manufacturers in low-wage countries, have traditionally been hostile to free trade. Financial industries, such as banking and insurance, have generally been enthusiastic about free trade, dealing as they do in a highly mobile commodity – money – and believing that they have exceptional skills that will allow them to thrive in foreign markets once they are opened to them. Yet, although there are still protectionist industries and although major industries, including automobiles, have demanded and received protection when threatened by vigorous foreign competition, the general sentiment of American business has become steadily more in favour of trade liberalization. Even the apparel industry, once allied with the textile industry in pursuit of protectionism, has now embraced globalization and supported NAFTA.[20]

For those who think that business always dictates to American leaders, it is interesting to note that American politicians were in advance of the business community's move towards free trade. Even before the end of the Second World War the then Secretary of State, Cordell Hull, was sure that the peace and prosperity of the postwar world was dependent upon increased trade. After the defeat of Germany and Japan, the United States played the leading role in creating international institutions that were dedicated to lowering trade barriers. The key institutions created were the World Bank, the International Monetary Fund (IMF) and the General Agreement on Tariffs and Trade (GATT). The World Bank evolved into an agency to facilitate lending to poorer nations while the IMF had the task of preventing international financial crises. The most successful of the international organizations created with American leadership, however, was GATT, which, before its replacement with the World Trade Organization (WTO) in 1995, had facilitated a reduction of 96 per cent in the level of average industrial tariffs.

American leadership in the international political economy was facilitated by institutional arrangements that were at odds with the general American constitutional principles of sharing power between different institutions (Congress, the President and the Courts). The President enjoyed unusual authority in foreign policy from American entry into the Second World War until the Vietnam War. In economic foreign policy, presidential dominance was reinforced and continued by the granting of 'fast-track' authority. Congress agreed that the president could negotiate reciprocal agreements for trade liberalization with other countries and Congress would guarantee him an 'up or down' (yes or no) vote within a specified time period without amending the agreement. This constituted a remarkable shift in power towards the president. Why did Congress cede so much power? In brief, even Congress believed that it had a chronic tendency to favour local over national interests. Congress, for this reason, had in the past had a clearly deleterious effect on trade policy. The worst example of this tendency was when a process of 'log rolling' between legislators had resulted in the Smoot–Hawley Tariff increase in the 1930s. Significant tariff increases by the United States invited retaliation by other countries, probably accentuating the worldwide Great Depression by reducing world trade. Fast-track was accorded to both Republican and Democratic presidents and was regarded by them as essential in securing approval of NAFTA and the last (Uruguay) round of GATT that established the WTO.

In the late 1990s, however, the dominant coalition in favour of free trade suffered significant setbacks. Unions, once supporters of trade liberalization, shifted into opposition. They were joined by most environmental interest groups, which were convinced that free trade and the international institutions (notably the WTO) that promote it were damaging to national environmental policies. In spite of this opposition, President Clinton secured Congressional approval of both NAFTA and the Uruguay Round. Clinton's struggle to obtain approval of NAFTA was epic and he was dependent for support on Republicans as a majority of his own Democratic Party in the House voted against the agreement. However, as part of his tactical manoeuvring to secure approval, Clinton let his fast-track authority lapse and was unable to revive it during the remainder of his presidency. On every occasion that Clinton tried to recover fast-track authority, he was placed in the odd position of receiving more support from Republicans than Democrats. Riots against the WTO in 1999 and the following spring against the World Bank and IMF illustrated the way in which trade policy had been popularized and was no longer the preserve of informed elites familiar with its arcane details. American leadership of international movement towards trade liberalization seemed in doubt. President Bush recovered fast-track authority in 2002 but only after making numerous concessions to uncompetitive industries, most notably steel and clothing. In order to obtain the necessary support for trade liberalization in general, the President increased tariffs on most imported steel to 30 per cent and revoked special arrangements to facilitate clothing imports from very poor Caribbean countries. The steel tariffs in particular so infuriated America's trading partners that Bush's victory seemed pyrrhic.

The most familiar way in which the American state engages in market-shaping activity is through macroeconomic policy. In common with the governments of most advanced economies, the government of the United States has attempted to promote economic growth and to avoid inflation and high unemployment. Characteristically, however, this responsibility has been exercised in the United States by a confused and confusing set of institutions. Voters have seemed to give presidents the credit or the blame for economic conditions; recent presidents who have been denied a second term (Carter and Bush) have generally sought it during or immediately after recessions. Since the Second World War, presidents have been well equipped with agencies to give economic advice – the Council of Economic Advisers (CEA) – and to develop budgets – the Office of Management and Budget (OMB). Yet presidents have never enjoyed the ability to raise or lower taxes and government spending quickly in response to economic conditions in the same manner as, for example, British governments. Congress shares the powers to tax and spend with the president, and has never rushed to give a president what he has requested in full. Until the mid 1970s, Congress's handling of macroeconomic policy was almost chaotic with little or no coordination between the committees that control taxation (the House Ways and Means, and the Senate Finance Committee) and spending (the House and Senate Appropriations Committees). Since the mid 1970s, a new set of committees, the House and Senate Budget Committees guided by Congress's own advisory agency, the Congressional Budget Office, have brought more order to proceedings. However, the inherent difficulty of varying taxation and government spending quickly in order to steer the economy, coupled with the limitations Congress imposed on itself in order to eliminate the budget deficits that plagued the USA in the 1980s and early 1990s, reduced the effectiveness of the classic Keynesian tools of economic management. Congress and the president were unable to vary taxation or government spending sufficiently and with adequate speed to move the economy in the necessary direction.

The growth in popularity of monetarism (which relies on controlling the quantity of money in circulation and interest rates) in academic circles also encouraged a shift towards greater reliance on the central bank of the United States, the Federal Reserve Board, to steer the economy. The 'Fed', as it is known, has the great advantage of not being democratically accountable. Its members are appointed by the president for extraordinarily long terms (14 years) while the Chairman, who is the real force at the Fed, is appointed for a four-year term of office that deliberately does not coincide with the president's, so that each new president must accept as Chair of the Fed someone appointed by his predecessor.[21] The Fed, however, is an institution created merely by legislation, not the Constitution; it is therefore vulnerable to changes in federal law that might reduce its powers or role. It is generally agreed, therefore, that in following unpopular policies, for example, exacerbating a recession in order to defeat inflation, the Fed must have the support of at least one of the elected branches of government. If the Fed were unpopular with the House, Senate and the President, it would risk its legislative mandate and powers being changed. This is, however, a very limited degree of political control and the Fed has long been regarded as one of the most independent central banks in the world. Ironically, the reduction of inflation in the 1980s followed by the long economic boom of the 1990s made folk heroes of chairmen of the Fed. Alan Greenspan, chairman from 1986 onwards, enjoyed a degree of esteem and popularity that most politicians could only envy and he was the subject of an admiring portrait by one time investigative reporter, Bob Woodward.[22] Greenspan's reputation even seemed to survive the downturn in the economy in 2001.

Even in a country celebrated for its commitment to free markets, the American state has enormous influence on business.

Government as Customer

The government of the United States, in common with the governments of other advanced industrialized countries, is primarily a transfer agency taking in money from one set of people (taxpayers) and sending it on to another (retirees, unemployed people and so on). Although a minority of government spending goes directly on goods or services, the vast scale of the United States makes government an important customer. The American government is the biggest and most important customer in the world, particularly for American firms manufacturing military equipment and aircraft.

How has the federal government used this influence? No one would suggest that the United States government has ever had a coherent, integrated approach to its relations with business. The fragmentation built into the American political system from its foundation is very evident. Dozens of different agencies interact with business, as do numerous Congressional committees. These agencies and committees may well be trying to move in different directions so that one agency (perhaps Commerce) is focused on making industrial production in the USA less costly while another (perhaps the Environmental Protection Agency) is preparing new regulations that will raise production costs significantly. In addition, Representatives and Senators are likely to approach decisions about the allocation of contracts by pressing for the money to go to their own district or state. Considerable political efforts are made to influence defence contracts. Legislators work closely with military contractors from their district or state to press their case in the Pentagon. On occasion, legislators working for their constituents have forced the military to buy planes or equipment it did not want.[23] The most careful studies suggest, however, that Washington folklore – that legislators who support military spending the most or who sit on defence appropriations subcommittees are better able to win contracts – is unfounded. Major contractors, however, do shore up their political position by dividing major contracts (such as the building of a plane) into hundreds of subcontracts that are distributed around the country.[24] The extensive use of subcontracting in military contracts ensures that a majority of members of the House have a constituency interest in a military project even though the major contractor may appear to be based in only a few districts. Thus voting against such a project amounts to voting against employment and prosperity in one's own district.

The highly politicized nature of defence contracting and subcontracting in the United States does, however, alert us to the problems that might have arisen if the federal government had attempted to adopt a more consciously interventionist role in the economy. In particular, it would have been extremely difficult to operate any version of the integrated industrial policies that were applied successfully in a number of other countries following the Second World War. A fragmented system of government heavily influenced by parochial interests is not well-suited to coherent industrial policy. Yet the importance, secrecy and widely supported character of national defence did allow the Pentagon to pursue more of an industrial policy, especially during the Cold War, than would have been possible for any other government agency. The Pentagon was able to nurture its key suppliers, working closely with them in a manner that had few parallels in other parts of the federal government. As we have seen earlier, military programmes had important civilian spin-offs for American industry, including the 747 jet, improvements in the microprocessor chip, the protection of the silicon chip industry from Japanese supremacy in the 1980s and, perhaps most important of all, the internet. Even though the USA has not attempted an integrated industrial policy, the size of government expenditure is so large (although small as a percentage of gross national product) that it inevitably has important consequences.

The Political Representation of Business

American business is represented politically through numerous different channels.[25] First, most large corporations now maintain their own lobbying offices in Washington DC. This has been true only since the 1970s, and the process is still incomplete. Corporations that are extensively involved with government, for example as contractors and suppliers, are particularly likely to have their own Washington offices.[26] However, Washington offices are not limited to lobbying for orders for their corporation and are probably more oriented to general policy issues than to merely expanding sales. Politically active corporations also try to exert influence through campaign contributions. The best-known technique for making contributions to politicians' campaigns is through Political Action Committees (PACs). Corporations, like unions, are allowed to pay the operating expenses of PACs that collect money from, in the case of corporations, executives and stockholders and dispense it to candidates in contributions that cannot exceed $5,000 per election and must be reported to the Federal Election Commission. PAC contributions are regarded by most lobbyists in Washington as an indispensable tool for gaining access to key legislators.[27]

Business PAC contributions have tended to be highly pragmatic rather than ideological in character. Corporations favour incumbents over challengers. To the dismay of conservatives, corporations have proved very willing to make contributions to liberal Democrats if they hold key positions in Congress, such as the chairs of committees and subcommittees controlling key legislation. Most businesses are Republican rather than Democratic in sentiment, however, and welcomed the opportunity to shift money to the Republicans when they took control of the House and Senate in 1994. In more recent years, corporations discovered that they could avoid the irritating limitations on campaign contributions to PACs by routing their money through the political parties. These 'soft money' contributions made through the parties, ostensibly for 'party-building' activity, could be of any amount and came from the corporation's general funds, not just from contributions by executives and stockholders. Instead of contributing a mere $5,000, corporations were able to donate hundreds of thousands of dollars. Soft money displaced PAC contributions as the most effective way for corporations to funnel large amounts of money into politics. PAC contributions remained useful, however, in making candidates aware of a corporation's support. In 2002, in the wake of revelations about the political operations of Enron Corporation before its high-profile bankruptcy, legislation was passed to end soft money contributions. As this book went to press it was unclear whether the law would survive constitutional challenges in the courts. It also seems highly likely that corporations will readily find alternatives such as making large contributions to political parties in the states (which were not covered by the new law), or to interest groups supposedly operating independently of the candidates.

We should not suppose, however, that corporations necessarily buy the votes of legislators who support them. Many legislators, including many Democrats as well as Republicans, are ideologically sympathetic to corporations' claims. More often, however, legislators help corporations active in their districts as a form of constituency service. American legislators devote enormous efforts to helping constituents in their dealings with government and would be politically vulnerable if they failed to do so. Even the most liberal of Democrats would feel a strong obligation to exert pressure on behalf of a corporation in her district that was seeking a federal contract, a more considerate response from government officials or a more helpful response from a regulatory agency. Legislators certainly take an active role in campaigns to attract investment, public or private, in their districts and states. Legislators will argue that it is wholly implausible to argue that they would not try to help a corporation that was a major employer in their district merely because it had not made a $5,000 PAC contribution to their election campaign.

Individual corporations also supplement the efforts of their own staff in Washington with lobbyists employed on a contract basis. For many years, prominent Washington law firms carried on a great deal of lobbying work, generally on behalf of business clients. In recent years, however, lobbying has emerged as a distinct profession. Contract lobbyists are employed by corporations partly in order to provide extra assistance when major issues arise but partly also to provide a centre point for the temporary *ad hoc* coalitions that are so much a part of the Washington lobbying scene. (A group of corporations and other interest groups comes together to campaign for a change in policy, works together to try secure passage or defeat of relevant legislation and then disbands.) During the period that the alliance is in existence, a contract lobbyist serves as its headquarters, coordinating meetings and strategy between the component interest groups. Contract lobbyists also have their own areas of expertise, often having contacts with politicians who may be little known by the corporation's own Washington lobbyists.[28]

Corporations are individual members of both trade associations representing specific industries and peak associations representing business as a whole. Some trade associations, such as the American Bankers' Association, have a high reputation in Washington. Most, however, have limited prestige and there is no doubt that the balance of power lies heavily in favour of the member corporations. Trade associations exist to provide corporations with a limited range of services such as monitoring legislation with potential impact on member firms. Corporations make the decision to subscribe or not to subscribe to the trade association depending on their degree of satisfaction with the level of services provided. Trade associations are not regarded as 'the' voice of the steel, automobile or any other industry and certainly lack the authority to make deals with government (or, for that matter, unions) on behalf of member firms. Trade associations thus enjoy much less standing than their counterparts in Japan or many European countries.

The contrast between peak associations in the United States and their counterparts in other advanced industrialized democracies is even more striking. As is the case with trade associations, individual corporations are unwilling to delegate much authority to a peak association. In addition, however, the standing of peak associations is reduced by the competition between them for members. The United States is once again exceptional, this time in terms of the number of organizations that claim to speak for business. Four organizations claim the title. The oldest is the National Association of Manufacturers (NAM), founded in the late nineteenth century. The second oldest is the U.S. Chamber of Commerce founded at the instigation of President Taft. The two most recent are the Business Roundtable and the National Federation of Independent Business (NFIB). There is some differentiation between these organizations. The NAM does not cover service industries and the Chamber of Commerce is heavily associated with small business. The Business Roundtable is limited to very large corporations and was created by Irving Shapiro of Dupont because he thought that the NAM and Chamber of Commerce were overly associated with right-wing, Republican Party politics. Yet there is also tremendous overlap and generally implicit, but sometimes explicit, competition between these organizations for members. As we saw in Chapter 1, competition has many virtues in keeping interest-group leaders attentive to members. It also, however, reduces the room for manoeuvre that interest-group leaders enjoy in reaching compromises with other interests or with government. Acts of interest-group statesmanship, such as reaching a compromise on health care, are harder to achieve when the interest-group leaders know that any departure from the preferences of their members or apparent signs of weakness are likely to result in a loss of members.

Business representation in the United States is therefore conducted in a manner that is very decentralized and fragmented. It is the individual enterprise, not the trade association or peak organization, that is paramount. This makes it difficult, if not impossible, for government agencies to develop close links with business organizations or to make them partners in governance, as has happened in other advanced democracies. Why has business retained this fragmented, decentralized mode of representation in the United States? After all, we might assume that fragmentation raises problems for any interest group as politicians and administrators are confronted with people arguing that they, not their rivals, truly speak for business.

One explanation for the fragmentation of business interest groups is that business has never confronted a serious challenge to its interests in the United States, as have its counterparts in countries with strong socialist and union traditions. Business mobilization tends to be reactive to challenges, even in the United States. The rise of consumer and environmental activism in the 1960s and 1970s prompted a significant upsurge in the political activism of business. Yet not even these crises prompted the multiple business interest groups that exist in the USA to consolidate into the sort of integrated structures found in continental Europe, Britain and Japan.

A more likely explanation of the fragmentation of business representation is that it reflects the fragmented character of American government. It is not just business organizations that are fragmented; many types of interest group share the characteristic. There are multiple competing (and bitterly antagonistic) farmers' organizations and ideologically distinguishable competing environmental groups that vie for popular support. Competing interest groups do not spontaneously unite, even in countries where they are less fragmented than in the United States. Governments in Europe have often worked to create more unified interest groups. The creation of the Confederation of British Industry (CBI) at the prompting of a Labour government is a case in point. Governments have encouraged interest groups to unite partly in order to avoid the difficulties that arise from receiving conflicting advice from competing groups and partly to make the interest groups more useful in helping governments to implement policies. Government departments in Europe have also maintained interest-group monopolies by giving privileged access to one major interest group and not to any competitors. But such tactics presuppose that government departments can limit or control interest-group participation in policy-making. This is not the case in the United States. The sharing of power among different agencies, congressional committees and the courts means that no interest group can be guaranteed a monopoly; a group denied a hearing in one venue, such as an executive branch agency, would be able to find an open door in another, such as a congressional committee. In the absence of pressure from government for interest groups to unite, the situation remains one in which interest groups – including business interest groups – are fragmented and competing rather than unified and monopolistic.

The Structural Power of Business

Two other well-known features of American government – federalism and the persistence of numerous units of local government – serve to increase the structural power of business. The United States has been called the land of ten thousand governments because of the multiplicity of political authorities that exist. In addition to the federal and state governments, around New York city, for example, significant power is held by municipalities, country governments and special authorities created for diverse purposes ranging from drainage to running the airports (Kennedy, La Guardia and Newark). Most metropolitan areas do not correspond to government boundaries; the New York metropolitan crosses three state lines, namely New York, New Jersey and Connecticut. More importantly, however, even modest-sized cities generally have a cluster of communities around them that are nominally independent but in fact are satellites with their inhabitants commuting into the core city for work and often travelling in for entertainment and major shopping. Generally, more affluent whites have left established urban areas, such as Milwaukee in Wisconsin, for legally separate governmental units, such as Waukesha County, from which they can commute into the city, leaving its problems and taxes behind when they return home at night.

The multiplicity of governments empowers business because it increases its exit options. Business can extract important concessions by moving, or even by threatening to move, from one state to another or even from a major city to a nominally independent small city outside its boundaries. In consequence, most states and large cities worry about their 'business climate'. If regulations are too strict and taxes too high, businesses may choose to not invest in a particular state. If local planning controls are irksome, businesses may relocate to another city. Particularly during periods of relatively high unemployment, competition for jobs between states can be intense. States have offered packages to attract new automobile plants such as those of the Saturn division of General Motors,

Honda, Mercedes Benz and BMW. There is some evidence that the price of attracting employment has escalated, with state governments spending ever more to attract (or keep) jobs. Whereas Pennsylvania had contributed $11,800 per job created to the costs of establishing an ill-fated Volkswagen plant in 1978, South Carolina contributed $65,000 per job created in a BMW plant in 1992 and Alabama a massive $200,000 per job created in a Mercedes plant in 1993.[29] Attempts by one state governor to obtain an agreement among states not to make such lavish offers to business were compromised by his own generous inducements to the makers of Tootsie Rolls and Fig Newtons to stay in his own home state.[30] Yet the ability of business to demand concessions is not unlimited. Some cities with high taxes, such as New York, may nonetheless be irresistible locations for certain types of business, such as finance, marketing and broadcasting. As we saw in Chapter 1, some industries may be more attracted by the prospects of a highly-skilled and educated workforce supported by research universities than by low taxes and lax regulations in a state with a poor educational system. Even the quality of cultural life may come into play. We discussed the use of the arts to attract Boeing to Chicago in Chapter 1. Another Midwestern example of corporations supporting the arts for their own interests is the generosity of corporations in Minneapolis which are eager to offset the disadvantage of cold winters in recruiting executives. A complex game is played out, therefore, between governments and business in which the ability to tax and regulate is constrained by the ability of business to relocate, and this, in turn, is constrained by the needs of some industries to cluster in particular locations.

It is also the case that an inevitable consequence of having thousands of governments is that there are hundreds of thousands of politicians running these governments who might launch initiatives of which business disapproves. This is the great disadvantage of decentralization for business. No matter how strong its grip might be on the federal Congress, there is always the risk that a state legislator might decide to make her reputation by promoting stricter standards in a field such as environmental protection. In fact federalism raises two dangers for business. The first is simply that measures it dislikes might be adopted at the state – or even local – level. The second is that a multiplicity of regulations might develop which confront corporations with many different requirements across the country. Business might prefer a moderately strict

federal law with national uniformity to a situation in which requirements vary dramatically from state to state, with some adopting
strict and others adopting lax regulations. Particularly during the
years of Republican strength in Washington (the Reagan and Bush
presidencies, the post-1994 Republican Congresses), business has
supported legal arguments that Washington, not the states, has power
to regulate in areas such as the environment.

Globalization has influenced the structural power of business in
the United States as in other countries. The United States has
always had very open capital markets with no controls over the
movement of capital in or out of the United States. It was thus a
realistic fear that employers might invest overseas in the production of goods requiring relatively low skill levels and import the
products into the United States. As we have seen, this risk was
avoided historically by the maintenance of high tariff barriers to
imports. In more recent years, however, as tariffs have been
reduced and transport costs have fallen in real terms, the trade
dependency of the US economy has increased considerably;
imports and exports combined are equivalent to over 25 per cent of
gross domestic product, still low compared with countries such as
Britain but a dramatic change since the 1950s when the equivalent
figure was about half that level. Increased trade dependency has
increased competitive pressures on American business but it has
also increased exit options. Businesses in the United States that
feel their employees are too expensive or government too demanding in regulations or taxation can relocate their production facilities more readily than ever before. The apparel industry provides
an interesting example. The industry, in alliance with the textile
manufacturers, was a strong long-term supporter of protectionist
trade policies. The industry has discovered more recently the
advantages of trade, contracting out production around the globe,
but especially to China and Latin America. In consequence, the
apparel industry, unlike textile manufacturers, has abandoned its
commitment to protectionism and instead supports free-trade policies that allow it to import its products from low-cost countries.

While it is important to bear in mind that many industries neither
wish to leave the USA nor possess the ability to do so because they
need to be close to skilled labour, scarce resources or markets, the
increased flows of trade in and out of the United States did change
the balance of power in favour of corporations. During the recession

of the 1980s, particularly when a strong dollar made imports cheap and American exports less competitive, employers were able to demand concessions from their workers in the 1980s so that they could survive foreign competition. Even during the economic boom of the Clinton years, workers seemed hesitant about reasserting their power, perhaps in recognition of the possibility that employers might move jobs overseas. There are indirect signs that workers recognized that the balance of power had shifted against them in the late twentieth century; economists were struck by both the slow rate of wage increases for blue-collar workers and by the mounting inequalities of income evident in the USA in the 1980s. It is possible that blue-collar workers fared better in the 1990s; whereas blue-collar wages in real terms declined by 3.5 per cent from 1982 to 1991, they rose by 12 per cent in the following ten years.[31] Some of the changes that occurred were subtle and little noticed. Not until after the collapse of the Enron Corporation in 2001 and subsequent revelations about its financial practices, did many Americans realize how far large corporations had retreated from the practice of providing employees with guaranteed retirement pensions. Such pensions had been the bedrock of the 'private sector welfare state' and had seemed a fixed element in American life in previous decades.

It is not surprising that American unions, which as recently as the 1960s had supported trade liberalization, moved into determined opposition to extending it in the 1990s. A new anti-trade-liberalization coalition emerged, based on unions and some environmentalists such as Ralph Nader, the minor party presidential candidate in 2000, and was strong enough to mobilize many Democrats in Congress to deny President Clinton (himself, of course, a Democrat) the authority to negotiate major new trade agreements during the last six years of his term.

Political Opposition to Business

People outside the United States commonly have the impression that it is a land of unbridled capitalism. This arises from the incorrect assumption that the weakness of the socialist tradition and the low level of unionization in the workforce means that there is no significant political opposition to business. In fact, unions are probably more important politically than industrially in the United States. They are the Democrats' major source of campaign contributions through PACs and soft money; very little union money flows to Republicans.[32] Unlike business, therefore, most unions do not divide their contributions between the two major parties and arguably Democratic dependence on unions has increased since they lost control of Congress in 1994 and consequently experienced a decline in the contributions they received from corporations. Unions also maintain a large and generally highly regarded lobbying operation in Washington. Unions are not by any means always on the opposite side to business, but they do come into political conflict with most corporations on a wide range of issues including trade, healthcare, occupational safety and health, taxation and consumer protection.

More surprising to foreigners is the intensity of anti-corporate sentiment found among the so-called public-interest groups that developed in the last third of the twentieth century. Although political scientists had predicted that it would be difficult to form interest groups to promote collective or public goods such as consumer and environmental protection, the late 1960s and 1970s witnessed an increase in the strength of public-interest groups. Numerous factors have been advanced to explain this increase. Some have associated the growth of public interest groups with the increase in post-material values that Inglehart[33] observed in richer industrialized economies such as the USA. Others, however, have pointed out that public-interest groups draw on a long tradition of reform movements in the United States stretching back through the Progressives of the early twentieth century (who shared contemporary concerns about the environment and consumer protection) to the Mugwumps of the nineteenth century (who, like Common Cause today, were focused on reforming government). Public-interest groups probably benefited from a combination of the upsurge in participatory politics among professional class people and the rejection of parties as a mode of political involvement.[34]

One of the most important factors in overcoming the collective action problems that Mancur Olson had identified[35] in fostering public-interest groups critical of business was ironically the great fortunes left by a previous generation of entrepreneurs. These fortunes had passed in part into the hands of foundations – non-party, non-governmental organizations of vast wealth controlled by boards that select their own members. Some of these foundations, although using the wealth created by conservative businessmen of the past, had a decidedly liberal philosophy. The Ford Foundation, for example, although funded by bequests from the very conservative Ford family, by the late twentieth century had become an advocate of liberal causes which it fostered in part by funding public-interest groups. Foundations' role in providing seed money was even more crucial, however, than their funding. What were their motives? Foundations were motivated in part by concern over the substantive concerns of liberal public-interest groups, such as protecting the environment, and in part by a concern to improve the quality and range of the entire interest-group system. Olson had identified a major shortcoming – the absence of groups that spoke up for common interests. Most important for our purposes, however, is the fact that the United States has generated a large and vibrant public-interest movement with large memberships, significant resources and a demonstrable capacity to make life in Washington difficult for business.

Regulation

One of the major ways in which business and government are connected in the United States is through the regulatory system. What is regulation? In brief, Congress usually passes legislation that commits government to a general goal, such as clean air or clean water, and commands an executive branch agency to turn this general commitment into a series of detailed requirements specifying how much of which pollutant will be tolerated in discharges into the atmosphere or water. The Administrative Procedures Act specifies an elaborate procedure for making these rules, providing numerous opportunities for public comment and criticism as well as review by the courts. If a corporation fails to comply with a regulation, the agency may levy sometimes very heavy fines through civil procedures that again are quite elaborate and provide many opportunities for review by the courts.

All advanced industrialized societies have some form of regulation. The regulatory system in the USA, however, is distinctive in surprising ways. In sharp contrast with the image of the United States as a capitalist heaven, most scholars have seen American regulation as more legalistic and adversarial than regulation in other countries.[36] US business and regulatory agencies have been more frequently in conflict over both the content of regulations and the ways in which they are enforced than regulators and business executives in countries such as Sweden and Britain. How can it be that relations between business and regulators can be more adversarial than in social democratic Sweden? Many different explanations have been advanced. Some contend that the United States has an inherently adversarial culture, which inhibits cooperation. Such explanations are hard to reconcile with the many complaints that were heard in the 1950s and 1960s that regulators were so closely tied to businesses they supervised that they were in effect 'captured'. Others have contended that people attracted to working in regulatory agencies tend for personal reasons or ideology to have an instinctive distrust of business. More convincing explanations derive from the law and politics. In the aftermath of numerous complaints in the 1960s of excessive business influence over regulatory agencies, Congress adopted regulatory laws going beyond preceding requirements (for example under the Administrative Procedures Act). These strategies to promote stricter regulation included specifying the content of regulations more closely and, most importantly of all, providing opportunities for public-interest groups to challenge regulations or their enforcement if it fell short of the targets that Congress had set. If regulatory agencies became stricter and more adversarial after the 1960s, this reflected exactly what Congress had attempted to achieve.

Politics has also affected the behaviour of regulatory agencies. Although generalizations about the character of the American regulatory regime are interesting, there is always the danger that they will suggest too much continuity and too little politics in the process. The style and approach of regulatory agencies has varied noticeably in Washington depending on the political balance of power. The tendency of regulatory agencies to be adversarial and confrontational reflected the strength of liberals in the late 1960s and 1970s. Studies of regulatory agencies such as the Federal Trade Commission (FTC), a consumer protection agency, suggest that an increase in Republican strength on Senate committees at the end of the 1970s prompted a speedy policy change in the direction of greater sympathy to business.[37] Most importantly, the election of Ronald Reagan as president in 1980 was followed by a sharp change toward more pro-business policies by agencies such as the Occupational Safety and Health Agency (OSHA) and the Environmental Protection Agency (EPA). Similar changes took place after the election of George W. Bush in 2000. The election of President Clinton in 1992, however, did not result in a clear switch back to stricter regulation. The administration instead explored new forms of regulation that might at least achieve a compromise between regulators, public-interest groups, unions and business. Whether these attempts to create more collaborative 'win–win' approaches could survive the arrival of the George W. Bush administration remains to be seen. Clearly some conservative business executives hoped that the new administration would roll back regulations rather than reforming their implementation. Business lobbyists were given privileged access to task forces, led by Vice President Cheney, that developed the new administration's policies on the environment and energy. Numerous Bush administration policies seemed to show a pronounced tilt towards business and away from environmentalists. Prominent examples included opening the Arctic National Wildlife Reserve (ANWR) to oil exploration, refusing to ratify the Kyoto Protocol on combating global warming and refusing to raise the mileage requirements for motor vehicles (the Corporate Average Fuel Efficiency or CAFÉ standards).

Conclusions

It should be clear by now that, not surprisingly, the vision of the United States as a business heaven is too simple. Business has enjoyed considerable advantages in the United States. It has never confronted a powerful socialist movement that has denied the very legitimacy of capitalism. Business has enjoyed considerable structural advantages, confronting numerous fragmented governments that it can play off against each other in a quest for more favourable treatment in return for subsidies or tax allowances. Yet business has not lacked political opponents notably labour unions and, in recent decades, the best organized public-interest movements in the world. The outcome of the struggles between business and its critics has varied. As David Vogel has argued, the power of business in the United States is not stable but varies.[38] Periods in which business was unchallenged, such as the 1950s, were followed by periods such as the late 1960s and early 1970s when environmental groups and other critics of business were very successful. The most notable development of the last few decades has been the way in which business, feeling unable to rely on the structural advantages attributed to it by social scientists, has felt obliged to emulate the techniques pioneered by interest groups such as unions and environmentalists. Once business mobilized, it possessed formidable advantages compared with other interests. The scale of business lobbying in Washington or, for that matter, business's payments to political parties and candidates for office, dwarfs those of any other interest group except for labour unions. Nonetheless, the very scale of the political efforts that business makes (not always successfully) to influence public policy suggests that the image of the United States as an uncomplicated heaven for capitalists is overdrawn. Business would not bother to try so hard if its position were unassailable.

The turn of the century witnessed a remarkable change in discussions of the relationship between business and government in the United States. For much of the 1970s and 1980s, the loosely-organized, ill-coordinated relationship between business and government in the USA had been the subject of much criticism. Admirers of neocorporatism or of the government-led growth policies of Japan and France had lamented the inability of American government, except in the area of defence contracting, to establish close partnerships with American business. The dynamic performance of the American economy in the last decade of the twentieth century prompted reconsideration of these criticisms. It became more common to contrast the United States favourably with the allegedly sclerotic European economies. The United States, it was argued, had been able to achieve higher growth and employment levels than Europe precisely because it had avoided large-scale government, rigidities in labour markets caused by excessive regulation and by powerful unions, and industrial policies that shored up declining sunset industries at the expense of growth sectors in the sunrise industries.

We have as yet little completed research on what the role of the American state was in achieving the boom of the 1990s. Perhaps the boom was in part the result of government policies, including defence related activities. The internet itself, for example, grew out of Department of Defense planning for communications systems in the event of a nuclear war. Perhaps the long-established American practice of investing heavily in higher education paid off in the era of a knowledge economy. Possibly the American state, belying its reputation for weakness, was unusually capable of withstanding demands for help and assistance from declining industries whose survival on economic life-support would have slowed economic growth. European attempts to support troubled steel mills, British attempts to keep alive its declining automobile industry and Japanese efforts to support inefficient retailing and agricultural units were all more determined than the assistance that was given to declining industries in the USA. Assistance to declining industries reduces growth both by imposing costs on more successful industries in the form of taxation to pay for subsidies and by locking economic resources, such as labour and capital, into low-growth, low-productivity activities. In this view, therefore, the American triumph was achieved not so much by successful state promotion of economic growth as much as by state avoidance of activities harmful to growth. Clearly, this debate cannot be settled here. Economists continue to disagree about the economic causes of the Great Boom of the 1990s, let alone government's role in bringing them about. Given the frequency with which the 'American model' is celebrated as a means of bringing about faster growth and prosperity, it would be useful to specify its nature. Unfortunately, the American model and the reasons for its apparent success are more complicated and confusing than many suppose.

Infectious Greed[39]

The success of the American economy in the 1990s was often interpreted within the United States and by conservatives elsewhere as demonstrating the total superiority of the American variant of capitalism. In this view, the genius of the United States had been to allow market forces to work more freely than in Japan or Europe. Government provided a strong framework of laws and regulations that collectively constituted the market but avoided detailed intervention in the market it had created. One of the lessons that

American advisers taught countries transitioning from communism to capitalism was that effective markets required a framework of firmly enforced laws and regulations. It would have been well for outspoken proponents of the American system to recall the Biblical warning: 'Pride goes before destruction and a haughty spirit before a fall.'[40]

It came as a considerable embarrassment, therefore, when in the early years of the new century a succession of scandals proved that the market creating and sustaining laws of the United States were not nearly as effective as had been supposed. The unexpected bankruptcies of high profile firms such as Enron and Worldcom posed questions about why accountants had certified reports indicating that these firms were in good health. The global accountancy firm, Arthur Andersen, received a devastating blow to its prestige and viability because it had given Enron a clean bill of health. As this book was going to press, a number of investigations were beginning into what had gone wrong. Popular concern about the consequences of a plummeting stock market was reinforced by anger as the public learned about the schemes that top executives had used to enrich themselves. The last two decades of the twentieth century had seen an enormous increase in the share of national income and wealth going to the very highest paid. A combination of increased income and tax changes in their favour resulted in the after tax incomes of the highest per cent of Americans rising by 119.7 per cent between 1977 and 1999; the after tax incomes of the poorest fifth (quintile) of Americans rose by 12 per cent and the incomes of the middle quintile by 3.1 per cent in the same period.[41] These vast gains for the very highest paid turned out to be linked to the financial crisis that hit in 2002. Highly paid executives had increasingly come to be paid in part in stock options – the opportunity to buy some of their business's stock at prevailing prices. If the stock price rose, the executives could exercise the option, sell the stock at the prevailing higher price and make a fortune. This gave executives an enormous incentive to inflate the value of their stock, which at least some did through dubious accounting methods. Accountants who, after all, are hired by the executives they inspect and who have increasingly diversified into selling services such as acting as consultants to the firms they inspect, had important incentives to remain silent about these practices.

It soon became apparent that far from being aberrations, the accounting abuses brought to light by the collapse of Enron were the tip of a very large iceberg. Moreover, not only were firms such as Enron very well connected politically (as we have seen) but newspapers were full of stories that many leading political figures had themselves while in business profited from some of the business practices now being criticized. It was widely alleged that President Bush himself had made over $800,000 some years earlier by buying stock in the company for which he worked with money loaned to him by the firm and selling it two months before the stock fell heavily when the firm reported disappointing figures.

Fearing a storm of protest from middle class Americans who feared the impact of the collapse of the stock market on their pension funds and savings, politicians rushed to compete with each other in the length of prison sentences they proposed for executives who misbehaved in the future. Arguably, however, the crisis pointed to deeply rooted failings in American capitalism. The first is that American firms have always been much more focused than, for example, German or Japanese firms on the price of their stock in the short term. The greed of executives who tried to artificially inflate the price of their stock merely reinforced this long-term problem. The second is that American capitalism has long seemed overly dependent on laws and regulations to ensure acceptable behaviour. Laws and regulations must always be part of securing acceptable conduct. Yet the capacity of law to regulate behaviour is limited; law enforcement works only so long as the authorities can concentrate on the minority who are lawbreakers because the majority are not. Even prior to the stock market crash of 2002, the United States had more comprehensive, intrusive and punitive laws governing financial dealings than other capitalist countries. The demands for more laws and even stricter punishments seemed to overlook this fact. What the United States lacked was a business community that was prepared to refrain from exploiting market opportunities to the full, in order to serve the longer term interests of the economy and society. The financial crisis of 2002 was therefore a salutary reminder that American capitalism has its failings as well as its strengths.

3

Government and Politics in Britain

Few countries have experienced such instability in the relationship between business and government as Britain. British governments since the Second World War have attempted to borrow from almost all approaches and models practised in other countries. A significant swathe of industries, such as steel, railways and coal mining, were taken into government ownership in the 1940s but were privatized in the 1980s. Neocorporatist partnerships between business, labour and government were attempted by both Conservative and Labour governments in the 1960s and 1970s, only to be abandoned within a few years. The strategy was explicitly repudiated by Margaret Thatcher's government in the 1980s which instead emphasized a market-orientated approach. Similarly, attempts by governments to coordinate strategies for growth (what has been termed 'indicative planning', for example in France) were started by a Conservative government, strengthened but then weakened by a Labour government in the 1960s and definitively ended by the Conservatives in the 1980s. Only since the Conservatives led by Margaret Thatcher gained power in 1979 has there been much continuity in relations between business and government in Britain. Thatcher's radical policies of privatization, reducing direct government involvement in industry, shifting away from fiscal to monetary policy and striving for competitiveness[1] were continued not only by her Conservative successor as prime minister, John Major, but, more strikingly, also by the Labour government of Tony Blair. Perhaps at last British policy had entered an era of stability.

The Context – Economic Policy, 1945–78

The instability in economic policy and business–government relations in Britain reflects in large part the struggle that the country has
faced to retain its economic standing combined with the fact that
policies (at least until the 1980s) had to be acceptable to unions as
well as business. British economic performance was notably worse
than its neighbours'. In consequence, Britain gradually fell down
the international league table of per capita income and as Table 4
shows is now less well off than major European rivals on a per
capita basis. Whether or not the policies followed since 1979 have
arrested, or even reversed, Britain's comparative decline is a controversial topic to which we shall return in the next section. It
should always be remembered, however, that Britain's problem
was *comparative*, not absolute, decline. Indeed, the British have
experienced a dramatic increase in their standard of living. All
sorts of things once rare or the preserve of upper income groups –
house ownership, car ownership, central heating and overseas
vacations, to name but a few – are now commonplace. Britain's
problem was that the tide of affluence was flowing markedly more
slowly than in other advanced industrialized countries. Although
Britain's decline was comparative, it became ever more painful
and in periods of global economic crisis (such as the 1970s) threatened to turn into absolute decline.

Policy-makers were genuinely puzzled about which policies
might best reverse comparative decline. Would government intervention to restructure failing businesses (as tried by Labour governments in the late 1960s and Conservatives in the early 1970s)
revive them, or merely funnel public money into dying 'lame
ducks'? Was government management of the economy using the
Keynesian techniques of varying government spending and taxation responsible for the long period of steady (if slow) economic
growth and high employment, or was it responsible for destabiliz-
ing the economy and increasing inflation? Were British unions
a major cause of poor economic performance because of their
resistance to technological change and employers' fears of strikes,
or were they the victims of slow growth themselves? Was the problem fundamentally – as the American Martin Weiner expounded[2]
to Margaret Thatcher's approval – one of attitudes so that slow
growth reflected the disdain that the British (or, at least, the

English) felt for manufacturing? If so, could governments do anything at all to change the prevailing culture? Or were the problems
of British industry due to the peculiar relationship between manufacturing and financial institutions in Britain (discussed further
below), which arguably starved British manufacturers of investment? No consensus existed on the answers to these questions,
leaving policy-makers perplexed about what the right approach
might be.

There was agreement, however, that any policy had to fall
within certain political parameters to be acceptable. The 'postwar
consensus' that prevailed from the 1940s until the 1970s rested on
a number of firm beliefs about the relationship between business,
society and government. The government was responsible for
maintaining full employment. A group of basic industries would
remain in government ownership. A comprehensive welfare state
would provide workers with a strong safety net. Government
would not intervene in the affairs of unions, including their
bargaining with employers. A government that ignored these
unwritten but binding commitments was asking for trouble. The
Conservatives, in particular, were under strong pressure to observe
the consensus. Remembered by many as the party that dominated
British politics during the Great Depression in the 1930s, Conservatives felt that their success was dependent on proving their commitment to the postwar consensus. Only as Britain's problems
progressively worsened did both Conservatives and Labour step
away from the consensus. In the 1960s both Conservative and
Labour governments intervened in industrial relations, trying to
maintain competitiveness by imposing limits on pay increases. The
Labour government also attempted (but then abandoned) a plan to
reform the unions; the Conservatives tried unsuccessfully in the
1970s, but successfully under Thatcher.

The intense sense of crisis in 1970s Britain made it possible for
politicians to move away from the previously controlling postwar
consensus. One important element was industrial unrest, particularly in essential services such as water, electricity supply and
hospitals. Roaring inflation contributed to talk of Britain becoming 'ungovernable'.[3] Why was the crisis so intense? In brief, the
long, gradual decline of Britain's comparative economic fortunes
was accentuated by developments in the world economy. The rise
of highly successful exporting countries, first Japan and later the

'Tigers', including South Korea, naturally placed greatest pressure on the weakest of the established centres of manufacturing, such as Britain, much as wolf packs pick off the weakest, straggling animals first. Another factor was the 'oil shocks' when OPEC was able, twice in the decade, to create artificial shortages and the resulting sharp price increases created problems for all advanced industrialized countries. Again, however, the crises had their sharpest impact on the weakest economies such as Britain's. The rapidly worsening economic conditions seemed to demonstrate the futility of all the policies that had been applied to arrest the country's comparative decline. Radical policy change began under the 1974–79 Labour government which abandoned the belief that government could guarantee full employment and switched the emphasis to monetary policy. It had done so with the pound collapsing on the foreign exchanges, the International Monetary Fund (IMF) insisting on changes as the condition for a loan to bale Britain out, inflation soaring and the authority of government itself in question. Policy changes that Labour accepted hesitantly and reluctantly under the pressure of crisis were adopted with enthusiasm by the Conservatives under Thatcher once they came to power.

The long period of almost desperate experimentation in policy predictably led different people to different conclusions. For many on the left, financial crises in the 1960s and 1970s had destroyed otherwise promising policies. The National Plan, Britain's brief experiment with indicative planning, had been destroyed in the 1960s by unsuccessful attempts to avoid devaluing the pound. It would have been wise, these critics contended, to abandon the pound and save the Plan. Attempts to use neocorporatist approaches and govern in partnership with the unions (and, to a lesser degree, with business organizations) had been disrupted by the financial crises of the 1970s that culminated in the need to seek emergency help from the IMF. Following its normal procedures, the IMF provided help with tight strings attached. The British government was required to make cuts in its expenditure plans, cuts that many members of the government, including moderate Labour politicians such as Anthony Crosland, found deeply painful. The conditions for the IMF loan ended the attempt to use neocorporatist techniques and govern in partnership with the unions.

Others concluded that these experiences showed that both indicative planning and attempts to develop neocorporatist approaches were ill-suited to British conditions. Whereas these approaches might have worked for other countries, they did not work for Britain. Both business organizations (as we shall see later) and the unions were incapable in practice of playing the roles assigned to them in both indicative planning and neocorporatism. The problem was not, as many commentators supposed at the time, that economic groups were too strong in Britain but that they were too weak. The Trades Union Congress (TUC) could not control individual unions, and individual unions often could not control their own members. An agreement by the TUC, often at the time called a 'solemn and binding undertaking', to limit wage increases had no serious impact on the behaviour of individual unions or, at the local level, their members. An agreement by the CBI to increase investment had generally not influenced the behaviour of individual businesses. Neither unions nor business organizations could make attempts at indicative planning or neocorporatism actually work.[4] The failure of neocorporatism and indicative planning led many to conclude that Thatcher was correct in her claims that 'there is no alternative' for Britain to seeking improved economic performance from greater efficiency through market mechanisms and shrinking the role of government. Britain's location in the international economy and the structure of its internal political economy precluded the successful adoption of any other strategy.

In the midst of the flux of changing policies, certain enduring structural characteristics of British business stood out and had major policy implications.[5]

The first, and arguably most important, was the division between finance and manufacturing.[6] In contrast to Germany, where individual banks have a close relationship with particular manufacturing companies, the British financial sector has long had a distant relationship with manufacturing. British financiers traditionally had a global perspective, lending to other countries and foreign enterprises. The 'City' (of London), as the financial sector is known colloquially, has not felt that its interests and those of manufacturing are related. On the contrary, the interests of the City and manufacturing diverged on some important policy issues, particularly the question of what exchange rate governments should attempt to maintain. The City tended to benefit from either a strong pound, which maximized its ability to invest in other countries, or from stability, which encouraged foreign confidence in the pound (and hence the City) for investments. Manufacturing, in contrast, needed above all to be competitive and required revisions of the exchange rate to maintain that competitiveness. As British inflation rates tended to be slightly higher (and in the 1970s, significantly higher) than other manufacturing countries' rates, the need for adjustments in exchange rates was considerable. British financiers tended to look with scepticism on proposals for investment in British manufacturing. Poor management and difficult labour conditions made British manufacturing enterprises less profitable investments than foreign enterprises or assets, such as property. British manufacturing industry was characterized by underinvestment, even while Britain was one of the largest overseas investors in economies such as the United States'.

Second, Britain's openness and vulnerability to the world economy was considerable. Britain's economy was too small and too dependent on trade to ignore problems of competitiveness. The 'balance of payments' problem – the difference between Britain's exports (including services) or net receipts in 'invisible earnings' from investments and its imports and payments to foreign countries – preoccupied British governments. Both Conservative and Labour governments pursued policies to tackle the balance-of-payments problem that caused them great political difficulty and cost them popularity, at least until the 1970s. A related problem was that when British governments were committed to maintaining a more-or-less fixed value for the pound against other currencies, they could be forced into sharply deflationary economic policies in order to convince investors at home and abroad that the value of the pound would indeed be guaranteed and not reduced in value against other currencies – a strategy known as devaluation. All Labour governments in this period faced the problem of maintaining confidence in the value of the pound, and were forced to make major changes to their policies in order to boost confidence.

The problem of managing the exchange rate (and therefore the balance of payments) seemed to disappear in the early 1970s with the advent of floating exchange rates by which governments allowed markets to set exchange rates. However, the problem resurfaced briefly, but with important consequences, in the 1990s. Thatcher had been persuaded to take Britain into the exchange rate mechanism (ERM) which fixed the value of the currencies of the European Union against each other. The Conservative government of John Major experienced a massive exchange-rate crisis in 1992 that completely destroyed its credibility in economic policy. Committed to maintaining the value of the pound at its set value within the ERM, the Major government found itself unable to convince investors that it could do so, even with help from other governments. After speculators, such as George Soros, had made a fortune betting on the inevitability of a devaluation, Britain was ignominiously obliged to leave the ERM. The reputation of the recently re-elected government was in tatters and the longstanding opinion of the Conservatives that they were the party better able to manage the economy was destroyed. Long before globalization was commonly discussed, therefore, British governments found that their goals and policies could be destroyed by international economic and financial circumstances. It is indeed ironic in view of all the trouble that foreign-exchange crises caused British governments that Conservatives fought to maintain the pound rather than adopting the euro.

Thatcherism, 1979 Onwards

No one would deny the importance of the shifts in policy that occurred during the prime ministership of Margaret Thatcher (1979–90), were continued by the government of John Major (1990–97) and consolidated under the Labour government led by Tony Blair. Some of Thatcher's policy changes had been (as noted above) anticipated on a small scale by the preceding Labour government. However, Thatcher clarified and intensified these changes and made new ones that had a profound impact. Several policy changes were central to Thatcherism.

The first was the withdrawal of government from direct involvement in business. Government-owned businesses were privatized, starting with the most potentially profitable, such as gas, electricity and telecommunications, and ending during Major's government with the most difficult to sell, loss-making enterprises, such as railways. Government also gradually drew back from subsidizing, reorganizing and directing privately-owned business, as both Labour and Conservative governments had attempted in previous decades. This process was not abrupt and simple; Thatcher propped up the declining British car manufacturing industry during her first years in office and, for much of her time in office, aided the coal-mining industry. Nonetheless, there was a sea change in expectations about government involvement in industry.

Second, a series of industrial relations (labour) laws shifted the balance of power against unions and in favour of management. Requirements for ballots of members before strikes and bans on 'secondary action' in support of another union helped to transform Britain from one of the most strike-prone economies to one of the least. Admittedly, economic change and high unemployment also weakened the unions. However, Thatcher's industrial relations laws did make a difference, as demonstrated by the unions' intense opposition to them.

Third, Thatcher developed a strategy to make Britain the least regulated, more market-driven of the major European economies. Restrictions on the ability of employers to 'hire and fire', for example, were much less onerous in Britain than in countries such as France. Thatcher's famous Bruges speech in 1986 is often remembered as simply 'anti European'. More importantly, however, it set forth an ideological difference between Britain and continental Europe. 'We have not rolled back the frontiers of the state in Britain only to see them advance in Europe', Thatcher proclaimed. Although her Conservative and Labour successors have used less strident language, they have substantively agreed with this position. The British industrial strategy was to attract investment by being a flexible market economy. Britain did, indeed, receive a disproportionately large share of direct foreign investment in the European Union, although the degree to which flexible labour-market strategies caused this has been debated.

Finally, Thatcher was clearer and more forceful than the preceding Labour government in repudiating government responsibility for full employment and in placing greater emphasis on monetary policy.

Tony Blair's Labour government left many of the policies adopted by Thatcher and continued by Major intact. There were some concessions to unions, such as the introduction of a (low) minimum wage. The framework of labour law that Thatcher had developed, however, was retained. The Labour government showed not the slightest interest in restoring either the powers of unions at the workplace or the privileged role in policy-making they had enjoyed under previous Labour governments. Blair strengthened the commitment to using monetary techniques to manage the economy by giving the Bank of England operational independence in its pursuit of economic stability; governments could no longer order the Bank to shift monetary policy, including interest rates, in ways that would be helpful to their electoral prospects. Labour never contemplated taking the privatized industries back into government ownership and even undertook modest extensions of privatization, for example of air traffic control. The government promoted 'public private partnerships' (PPPs) bringing private capital into public-sector projects, such as improving hospitals and the London Underground. The government pledged not to increase either government expenditure or income taxes beyond the levels set by the Conservatives during their first years in office. In fact, government expenditure as a percentage of GDP declined slightly during the first years of Labour government and the Chancellor of the Exchequer, Gordon Brown, became the first Labour holder of that office to cut rather than increase income tax. The government's performance in economic policy was highly regarded, earning Labour for the first time ever the reputation of being more competent in this sphere than the Conservatives. Perhaps more importantly for our purposes, Blair's acceptance of key components of Thatcherism marked its ultimate consolidation.

It would be incorrect, however, to assume that policies such as privatization have simply ended or sharply curtailed the impact of government on business. In general, privatization was followed by the creation of regulatory bodies that were intended to protect consumers from exploitation by what are in effect privately-owned monopolies. Just as Americans had long expected to be protected by regulatory agencies, now the British came to rely on inelegantly named new agencies such as OFGAS (covering natural gas). The electricity and gas industries are now regulated by a combined agency, OFGEM. OFWAT covers water supply industry. As in the United States, regulators were often accused of being too sympathetic to the companies they regulated rather than their customers. It also became apparent that the political imperative to make government-owned industries saleable had prompted the Conservative governments to privatize industries structured in a way that was more favourable to shareholders than customers; particular concerns were expressed about the way in which the railways had been privatized.

One further background factor must be mentioned. The European Union took on greater and greater significance for British industry. When Britain entered what is now the EU in 1973, it had become clear that British trade in goods was largely now with Europe; most British exports went to Europe now rather than to 'deep water' destinations such as Latin America. This fact was one of the most powerful arguments for joining the EU. The large European market would provide British industry both with opportunities and with a 'cold shower' of competition that would improve its performance. However, since the 1970s, 'Europe' has become an ever-more-present institutional fact for British industry. As Majone has noted,[7] the EU has expanded its authority by issuing regulations and many of these regulations, for example on the environment, affect industry directly. The EU makes trade policy on behalf of Britain and its other members and the campaign to create a truly integrated European market (the Single European market) required a blizzard of regulations from the EU in Brussels to sweep away national barriers to trade. It was a debatable question by the early twenty-first century whether the EU in Brussels or the government in London was a more significant source of regulations affecting British industry, for example, in areas such as environmental protection. An official in the Environment Agency told the author in 2002, 'It is Brussels, not Whitehall or Westminster, that is the driver of change in this area now.' Two very different scenarios for the future impact of Europe on British industry have been suggested.

The first is that Britain, as the least regulated economy, will pull other European countries in its direction. Afraid of losing investment to Britain, other members of the EU will be obliged to move their own policies in a market-oriented direction. Regulations protecting, for example, the rights of workers will be relaxed in a 'race to the bottom' to be most attractive to investors. Wolfgang Streeck[8] argued that in the contest for the future of Europe, the former head of the EU Commission, Jacques Delors, who favoured stricter regulations, had lost and Thatcher had won; Europe as a whole would become more Thatcherite. The other scenario is that members of the EU with stricter regulations, such as France and Germany, will force Britain to match those regulations in order to reduce the competitive disadvantage that results from their costs. Struggles to oblige Britain to adopt policies such as stricter limits on maximum hours of work are part of this process.

The Organization of British Policy:
An 'Anglo-Saxon' Model?

The emphasis on market forces in British policy in recent decades has encouraged a tendency to group Britain with the United States. Certainly there are similarities. Companies are generally separated from banks and other financial institutions, and not linked to them as in Germany or Japan. Managers are acutely aware that they must satisfy shareholders or they will be removed or will be subject to a hostile takeover bid. The harder question to answer is whether the structure and standing of business interest groups in Britain is at all similar to those in the United States.

Studies of the relationship between interest groups and government in Britain have long emphasized several features of governance practices in Britain that have favoured interest groups, or at least those representing sectors of society, such as business, whose cooperation governments have sought.[9] Government departments were expected to consult with interest groups. Favoured interest groups which enjoyed 'insider status' were given the opportunity to comment on policy issues and proposals in confidence before they were made public and it became harder for the government to modify them. In return, interest groups often carried out tasks that were useful for government, thus saving it the expense and trouble of conducting the task itself. Perhaps the most striking examples of helpful activity by interest groups are the child protection and animal welfare activities of the National Society for the Prevention of Cruelty to Children (NSPCC) and the Royal Society for the Prevention of Cruelty to Animals (RSPCA). Both maintain quasi-governmental inspectorates that are the leading enforcement organizations for laws against cruelty to children and animals.

A particularly close partnership existed between the Ministry of Agriculture, Fisheries and Food (MAFF) (since 2001, Department for Environment Food and Rural Affairs (DEFRA)) and the National Farmers' Union (NFU).[10] Generally, government departments preferred to have one interest group per sector which was clearly identified as its representative. For much of the era after the Second World War, departments and ministries such as MAFF have taken clear action to discourage competitors to the dominant interest group from gaining stature because it was advantageous to have a single interest group to do the work of balancing contending interests within an industry or, in the case of the peak association for business, between different industries. An interest group that dominated its field was also more likely to provide help in gathering information and assisting in governance than an interest group struggling to compete with others. Government departments generally favoured and promoted the presence of a single, monopolistic interest group with which they could consult and cooperate closely. It was clear that the business interest groups have shared fully in this practice of close relations between interest groups and government. Links between trade associations and government departments, in particular the Department of Trade and Industry (DTI), are extremely close.

This practice seems so much at odds with the picture of the United States, presented in the previous chapter, with its numerous overlapping and competing interest groups that one might wonder how the idea of there being an Anglo-Saxon model ever arose. The answer is in large part because of the character of British business organizations.

At first glance, British business organizations are impressive. The Confederation of British Industry (CBI) has been recognized as the spokesman for industry since its creation in the 1960s (although as we shall see below, its status has been less secure in recent years). Indeed, as already noted, the creation of the CBI was encouraged by the Labour governments of 1964–70 that sought a reliable spokesman for business, particularly in the indicative planning process.[11] The CBI has regular and privileged access to all government departments whose work affects its members: the Treasury as well as the Department of Trade and Industry. Its staffs include respected economists and other experts, and its pronouncements on the state of the economy and problems facing business are treated with respect by the media as well as by politicians. Compared to the American business organizations, such as the National Association of Manufacturers, that are locked in a struggle for status and influence with rival interest groups, the CBI seems to occupy a lofty and secure position. Similarly, most industries have a trade association to speak for them that is untroubled by challenges or competition from rivals. The trade associations have also had privileged access to the DTI although they would not normally seek access to other government departments. Trade associations would be on the list of organizations to be consulted about policy proposals that civil servants maintain and use. The CBI and trade associations are also linked to their counterparts in the European Union through general employers' organizations and EU trade associations.

Why, then, has it been suggested that British business organizations are at all similar in nature to American ones? The answer is in large part because of the distribution of power within them. In Britain as in the United States, authority resides in the individual company and not the trade association or the peak association (CBI). Unlike the situation in Germany, trade associations are rarely responsible for negotiating wage agreements with unions; industrial relations are handled much more at the level of the individual enterprise. Similarly, again in contrast to their German counterparts, trade associations have few governance responsibilities; they are not involved in running health-care or apprenticeship programmes.

In countries that have a genuinely powerful peak association, its membership is generally composed of trade associations. Companies are usually members of trade associations, which in turn are members of the peak association. It is expected, and possibly even legally required, that individual companies join their trade association. The peak association therefore has tremendous authority and can claim to speak for industry as a whole, its views and interests having been defined and codified first at the level of the individual industry by the trade association and then at the level of the whole industry by the peak association.

In contrast, the membership of the CBI is an uneasy mix of trade associations and individual companies. As in the United States, there is no legal or even moral requirement for individual companies to belong to their trade association or the CBI. Individual companies, as in the United States, can therefore exert leverage by threatening to leave if they are not totally satisfied by policies that are adopted. In the early 1980s, after the then Director General of the CBI had threatened a 'bare knuckle fight' if policies of the Thatcher government (such as keeping the pound at an uncompetitively high level) that were harming manufacturing industry were maintained, several companies having close relations with the Conservatives resigned or threatened to resign from the CBI. The CBI soon backed off.

An important consequence of this distribution of power for business organizations has been that they lack the authority to commit their members. Governments that have made agreements with business interest groups such as trade associations or with the CBI have been disappointed to discover that those agreements are not necessarily honoured by individual businesses. In the mid 1960s, for example, after a National Plan was negotiated between business, unions and government to provide for sustained economic expansion, the CBI's commitments on increased investment did not translate into actual increases in investment by individual companies. They continued to base their decisions on anticipated levels of return, not the undertakings of those who represented them. The same was true for trade associations. Their limitations therefore reduced the incentives for governments to negotiate with them and to make concessions.

Modes of Business Representation

So far, we have discussed the representation of business in Britain largely in terms of the links between trade and peak associations and government departments. That emphasis is appropriate because in Britain (as in most parliamentary systems) the power of the 'executive' part of government makes it the natural focus for interest groups, including business. The best time to influence policy and legislation is when it is being drafted in a government department, not when it is under consideration in the Commons where the government's disciplined majority is likely to ensure its passage and the government will not wish to be embarrassed by withdrawing or modifying its proposals. British interest groups that are afforded the opportunity for 'insider status' – having friendly, confidential discussions on policy proposals before they are announced – are almost always well advised to take it.

Yet business representation in Britain is by no means limited to confidential and cosy chats between its interest-group officials and civil servants. Since the late nineteenth century, the Conservative Party has been considered the natural party of business. Although British levels of campaign spending are puny by American standards, British campaign finance laws have, until recently, also been very permissive. Companies have been allowed to contribute funds from their regular accounts to political parties, and only since the 1960s have they even been required to disclose these contributions. Following the wave of scandals in the declining years of Conservative government in the 1990s, the Nolan Committee on Standards in Public Life suggested limits on contributions, as well as requiring them to be reported. Until the late 1990s when a few companies made headlines by giving money to Labour, business contributions invariably went to the Conservatives. This is not to say that the Conservatives always adopted policies favourable to business. As we saw above, the CBI in the early 1980s thought that some of Thatcher's policies had a pronounced and negative effect on industry. The anti-European policies of the Conservatives under William Hague worried many industrialists who felt that continued non-adoption of the euro by Britain harmed their prospects for competing in Europe. The industrialists knew that leaving the EU – as some Conservatives favoured – would have been a complete catastrophe, given the importance of its markets for them. On many other issues however, such as taxation and labour laws, the Conservatives have clearly pursued policies that business executives favour. The difficulty for business has been to preserve adequate distance from the Conservatives to have credibility in its dealings with a Labour government. Organizations such as the CBI carefully avoid any overt ties to the Conservatives. An increasing proportion of companies in Britain also refrain from making campaign contributions. The Conservatives were always dependent financially on a limited set of businesses, historically particularly in brewing and construction, which gave the largest contributions. Their financial dependency on a limited number of companies and industries has increased in recent years. The assiduous courting of business by Labour under the leadership of Tony Blair must also have worried the Conservatives. Although there were several damaging scandals associated with gifts from rich business people to Labour, the party did receive large and entirely legal contributions from firms such as Sainsburys (the supermarket chain) and Marks & Spencer (the high-street retail chain). Indeed, allegations of 'sleaze', previously common in connection with contributions to the Conservative Party, arose around some of Labour's contributions from businesses such as the Enron Corporation and the owner of an international steel firm that enlisted Tony Blair's help in buying a steel-mill in Romania. As the Conservatives depend on business contributions for over half of their income, Labour's increasing success in attracting business money must have worried them deeply.

Business organizations do not neglect Parliament entirely. Trade associations and the CBI regularly brief Members of Parliament and appear before their Select Committees. Trade associations also take advantage of the rather peculiar procedure under which interest groups can pay Members of Parliament to represent them in Parliament so long as the relationship is fully acknowledged. A Parliamentary strategy for influence is, if handled with care, a valuable supplement to an 'insider' strategy. It can be very useful if its backbenchers start to express concern about the government's policies in line with the opinions being expressed in private by the CBI or trade associations.

Individual companies also employ their own lobbyists. There has been a trend towards companies having their own political representation rather than relying on business organizations. Individual companies have also retained the services of contract lobbyists to forge links with parliament. Contract lobbyists are not nearly as numerous or as well paid as in the United States. Again, however, they are growing in number and stature as we shall discuss later. Sometimes companies have also used public relations consultants to promote their cause with the general public.

In practice what weights do British businesses place on these different modes of representation? In an important book, Neil Mitchell answers this question using interesting and illuminating information derived from a survey of British businesses and their organizations.[12] Reflecting the more limited power of British business interest groups than initial appearances might suggest, businesses were more likely to say that they were in contact with government directly (68 per cent) than through their trade association (46 per cent) or the CBI (24 per cent).[13] Rather surprisingly again, only 65 per cent expected that they would be generally in agreement with the CBI on disputes involving their firm.[14] However, businesses seemed to feel by and large that they had good opportunities to influence policy. Companies expected to be involved in discussions with government on proposed policy changes both when the policy was being discussed in principle and when it was being developed in detail; this was true almost as often under a Labour government, when 66 per cent of companies expected to be consulted on both principles and details of policies, as under a Conservative government when 71 per cent did.[15] Business organizations themselves continued to believe in the traditional 'insider group' tactics. By far the most commonly used for business organizations was meeting with civil servants (used by 86 per cent), followed by making written submissions (78 per cent), lobbying (57 per cent), meeting ministers (55 per cent) and staging a public relations campaign (21 per cent). When asked which tactics were effective, businesses placed meeting civil servants first, meeting ministers second and both far ahead of lobbying Parliament.

Trends since Thatcher

Neil Mitchell's survey was conducted midway through the 18-year period of Conservative government in the late twentieth century. That long period of Conservative government had important consequences for the relationship between business and government in Britain, along with much else in British politics and society. Thatcher herself had an intense suspicion of business executives who, as she saw it, sat around on consultative committees instead of getting out and making money. Although Britain has never been regarded as a highly corporatist country, Thatcherites somehow convinced themselves that the country's economic problems were caused by the impact of corporatism. In addition, as we have seen, relations between Thatcher and the Director General of the CBI were notably poor in the early 1980s. It was not surprising, therefore, that the Thatcher government followed a policy of deliberately weakening links between business organizations and government. The Department of Trade and Industry was reorganized in a way that made close partnerships between its divisions and trade associations less likely to occur. The CBI, almost as much as the Trades Union Congress (TUC) representing unions, found itself much less welcome in the corridors of power (including in the prime minister's office in 10 Downing Street) than it had been under the previous Labour government. A rival organization, the Institute of Directors, which was more in line with Thatcherite thinking, was given increased attention and status, a move that was very much at odds with the traditional practice of dealing with only one organization per sector.

The frictions between Thatcher and the CBI were partly due to her personality and views. These changes masked, however, a more fundamental shift in the standing of business organizations. Government simply needed business organizations less than in the past. During the 1960s and 1970s, for example, both Labour and Conservative governments had eagerly sought the assistance of business organizations and unions in implementing key economic policies. The National Economic Development Council (NEDC), a forum in which government, unions and business could meet to try to develop agreement on measures to promote economic growth, was created by the Conservatives in the early 1960s and clearly required the participation of business organizations. Subsidiary organizations (the 'little Neddies') were created on an industry-by-industry basis. Again, they required the cooperation of business organizations and unions. The development of the National Plan in the 1960s could be accomplished only with the help of business organizations, which explains why the CBI was created at that time with the active encouragement of a Labour government. The prices and incomes controls through which both Conservative and Labour governments attempted to limit inflation and balance-of-payments problems in the 1960s and 1970s could not be attempted without the participation of business organizations and unions. Thatcherism swept away all these policies. Prices and incomes policies contradicted her belief in market mechanisms. National economic planning was equally abhorrent. The NEDC lingered on, to be abolished during the Major government. Even if Thatcher and Major had been particularly fond of the CBI's officials, they would still have consulted them less than their predecessors, simply because they needed their help less.

The profound policy changes during the Thatcher/Major years had profound implications, therefore, for the relationship between business and government. Moreover, these changes seem to be permanent. The Labour government elected in 1997 under the leadership of Tony Blair based its economic policies on accepting these changes with minor modifications.[16] The Labour government promised explicitly not to reverse the approach to economic policy set by the Conservatives and in some respects (such as giving greater independence to the Bank of England) extended those policies further. The Blair government did show signs of wanting to work more closely with the CBI and trade associations in some areas. The minimum wage it introduced to Britain was set at a level determined by a commission which was dominated by the CBI and TUC. In an interesting innovation in environmental policy, the government introduced taxes on energy consumption (associated with generating greenhouse gases) that could be reduced for industrial sectors that negotiated an agreement to improve their environmental performance with the government. Crucially, however, the Blair government set its face against any return to prices and incomes policies used by past Labour governments – policies that require a close partnership between business, unions and government – and against any revival of attempts to create neocorporatism in Britain more generally. Thus, while the Labour government lacked the ideological antipathy to business organizations (or unions) of the Conservatives, it still had no need for a relationship as close as had existed in the pre-Thatcher era.

The Overall Power of Business in Britain

How powerful, then, is business in Britain? Answering that question requires attention to the strength of challenges business has faced, the strength of business organizations and the structural advantages business enjoys in Britain, as in all market economies.

Clearly, business in Britain has been faced with more developed challenges than in the United States. The Labour Party has shared power in the modern era with the Conservatives, holding office for twenty years of the period from 1945 until the end of the twentieth century. Until the early 1990s, the Labour Party was, in theory, committed to the creation of a socialist society. While this commitment was almost entirely theoretical, the party did contain an influential left wing, which held sharply anti-business attitudes explicitly rejecting the legitimacy of capitalism. Unions in Britain are much weaker today, recruiting only about 33 per cent of the workforce, than in the 1970s when just over half the workforce was unionized. However, British unions have organized a higher proportion of the workforce than in Germany, France, Italy, the United States or many other countries. Yet the problem that has faced British business – and the nation as a whole – is that this strength has never coalesced into a centralized, disciplined organization with which business or government could make compromises. British unions, unlike their American counterparts, were strong enough to be a problem but, unlike the far stronger unions of northern Europe, were not sufficiently strong to be capable of working in partnership with business and government. Unions in Sweden, for example, were far stronger than British unions, but this strength allowed them to play a much more constructive role in the Swedish economy. British unions always faced the risk that if they agreed to a moderate wage increase with their own employers, they would seem weak and ineffective compared to unions that insisted on large increases. The TUC lacked the authority that, for example, the Swedish and German union federations enjoy, to control the wage claims individual unions make. Moreover, power in many unions is decentralized so that if national leaders agreed to wage restraint, local shop stewards could step in and lead local campaigns for increases. Conservatives feared the power of unions. Ironically, the weakness of the TUC and central union leadership made it hard for their leaders to be economic statesmen.

Attitudes to business in Britain are complex. The British do not have the Americans' enthusiasm for capitalism as such, though as Richard Rose noted,[17] most of them see it as a practical necessity. Yet British culture, as Martin Weiner and Mrs Thatcher both noted with regret, places commercial success behind other values. Labour leaders were often torn between support for manufacturing industry, on which the prosperity of many of their supporters depended, and a desire to promote the rights of unions and equality in society as a whole, through measures that might impede economic growth. Even the Conservative Party historically contained a minority who were worried that the pursuit of profit might undermine British culture and national identity.

Many British Conservatives in the 1950s were convinced, for example, that commercial television would undermine culture and therefore supported a continuing monopoly for the BBC. It can even be argued that the British Right, unlike its counterpart in the United States, has sometimes held attitudes unsympathetic to capitalism because of the continuing influence of pre-industrial traditions. Only in the Thatcher era did this scepticism about commerce disappear from Conservative thinking.

The CBI and British trade associations appear at first glance to be impressive, at least compared with their American counterparts. However, in practice, British business organizations are less impressive than they seem. Not every industrial sector in Britain has a strong trade association. Neither trade associations nor the CBI have the authority to commit their members to agreements supposedly made on their behalf. Civil servants and ministers are more likely to be concerned about the limitations of British business organizations than impressed or intimidated by their strength. Moreover, business organizations have generally been seen as representing primarily manufacturing, not finance. This has been an important limitation on their standing. Financial institutions have had less formalized links to government and to the Conservative Party. As we saw earlier, the Bank of England has long considered one of its responsibilities to be representing the needs of the financial sector to government. As the Governor of the Bank of England has regular and easy access to one of the most powerful ministers (the Chancellor of the Exchequer) and the prime minister, this is a considerable advantage. Backbench Conservative MPs have also frequently been members of the boards of directors of companies in general and financial institutions in particular. While it would be naive to suppose that the behaviour and decisions of MPs are shaped by these links, their existence provides another means by which the concerns and interests of business can be communicated to government.

It would be hard to argue that, even before the Thatcher Revolution, British policy was systematically unsympathetic to the needs of business, even if it was ineffective in strengthening the British economy. How has British business avoided severe political setbacks if its interest group organizations are of limited strength and the apparent challenges from the unions and left wing of the Labour Party appear to be far greater than in, for example, the

United States? Once again, we must turn to the structural advantages that business enjoys and take care to distinguish between the power of *business* and the power of *business organizations.*

As we discussed in Chapter 1, business enjoys some structural advantage in any market economy. Ironically business in Britain has enjoyed particularly strong structural power because of the comparative weakness of the British economy until the Thatcher era. British governments until recently have been confronted by the constant struggle to improve Britain's comparative economic performance. The now familiar argument (discussed in Chapter 1) that the future employment and prosperity of the country as a whole is dependent on keeping business happy has had special resonance in Britain. British manufacturing has struggled throughout the modern era. Immediate pressing problems, such as the balance-of-payments crises, focused the attention of both Labour and Conservative governments on the question of how the British people could continue to enjoy a standard of living comparable to the rest of Europe. Arguments from business in favour of a policy that helped it grow – or against a policy that hindered it – were likely to be successful. Thus the British example is consistent with the argument that David Vogel makes about business in the United States; when the economy is weak, it may be more likely to influence public policy than when it is strong.[18]

The threat that, if business is treated badly, it will relocate elsewhere or, more probably, shift its investment into more sympathetic countries has had special significance for Britain. Britain has been in the ironic situation of having a relatively unsuccessful manufacturing sector and a highly-developed, sophisticated and internationally-minded financial sector. British bankers were lending money around the world in the nineteenth century, to Latin America and the United States as well as to parts of the British Empire. British investors who were prepared to shift money overseas in the quest for a higher rate of return have been well served by the financial sector. The threat of 'anti-business' policies or conditions resulting in a quick loss of funds overseas has been particularly real for Britain. Politicians have been well advised to avoid placing business under stress.

Might British business face the danger that Vogel sees for American business: that a period of greater success results in increased political vulnerability? The comparative performance of the British economy in the 1990s was much improved. Britain was no longer the economically sick man of Europe. Unemployment was lower than in other major European economies and, while economic growth was not stellar, it was often higher and always comparable to growth in France, Germany and Italy (see Appendix Table 4). Yet the danger that this would result in an upsurge of anti-business policies seemed unlikely while the memory of Britain's humiliatingly slow growth and economic decline in the decades following the Second World War remained so vivid.

4

The Decline of the Developmental State

A strong case can be made that the countries that advanced the most economically after the Second World War did so with government playing a major leadership role rather than relying on market forces. Many British commentators in the 1960s compared the slow growth of their own economy with the dynamism that was evident across the Channel as France was transformed from a relatively backward European economy to one of the Continent's leaders. In the 1980s, some American commentators contrasted the poor growth levels of the United States with Japan's high growth rates. France and Japan, some contended, had succeeded because the state had been the driving force behind economic growth.[1] Whereas traditional economists in the USA and UK portrayed the state as a drag on economic growth and efficiency, both the French and the Japanese had realized its potential for economic leadership and development. By the late 1990s, however, traditional economists could feel vindicated as it was Japan's turn to be associated with weak growth and France struggled to reduce its high unemployment.

Why had the model of state-led economic growth that had seemed so promising in the past apparently failed? Had the model been rendered obsolescent by globalization, or had its inherent limits merely been slow to emerge?

The decline of the developmental state is a political as well as an economic puzzle. The pursuit of growth at all costs required a favourable political setting as well as the mobilization of economic resources. This favourable political setting could be achieved partly through the mobilization of economic support and partly by restricting the ability of those whose interests were harmed by industrialization to impede the process through political means. The Asian developmental state in particular was often portrayed as subordinating everything to economic growth. The object of the exercise was to catch up with the developed world. Developmental states were able to maintain high-growth policies partly by eliciting the support of the population for the goal and partly by repressing demands that were thought to conflict with it, such as pressure for aid to declining industries, increased rights for unions or the development of a welfare state. Of the famed four Tigers of Asia (South Korea, Taiwan, Hong Kong and Singapore) two (South Korea and Taiwan) were clearly undemocratic until recently and sometimes endowed forcefully repressive regimes, Hong Kong was a colony and Singapore was perhaps best described as an authoritarian democracy. The model Asian developmental state, Japan, had been endured with democratic institutions by the Allies after the Second World War. In contrast with Britain, whose institutions Japan's otherwise so much resembled, the political system was dominated by a single party, the LDP, which held power continuously from the commencement of elected self-government until the 1990s and then again after a brief interruption. In Asia, therefore, repression and imperfect democracy had helped to maintain growth policies. What would happen if repression ended and democracy increased? Could high-growth policies be maintained? In fact we shall see, by the end of the twentieth century, the political as well as economic underpinnings of the developmental state had frayed. Three of the four Tigers (Hong Kong, Taiwan and South Korea) had experienced significant democratization and in Japan the unbroken reign of the LDP had ended. The ability to repress popular demands that conflicted with the goals of the developmental state had diminished. The problem of combining greater democracy with the developmental state will be apparent in the examples that we shall now explore.

France

The period from the late 1940s to the late 1970s is known in France as the *trente glorieuses*, the thirty glorious years of growth, expansion and catching up with the former economic leaders of Europe, Britain and Germany. The decades after the Second World War, therefore, contrasted forcefully with the decades after the First World War when the French economy, and indeed the entire society, had seemed stagnant, deeply conservative and inefficient. The French state had been fully complicit in this stagnation, both reflecting a conservative society resistant to change and serving interests that stood in the way of progress. Governments were composed of unstable coalitions of parties in Parliament; coalitions that were always collapsing or about to collapse, were always willing to extend protection or subsidies to economically troubled sectors – steel, agriculture, wine producers, small shopkeepers – or whichever minority group could claim to have the ability to determine who held power in Paris.

At first it seemed that this pattern would continue after the Second World War.[2] Popular accounts of French life and culture such as Lawrence Wylie's *Village in the Vaucluse*[3] suggested that French society was as resistant to change and innovation as ever. The transition from the Third to the Fourth Republics in 1947 changed the practices of French party politics and their pathologies little. The clamour for protection and subsidies from numerous interest groups continued. Yet below the surface, a group of gifted administrators such as Jean Monet, who went on to become the father of the European Union, were working to ensure that the future would not be like the past and that stagnation and drift would not continue.

The ostensible instrument for the transformation of the French economy was to be a new agency, the *Commissariat du Plan*. The Commissariat produced and implemented a series of five-year plans setting out the steps for French economic growth and development. These plans were not like those of the Soviet Union that used state power to command investment and production. They were to be produced in collaboration with major economic groups and were to be *indicative* of desirable developments; French planning therefore became known as the leading example of *indicative planning*. It was not intended to impose outcomes that diverged from market forces; it was, rather, an attempt to identify and anticipate market forces. The role of the state was not so much to defy markets as to shape them and position French enterprises to take advantage of economic opportunities. The French state did not plan alone. The planning process theoretically provided for participation by a range of economic and social interests including unions. In practice, however, the planners selected, encouraged and, in some instances, created what they saw as the most suitable interest groups to work with them. Defensive, backward-looking interest groups that sought to maintain outmoded practices or industries through government subsidies as well as communist-inclined groups were not taken seriously by the planners.[4] In the cases of both agriculture and industry, the state promoted new interest groups that were sympathetic to change and development and willing to work with government to achieve them. Those interest groups that were involved in serious consultation and partnership were committed to economic change and modernization in their sectors. French planning involved partnership between the state and interest groups but it was a highly unequal, state-dominated partnership.

What was the impact of indicative planning?[5] For its proponents, there was no doubt that it was the means by which France had been transformed. Indicative planning brought enterprises together to consider potential developments. This process attacked the caution and conservatism of French business by setting out possibilities for growth. It also facilitated growth by making businesses aware of each others' plans. Plans for growth in the automobile sector might have been hindered by shortages of raw materials such as steel had steel mills not been made aware of likely developments through the planning process. More sceptical studies, perhaps predictably written by American economists, suggested that the apparent relationship between economic growth and indicative planning was purely coincidental. Market forces had transformed France, not government. The Five Year Plans were frequently ignored by both companies and government departments. Companies, fortunately, relied on economic judgement, not government guidance in making investment decisions. France's relatively backward status in the 1930s had become an advantage because it provided a large pool of labour underemployed in small-scale agriculture to work in industry.

Much discussion of indicative planning failed to take account of the real leverage that the French government had to secure compliance with the general strategy of the Plan if not the detail of each part. This ability to secure cooperation derived from several features of France's economy and society. First, the state-owned sector in France was relatively large. Government owned not only the railways, the airline (Air France) and the utilities but important manufacturing enterprises such as Renault, the automobile manufacturer. Government-owned industries could be ordered to comply with the general direction of the Plan. Second, the elite of French society had many connections forged through their common education in the famous schools (*grandes écoles*) and membership of the top professional organizations (*grandes corps*) thereafter. French government officials tended to move from a successful career in government to one as a top executive in the private sector – a career shift so common that it had a well-known name, *pantouflage*.[6] This career pattern forged close relations between the senior bureaucracy and their predecessors who had moved into key positions in the private sector. Third, the French financial system, as John Zysman explained, gave teeth to the state's economic strategy.[7] In brief, the supply of scarce credit came largely from government-controlled financial institutions that were guided by the state's economic strategy.

A crucial problem for any economic strategy in which the state plays a leading role is avoiding the subordination of long-term economic goals to short-term political pressures. Critics of industrial policy in the United States argued plausibly that legislators would turn government intervention into a form of pork barrel for their districts and states. In Britain, too, government aid to industry in the 1960s and 1970s too often went to declining 'lame duck' industries; the governing party would use industrial policy as a means of subsidizing failing industries in a quest to buy votes in key constituencies. How were these problems avoided, or at least contained, in France? As we noted earlier, in Asia these political problems did not arise in the Tigers, which had undemocratic regimes in power, or in Japan, because of the overwhelming dominance of the LDP. France had its deeply-rooted democratic values and numerous competing political parties. Against the odds, means were found to limit the impact of electoral politics on political development for nearly all of the *trentes glorieuses*.

Monet and his fellow pioneers of indicative planning operated within the bureaucracy. The senior French bureaucracy contrasted favourably with politicians in terms of their education, prestige and cohesiveness. Selected according to the French republican principle of recruitment through rigorous selection on the basis of merit, united by their common education in the 'great schools' such as the Ecole Normale d'Administration or, for civil engineers, Ponts et Chaussées, the French bureaucracy towered above the petty feuding politicians of the Fourth Republic.[8] The frequent changes of government in that regime further diminished the ability of politicians to 'interfere' with the Plan. Governments came and went with such frequency (even though individual ministers might keep their jobs under several different prime ministers) that the capacity of politicians to control or initiate policy was seriously impeded. The Fifth Republic, particularly during its first twenty years, provided an almost ideal setting for the bureaucratic policy-maker. The utter dominance of the legislature by the President, then elected for the unusually long term of seven years and, until the 1980s, always from the same party grouping, provided a high degree of insulation for bureaucratic policy-makers from electoral pressures. For its first decade, the Fifth Republic was truly an elected monarchy with President de Gaulle as its king and the senior bureaucracy as his capable servants.[9] De Gaulle recognized that in the modern world, the power and prestige of nations was dependent on their economic strength. Accordingly, he supported the efforts of the modernizing bureaucrats to move France into the premier division of economies: as we have noted, this effort was largely successful.

How, then, did the French developmental state come to decline? The two most obvious explanations are that it outgrew itself and that domestic political circumstances changed. We noted earlier that the French economy used to be one of the weakest in Europe. Slow growth and regular devaluations of the currency seemed to be its lot. The enormous success of the French economy may have been caused by the growth policies of the French state. However, the success of those policies decreased its capacity. The French economy became more integrated with the rest of the world, thereby reducing the capacity of the French state to steer investment towards industries that it favoured. To the degree that French firms operated in an international market – a market that was, by definition, beyond the capacity of French governments to control – governments were obliged to accept that growth and investment would be determined by market forces, not by government. In 1955, exports had been 15 per cent of French GDP: in 2000, they were 28.7 per cent.

The enormity of this economic change was reinforced by the European Union and by international trade liberalization. EU rules made it much more difficult – if not impossible – to continue the strategies of the developmental state. The allocation of contracts by nationalized industries as well as by government, selective subsidies, selective enforcement and non-enforcement of administrative rules to assist favoured industries and the allocation of low-interest credit to favoured companies were all familiar tactics to French officials. They were all, however, contrary to the rules of the European Union which were designed to ensure fair competition between companies based in different member states. While it would be naïve to think that these practices were ended merely because the EU said they should cease (Air France benefited from large-scale low-interest loans in the late 1990s, for example), the EU did notably diminish the frequency and openness with which such tactics could be used. Similarly, international agreements, such as those enforced by the World Trade Organization (WTO), and more specialized agreements (for example, with the United States on competition in selling commercial aircraft) reduced opportunities to use the cruder forms of state intervention.

These changes in the international environment coincided with several changes in domestic politics that also made it harder for the developmental state to operate without political interference. The Fifth Republic became more democratic. Effective competition developed between the left and the right culminating in the election of a Socialist President, Mitterrand, in 1982 in partnership with a Socialist majority in the National Assembly. Thereafter, competition between left and right was sufficiently keen and close to result in repeated periods of 'cohabitation' during which the left would control the Presidency, the right the National Assembly or vice versa. Even before the 1982 election, however, it had become apparent that the competition between left and right had diminished the opportunities for economic policy-makers to act without regard to electoral consequences; enormous subsidies were paid to the steel industry, for example, not because it was identified as a future growth prospect but because closures of steel mills might have adverse political consequences. Similarly, in the 1990s, protests against the rationalization of state-owned firms, such as Air France, soon forced a change of policy. The increased significance of electoral politics was given institutional and symbolic recognition in 2001 when the constitution of the Fifth Republic was amended to reduce the Presidential term of office from seven to five years.

The French bureaucracy also saw its prestige diminish. The 1980s and 1990s witnessed an upsurge of anti-statist sentiment among French intellectuals, not so much as a reaction to the Fifth Republic but to (belatedly) the Soviet system. The higher bureaucracy was no longer universally considered to be the best possible career, and applications to the 'great schools' fell considerably.

France had also received a sharp lesson in the realities of global markets in the 1980s – a lesson that changed the thinking of all politicians about what was feasible policy for a single nation-state. In particular, the 1982 elections also led to another sharp lesson in the importance of external economic constraints. The Socialists' majority in both the National Assembly and Presidency naturally encouraged them to attempt radical change. The first left-wing programme of the Fifth Republic was soon abandoned however, not because of political opposition but because of international financial pressures. A massive flight of funds out of France obliged the Socialist government to execute a U-turn in policy.[10] Thereafter governments would accept that markets were too hard to defeat and that policy must be 'market-conforming'. By the 1990s, France had joined the vogue for privatization and its Socialists were no more of a threat to capitalism than Schroder's Social Democrats in Germany or Blair's Labour Party in Britain.

Yet it would also be wrong to come to the conclusion that France had embraced *laissez-faire* economics in the footsteps of Reagan and Thatcher. Attempts continued to build up 'national champions', successful French firms in growth industries, through government policy. They were not generally successful, the example of the unsuccessful attempt to create a strong French computer firm, Machines Bull, being a conspicuous example of failure. As we have noted above, generous government 'loans' to troubled firms such as Air France continued, though more because of political pressure than because of economic planning decisions. Finally, the Socialist government headed by Leonard Jospin adopted a number of measures to counteract unemployment, such as reducing the working week to 35 hours, that were clearly contrary to the recommendations that traditional, market-oriented economists would have made. Even privatization had a particularly French character as the state retained a 'hard core' of stock that enabled it, among other things, to prevent control of the firm passing into foreign hands. Nonetheless, the days of bold planning had passed. Governments might provide marginal assistance to firms but they no longer thought that state action could bring about prosperity. As Vivien Schmidt summarized the changes:

Although relations between business and government remain close, the ties that bound them inextricably to one another through the postwar period, first through planning and then through industrial policies, have been loosened. Ministries have become partners rather than leaders of industry, while industries that used to look almost exclusively to the state for guidance now turn to one another for strategic advice and equity investment and to the enlarged stockmarket for funds. Even the nationalized industries have become mostly autonomous.[11]

Japan

France had been a successful developmental state. In the same era, however, the Japanese had achieved miracles, rising from poverty to become the second largest economy in the world.

One of the problems that can result from thinking of countries as 'models' is that we overlook the important changes that take place within them. Political economies are rarely stable for more than a few decades. Change can be more or less rapid, and more or less intentional. Although it is common to talk about the Japanese model as though it was unchanging, we can distinguish at least three phases in the Japanese political economy since 1955. In general, the trajectory of the Japanese developmental state was similar to the French experience but in a more extreme form, passing from state leadership of economic development to an era of stagnation in which the state conspicuously failed to lay the groundwork for further development. Before tracing this trajectory, it is necessary to give some background on the political context of the Japanese developmental state.

The development of Japan as a modern nation had been based on a partnership between the state and business. The Meiji Restoration created a stronger monarchy that was able to assert power over the previously dominant nobility and promote Japan's parity with the western states who had asserted their power so vigorously by the appearance of Commodore Perry's 'black ships' in Tokyo Bay in 1867, thus ending Japan's self-imposed isolation from the world. In Japan, as in France, the notion that the state should stand back and allow market forces to bring about industrialization and development would have seemed very strange.

The Japanese government prior to the Second World War worked in close partnership with a limited number of very large enterprises that were involved in different industries, known as *zaibatsu*. These giant enterprises were seen by the Allies (and in particular by the Americans) as a cause of Japanese imperialist sentiment and were, in theory, broken up during the occupation of Japan after the Second World War. In practice, however, they re-emerged in a slightly altered form and with a different name. Japanese big business in the modern era has comprised networks of large firms clustered around a large bank that supplies most of their credit needs. Officials from the bank sit on the boards of member firms, which have similar links to each other. The very large companies, such as Toyota, are well-known in Europe and North America. Their management styles are also known, and often mocked, in the west: lifetime employment and paternalistic arrangements to provide for the health, welfare and housing of employees coexist with expectations of total commitment and loyalty from workers. Of course, these companies also pioneered manufacturing techniques such as 'just in time' production that have since been emulated by North American and European companies. It is less well-known that the giants of the Japanese economy rest on a bedrock of small to medium-sized companies that supply them with components. Workers in these firms do not enjoy the lifetime employment or paternalistic welfare benefits that workers in the very large companies enjoy. The small to medium-sized sector provides the flexibility required to cope with downturns in the economy.

The Japanese bureaucracy survived the war more or less unchanged and with its power enhanced by the fact that the military, one of its main rivals for influence, was weakened by the American occupation. The Japanese bureaucratic model was much more familiar to Europeans than Americans. It recruited from a limited number of the most prestigious and selective universities, particularly the Imperial University of Tokyo, and, as in

France, the higher bureaucracy was considered to be the most prestigious career possible. Retirees who moved into executive positions in the private sector were said to have experienced 'the descent from heaven'. While constitutionally subordinate to the politicians who held the key government positions in the Cabinet, in practice senior bureaucrats expected to make most policy decisions.[12] 'I don't understand why politicians would expect to make policy', one experienced senior official remarked to the author, 'What do they know or understand about the issues involved?'

The politicians who, in theory though probably not in practice, decided policy in Cabinet or in the Diet (parliament) were, as noted earlier, drawn exclusively from the Liberal Democratic Party (LDP). This was, in the contemporary western sense, a conservative party, an alliance of farmers (whom the political system overrepresented), business and above-average-income citizens. Corruption and pork-barrel politics were important in maintaining the dominance of the LDP. Concern about corruption in Japanese politics mounted in the 1990s. As the NGO that specializes in combating corruption globally, Transparency International reported in 2001, 'Japan's ten year economic crisis fostered a succession of allegations of corruption and electoral campaign scandals'. Three cabinet ministers were forced to resign from the 2000/2001 Yoshiro Mori government including the State Minister of Economic and Fiscal Policy following allegations of bribery by an insurance company with the intention of influencing government decisions.[13] Some of the corruption is in the straight forward form of payments by business executives to influential politicians. More systematically there are numerous examples of pay-offs to key constituencies to keep LDP supporters happy. For example, there are many bridges and highways that lead nowhere in particular or, to be more precise, lead into lightly-populated areas represented by powerful politicians. The prevalence of pork-barrel politics explains why spending on infrastructure is unusually high as a percentage of GDP in Japan compared to other OECD nations.[14] Similarly, Japanese farmers have been lavishly subsidized. The LDP has also been helped, however, by the almost suicidal strategies of the Socialists. While not arguing for radical change domestically, the Socialists' pro-Soviet, anti-American policies during the Cold War destroyed their credibility. Contrary to western belief, the Japanese have not always been pro-business workaholics. Immediately after the Second World War, Japan experienced a wave of labour militancy that was defeated in part by the opposition of the American occupation authorities and the Japanese government they controlled. Thereafter, the ineptness of the left contributed considerably to its marginalization in politics.

The Japanese developmental state therefore consisted of an alliance between the LDP, bureaucracy and big business. Political scientists have given much attention to the relative power of these elements (with most agreeing that politicians ranked lowest). It is more useful to think of the relationship as a mutually beneficial alliance. The state and business wanted growth. The politicians sought office and the perks that came with it. So long as business and the bureaucracy in partnership could deliver growth, politicians were content to leave them alone while they concentrated on political games such as who would be the next Prime Minister, and on securing benefits for rich supporters or their constituencies. The LDP did provide one vital service, however. It insulated the developmental state from the political pressures of interests, such as declining industrial areas, that might have interfered with growth strategies. While the politicians focused elsewhere, the senior bureaucracy and large businesses in partnership pursued the economic construction of Japan.

As in the case of French indicative planning, there has been much debate about the importance of the state in Japanese success from the 1950s to the 1990s.[15] As we noted earlier, any assessment of the role of the Japanese state has to recognize the changes that have occurred during the three periods of the postwar Japanese political economy.

The Era of Government Domination, 1955 to the 1970s

From the end of the Occupation to the oil shocks in the 1970s, the Japanese government enjoyed very considerable power over industry. As in France, the Japanese government had control over a major source of capital through the post office bank. Capital was allocated according to the priorities for development established by the Ministry of International Trade and Industry, MITI, supported by the Ministry of Finance. This channel of influence was reinforced, however, by direct, physical controls that were more extensive and complete than the French government wielded. Firms wishing to import goods or machinery, for example, needed a permit from MITI and permits could be denied to those whose plans did not accord with the government's. In practice, however, there was little conflict. MITI's plans were 'market-conforming', seeking to accelerate the movement of firms up the product hierarchy into more profitable, higher-value-added industries rather than trying to impose commercially unsound decisions on them.[16] MITI always recognized the importance of competitiveness. In most major industries, MITI ensured that there was competition between large firms rather than relying on the development of a single 'national champion'. In the automobile industry, for example, MITI wanted to see both Nissan and Toyota strive for larger shares of the domestic market as a preparation for international competition. MITI's strategy of promoting export-led growth, rather than following the Latin American strategy of import substitution, also promoted competitiveness. Whereas an import-substitution approach fosters inefficiency by excluding foreign competition, a strategy of pursuing growth through exports requires competitiveness, because foreigners cannot be forced to buy Japanese goods. The Ministry of Finance also aided Japanese competitiveness abroad by keeping the value of the Japanese Yen low on the foreign exchanges.

Close collaboration between MITI, trade associations representing individual industries and the peak association to which they are affiliated, the *Keidanren*, ensured that conflict was kept to the minimum. Politicians interfered little in the process. A crucial international factor at work was the willingness of the United States to tolerate a very unequal trading relationship with Japan. Japan could export relatively freely to the United States while American and European companies were excluded from Japan. A huge trade imbalance in Japan's favour developed.

A More Equal Partnership; the 1970s and 1980s

Japanese success brought its own problems. American economic crises in the 1970s ended the era in which the United States would tolerate an unequal trading relationship. Japan joined GATT and, although it did not hasten to follow the organization's liberal trade rules, it was obliged to discard gradually the more egregious breaches such as requiring import licences. Companies attempting to export to Japan complained, however, that the Japanese government was adept at developing health and safety requirements that continued to exclude foreign goods.

MITI continued to guide economic development. Its ability, in partnership with the Ministry of Finance, to influence investment decisions through the allocation of credit remained. Moreover, the extraordinary success of Japan gave MITI a degree of moral authority that helped secure cooperation. Yet there were important examples of companies defying MITI's wishes. A celebrated example is Honda's decision to move into manufacturing automobiles. MITI believed that there were already more than enough Japanese automobile manufacturers, yet Honda ignored MITI's advice with impunity – and great commercial success. Domestic politics continued to encroach little on the partnership between MITI and industry. However, external circumstances started to change the balance of influence between business and government in business's favour. The United States and the European Union had shown significant signs of becoming more protectionist under the impact of adverse economic circumstances. Japan was required to accept limits on the amount of politically-sensitive goods, such as steel and automobiles, that it could export to the USA and EU. Fearing that this trend might continue, Japanese companies established overseas factories in the United States and the EU (chiefly in Britain). Japanese companies also moved production to lower-cost countries in Asia. Overall, Japanese companies became notably less Japanese and susceptible to government influence.

*The Decline and Fall of the Developmental State,
1990 Onwards*

The final and most recent stage has created a situation very different from the situation described and celebrated by authors such as Chalmers Johnson. Government influence over industry continued to decline. Continuing pressure on Japan to comply with the rules of GATT and the WTO inhibited the exercise of government influence on investment decisions. Both Japanese manufacturers and banks had outgrown the domestic economy and their overseas development had moved them beyond the control of MITI or the Ministry of Finance. At the same time, however, the lack of adequate rules to ensure the accuracy and transparency of company financial rules meant that Japanese companies were not subject either to full market disciplines. The situation of being subject to neither the government nor the market created irresponsible capitalism. Japanese banks gave massive loans to companies that had little chance of repaying them and making a profit on the investment. The rapid economic growth and movement of Japanese companies up the product hierarchy gave way to stagnation, banks saddled with massive bad ('non-performing') loans and the destruction of confidence in government, particularly the bureaucracy. The senior bureaucracy ceased to be regarded as the custodian of the national interest and instead was criticized not only for inefficiency but for corruption. Politicians and electoral politics became much more prominent. The temporary loss of power by the LDP in the early 1990s increased the importance of electoral and Parliamentary politics; bureaucrats and business could no longer assume that the LDP would provide a buffer to shelter them from pressures while they planned the economic future. Politicians became much more assertive. An extensive reorganization of government was launched, though not fully implemented. The collapse of the old order was illustrated vividly when MITI was renamed and reduced in status. Other proposals aimed to strengthen the power of ministers, and particularly the prime minister, over the bureaucracy. Yet there were few if any signs of major reform. Japan seemed no longer the economic growth machine but a stumbling giant. By the early years of the twenty-first century, the Japanese economy was, in terms of GDP per capita, contracting at a significant rate. Yet no one seemed able to push through a reform package that would deal with the fundamental problems of the Japanese system. The Dutch journalist, Karel van Wolferen, argued, that even in the glory days of rapid growth, the Japanese political economy was one with no one in charge.[17] It was a machine that lacked a drive, which functioned well until a change of direction was required. That description seemed all the more apposite in the early twenty-first century when it became apparent that a change of direction was indeed necessary.

The downfall of the Japanese developmental state shared several features with the pattern we saw in France. Both developmental states were weakened by their success. As they became major and successful exporters, the governments of Japan and France became less able to steer their economies and control industrial development. In both countries, the influence and authority of the bureaucracy declined while the influence of politics and politicians increased. While France experienced real problems, particularly high unemployment, in the early twenty-first century its economy seemed to have adapted to new conditions. In Japan, however, the end of the developmental state left behind a more serious crisis. Ironically, the Japanese state seemed to lack the vision and political ability to break out of its crisis.

South Korea

The success of South Korea is perhaps an even more remarkable story. Between the early 1960s and the late 1980s, South Korea experienced a forty-fold increase in per capita GDP, a change that took it from the ranks of the poorest countries to membership of the 'rich nations' club' of the OECD. Growth was based on exports, which increased from $40.9 million in 1961 to $15 billion in 1979. Growth fluctuated in the 1990s; double-digit growth rates gave way in the late 1990s to a contraction of the economy. More recently, growth has resumed, although at more modest levels.

Korea had always been a predominantly agricultural country. The Japanese during their occupation made a few attempts to create industry but these efforts were modest and soon overtaken by the Second World War. After independence and the Korean War, Korea – henceforth, meaning 'South Korea' – was ruled by a series of authoritarian regimes. The first of these was headed by Syngman Rhee who combined strident anti-communism with anti-Japanese nationalism. A military coup brought Park Chung-Hee to the presidency who continued authoritarian rule. His rule rested in part on popular support for economic policies that promised economic growth fast enough to catch up with Japan. Park believed that decisive action was necessary to break the corrupt partnership between business and government that had existed under Rhee. Park ruled with the aid of an elitist, meritocratic bureaucracy recruited from the most prestigious university, Seoul National. The Korean model was, in this respect, similar to the French and Japanese.[18]

The similarity with the French case is strengthened by the use from 1962 of five-year plans, crafted by the Economic Planning Board (EPB). The EPB had a very broad remit, covering budgeting, macroeconomic policy-making, control over foreign investment and even the power to set prices for a range of goods. The head of the EPB was the deputy prime minister and chair of the Council of Economic Advisers. The EPB dominated other ministries, partly by placing its own officials in senior ministry posts, partly by controlling the budgets of other key departments, such as the Ministry of Finance and Ministry of International Trade and Industry (MITI), and partly through a network of informal contacts. The EPB was known to have the strong support of the President and of the economic advisers within his office (the Blue House). The Plans that the bureaucracy developed, in a more formalized but comparable way to MITI in Japan, established a series of priorities for industrial development. In the early 1970s, for example, President Park proclaimed the Era of the Heavy Chemical Industry. This was followed by steel and other metals, machine-building, shipbuilding and electronics in a deliberate move away from lower productivity, labour-intensive industries. Some of the more visible of Korean imports into Europe and North America that resulted from this process were automobiles, notably Hyundai and Daewoo, and consumer electronics such as Samsung.

Park also created a compulsory, state-controlled pattern of corporatist linkages to both unions and employers. Unions were reorganized by the KCIA, the state security agency, with the Federation of Korean Trade Unions at their peak. All businesses were required to join a state-sponsored organization that brought the EPB important information on the state of industry as well as a means to pass down government policy to business. There was no doubt, however, that both unions and employers' organizations were dominated by the state. They existed to assist the state in its policies of economic development, not to make demands upon it.

State dominance over industry was reinforced by the pattern of economic development in Korea. Rhee had started a typically nationalist import-substitution policy that, while redistributing land more equitably, discriminated against agriculture in order to fund industrial investment. Because of nationalist concerns that foreign, especially Japanese, investors might control Korean industry, Rhee initiated the practice of funnelling foreign investment through the state to industry. In practice, as time passed, Koreans took the view that industrial investment was best directed to a limited number (five) of very large firms that operated in different industries. These were the famed *chaebols*. Government provision of credit to the *chaebols* was reinforced as a tool for shaping expansion by tax credits, exemptions from tariffs on necessary imports and protection from foreign competition. While government thought that they were minimizing risks and securing economies of scale by investing in very large companies that operated in different industries, the Korean pattern of development had its disadvantages. First, the very large firms were soon 'too big to fail': their bankruptcy would have created an enormous crisis of the entire regime. The state was therefore obliged to rescue *chaebols* that got into commercial trouble. Second, Korean development created a feeling among many workers that they lived in a hierarchical, inegalitarian society. In consequence, and in spite of severe repression they have often undertaken militant, even violent, action in support of their demands.

The Crisis of the Korean Developmental State

In spite of its successes, the Korean developmental state has also experienced a crisis in recent years. In the late 1990s, in particular, a financial crisis precipitated a fall in GDP and a surge in unemployment – unprecedented conditions for the country. A number of factors had changed considerably the options for the developmental state.

First, the authoritarian state had been transformed into a democracy. Rising discontent, in part due to the social dislocation caused by the success of the economic development policies of the authoritarian regimes had followed, weakened their support. This discontent surfaced in 1980 in protests that were repressed savagely, notably in the Kwangju Massacre in which hundreds died.[19] Protests died down, only to resurface in the mid 1980s and this time expanded support from workers and students from the middle classes. In 1987, Park's successor, Roh Tae-Woo, conceded to many of the protesters' demands and allowed free elections.[20] By the end of the century, the one-time dissident, who had come close to being executed,

Kim Dae-Jung, was President. Korea no longer had an authoritarian state that could control society in pursuit of economic growth.

Second, Korean economic success, like French and Japanese, brought the economy into the global economy. Korean exporters had to respond to markets, not government plans. Korean firms, like Japanese, moved production overseas. The British government in particular eagerly courted Korean investment in plants to manufacture microchips and to conduct research in computers. As in Japan, the movement of companies overseas reduced the capacity of the home government to control them. Full membership in the elite of the global economy (reflected in membership of the OECD) also brought demands for Korea to abandon the techniques used to enforce economic plans. Overt discrimination in the imposition of tariffs, subsidies and the provision of cheap credit were contrary to the rules of the WTO. Other countries (particularly the United States) and international organizations (the IMF, the World Bank) pressed for a liberalization of controls on capital movements. Nothing could have been more out of line with the campaign the USA and international organizations waged for capital liberalization than the Korean practice of the government borrowing overseas to lend to selected, favoured companies at home.

The Korean developmental state was therefore undermined by a combination familiar to us from the French and Japanese cases. Democratization reduced the opportunities for rule by the bureaucracy. Economic success reduced the degree to which the economy was self-contained and amenable to government manipulation, especially as successful companies invested overseas. Perhaps the most important development, however, was the uneasy compromise that developed between government and market control over investment. Government has less ability to control investment than in the past. On the other hand, the conditions for market controls – transparency in accounts, regular reporting of results in company documents and so on – are not present either. The *chaebols* developed in sprawling, financially ill-disciplined enterprises laden with debt and unproductive investments. The result was the financial crisis of the late 1990s.

The intensity of the crisis in a country that had based its national self-esteem on high economic growth rates prompted consideration of whether the *chaebols* should be broken up. Pressure for such fundamental change was reduced, however, by the recovery of the economy in the new century. What had changed, however, was the willingness of the Korean government to see *chaebols* fail. The argument that *chaebols* were too large to be allowed to become bankrupt was invalidated by the fact that some did fail. In order to survive, *chaebols* were forced to focus more on profitability and less on growth at all costs. Some abandoned unprofitable investments or sold them to other companies. Other *chaebols* in effect broke themselves up. The different parts of Hyundai have passed into the hands of different heirs to the fortune; the integrated commercial empire is coming to an end.

The Future of the Developmental State

There are, of course, many other examples of developmental states that present interesting variations on the themes we have identified. Taiwan's system, for example, has been complicated by the influence of the political party, the Kuomintang, whose leaders fled to the island following the Communist triumph on the Chinese mainland in 1947.[21] Taiwan has also relied on economic strategies that have encouraged small and medium-sized enterprises more and very large firms less than in the Korean case.[22]

Nonetheless, the developmental states that we have studied had a number of common features. First, an elite bureaucracy was able to target promising industries for development without political 'interference' at levels that ranged from the relatively benign (as in France) to the sometimes severely repressive (Korea). Second, the government held a number of policy weapons (notably control over the availability and cost of credit) to ensure that its priorities for economic development were turned into reality. Third, the developmental states were able to take advantage of several important, favourable international conditions. The first of these conditions was an international trading system that facilitated exporting because major economies (especially the United States) were open to imports. The second was a willingness to tolerate unbalanced trading practices by developmental states (which were willing to export but not import). This reflected Cold War politics, particularly in these cases of Japan and Korea, which the United States needed as strategic allies. The third international condition was the continuing economic growth experienced by the advanced economies which made them more tolerant of increased competition from the developmental states.

All the developmental states that we have studied have experienced changes that undermined their ability to continue the approaches that brought them such success. The combination of stagnation, or even decline, of the Japanese economy and the financial crises of the Asian Tigers in the 1990s demonstrated powerfully the problems that the previously most dynamic developmental states faced.[23] What is less clear, however, is whether the decline of existing developmental states reflects merely a stage in their own development or whether the developmental state itself is no longer viable. Some of the changes that we have identified are probably part of the developmental process. The decline in the capacity of French, Japanese and Korean governments to control their economies as they become more integrated into global markets and their companies invest overseas suggests that successful developmental states, by their own success, make it unlikely that they can continue to operate as developmental states. This would leave the possibility that we shall see other, as yet unidentified, countries go down the same path as Japan or Korea. An alternative perspective might suggest that the developmental state option is no longer available. Stricter rules set by international bodies, such as the WTO, largely prohibit discriminatory policies that would foster growth. International pressures to liberalize capital markets do the same. Rich countries such as the United States are no longer willing to tolerate countries that are willing to export but not to import. In short, the developmental state that has transformed countries' economic prospects in the past may not be an option available to other countries in the future.

5

The Past, Present and Future of Neocorporatism

Introduction

All capitalist systems must establish some form of relationship between the state, capital and labour. A distinctive aspect of European capitalism is that the balance of power between these interests has been more equal than in the American or Asian variants. Labour has been better organized and has wielded more influence in both industry and politics than in, for example, the United States or Japan. This is, of course, a generalization. There are important differences between the European countries. The percentage of the labour force in Britain that is unionized is higher than in Germany, and higher in Germany than in France or Italy. Yet even in those countries such as France with low workforce unionization, the percentage of the workforce whose pay is determined by union rates and negotiations is relatively high and the political power of labour is considerable. Establishing a settlement between the state, capital and labour has been a central issue in European politics and society. On the one hand, organized labour has been too firmly established and powerful for employers to overcome it. On the other hand, these countries have to be competitive internationally if they are to maintain their standard of living. The neocorporatist countries, which are all European, are the countries in which this settlement has been the most explicit.

What is meant by the word 'neocorporatist'?[1] Neocorporatism is a form of governance in which organizations representing major economic interests, usually unions and employers' organizations, are given major, privileged opportunities to participate in

102

policy-making in return for accepting responsibilities to assist the state in the governance of society. Corporatism is the view that people should be partly or wholly represented on the basis of their occupations or economic role and can be traced back to the crafts-man's guilds of the Middle Ages. This combination of sharing in representation and governance is at the core of corporatism. Corporatist bodies were not simply organizations for voicing common concerns or attitudes but were also involved in setting standards and conditions for the craft. Perhaps because of the governance role played by the guilds, they were recognized by the crown and rival bodies could not be established. This idea that organizations that participate in corporatist arrangements are given a guaranteed monopoly status by the state is fundamental to the concept today, and contrasts with the standard expectation in pluralist politics that new and competing interests will always be emerging. In modern times, corporatism has been associated with fascism and the corporatist bodies were used as part of the apparatus of fascist rule.

The term 'neocorporatism' has been used more recently to describe the voluntary cooperation between major economic interest groups and the state. Scholars have been eager to distinguish it from the coerced forms of corporatist organization imposed by some authoritarian regimes. In neocorporatist societies, long patterns of historical development have produced strong, centralized unions and employers' organizations that make very attractive partners for government. Individual unions have yielded significant powers to their federation, not only to represent them but also to control wage bargaining and strikes. Employers have entrusted their trade and peak associations with significant powers too, not only in wage bargaining but also in areas such as environmental policy. Although voluntary or societal neocorporatism is not *compelled* by the state, most scholars believe it is *encouraged* by the state and does not simply arise 'naturally'. Governments, as we have seen in our discussions of France and even Britain can strengthen and support a particular organization by making it clear that they regard it as the only authoritative voice for the interest it seeks to represent. Alternatively, governments can encourage rival organizations as in the 1980s when Margaret Thatcher started to treat the Institute of Directors as being at least equal in standing to the Confederation of British Industry (CBI). The strength of neocorporatism is therefore explained as a balance between the relative importance of long-term, sociological factors in strengthening organizations on the one hand and on the other hand, the role of the state in building up unions and employers' organizations as potential partners. The relative importance of these factors in creating neocorporatism is an issue to which we shall return below.

Political scientists agree that neocorporatism has existed in its fullest form in relatively few countries. The most commonly cited examples are the Netherlands, Norway, Sweden, Denmark and Austria. Yet political scientists have also suggested that tendencies towards neocorporatism have appeared in other countries not normally associated with the practice. The Republic of Ireland has recently emerged as a highly neocorporatist state, something that would not have been predicted in the past. At certain times, usually during economic crises, Britain and even the United States have toyed with neocorporatism. In Britain, both Conservative and Labour governments created neocorporatist institutions such as the National Economic Development Council (NEDC) which brought government, unions and employers together to discuss economic policy. In the 1970s, British governments made particularly strong efforts to govern the economy in partnership with employers' organizations and unions. In the United States, both during the crisis of the Great Depression in the 1930s and the financial crisis of 1970s, some efforts were made to adopt neocorporatist practices. Obvious questions for us to explore are where, when and why neocorporatism operates.

Another obvious question concerns the consequences of neocorporatism. It is an article of faith among many traditional economists, as well as conservatives, that strong labour movements are a fundamental barrier to economic success. They consider that economic success depends on efficiency; efficiency can be attained only if markets are allowed to operate freely and unions, by their very nature, impede the workings of the labour market. Whatever the political views of the union, it exists to drive up the wages of its members, perhaps beyond the level that the market establishes. Thatcherites in Britain believed that the economy could prosper only if the power of unions were sharply reduced. People who support this view, which has become almost conventional wisdom, should be amazed by the power of unions in neocorporatist countries and puzzled by the fact that these are among the most prosperous countries in the world. As we shall see, neocorporatism has given unions a remarkable degree of power and influence. Conservatives might respond, however, that in the 1990s the hour of reckoning struck. Neocorporatist countries might have coped in spite of their practices in the past; but they could no longer maintain their systems in the face of the increased competitive pressures resulting from globalization.[2] Others have suggested that neocorporatist countries have in fact not only adapted to globalization without sacrificing their neocorporatist practices but have used those practices to make a relatively smooth adaptation to new economic circumstances.

How Does Neocorporatism Work?

Neocorporatism is then the sharing of governance between economic interests, generally business and labour on the one hand and the state on the other. What does a neocorporatist arrangement cover, and what does it look like in practice?

Most neocorporatist arrangements have involved agreements on wage bargaining.[3] This has been true of the long-established Scandinavian variants (such as Sweden) and the newest examples, notably Ireland.[4] In neocorporatist countries, unions, employers and government agreed a common and universal percentage wage increase covering all workers in all industries. The percentage wage increase would be set at a level that would not damage the economy and, in order to increase competitiveness, below the increase that unions could achieve under current market conditions. Yet workers have been well served in the long run by the agreements made by their unions. The most neocorporatist countries were typically small and had a very high dependence on international trade. Had unions fully exploited the bargaining power that full employment gave them in the short term, their members would have suffered in the long term as their employers were priced out of foreign markets. Unrestrained wage demands would result in either a lack of competitiveness in foreign markets or a steady deterioration of the value the currency. Agreement on wage restraint therefore became essential. Neocorporatist countries, which were heavily dependent on international markets, needed a national bargain between government, unions and nationally-oriented capital to promote growth and efficiency. Only unions in countries with highly centralized wage bargaining could show such restraint. If union power was decentralized (as in Britain), the willingness of any one union to forgo a wage increase in the cause of economic stability and competitiveness was not necessarily matched by other unions. In decentralized systems, therefore, restraint by any one union might result merely in its members seeing their incomes decline.

However, although unions in neocorporatist systems were acting in their members' long-term interests, they still expected to receive benefits in return for their short-term concessions, particularly their restraint in wage demands. Some of the pay-off came in the form of government policies. Governments kept employment high, if necessary through stimulating the economy. Unions did not restrict their bargaining to wages, however, but looked for compensation in the 'social wage' for limited increases in regular wages. Social wages would include welfare-state benefits, retirement pensions,[5] improvements in working conditions and childcare. Neocorporatist states are all relatively generous welfare states and this is no coincidence – improvements in the welfare state have been used to lubricate talks about income restraint. For their part, employers promised to continue to invest domestically rather than moving capital overseas in return for the unions' forbearance in the use of their power.

Neocorporatist arrangements have been used to provide governance in policy areas other than national-level wage bargaining and industrial relations. Indeed, a powerful school of thought has suggested that we should look for neocorporatism not at national-level but at the meso-level of particular policies or industrial sectors. Neocorporatist patterns of policy-making can then be found in countries that are not generally placed high on the scale of neocorporatism. Thus, while the UK has not in general been regarded as highly neocorporatist, policy-making on occupational safety and health since the 1970s has been handled by the Health and Safety Commission, an almost textbook example of a body dominated by representatives of employers and unions working in a highly collaborative, consensual style. The dairy industry in the United States has operated under a neocorporatist governance structure. In continental Europe, neocorporatist arrangements cover areas such as training and apprenticeships, and the administration of health insurance. Incomplete neocorporatist arrangements can also be found in areas such as environmental protection where trade associations accept responsibility (as in the German EMAS scheme, discussed later in this chapter) for ensuring that their members are minimizing pollution. These are examples of incomplete neocorporatism in the sense that only employers and the state are involved. Nonetheless, the principle of partnership between the state and a major economic interest is evident.

Neocorporatist countries have formal institutions such as councils on economic policy in which government, unions and employers meet. But neocorporatism is also a state of mind, a habit of consulting and seeking compromise. It is characterized by a high degree of trust and wish for partnership between government, unions and employers' organizations, and these attitudes find expression in informal as well as formal meetings.

Why Does Neocorporatism Occur in Some Countries but Not Others?

There is widespread acceptance of Schmitter's[6] ranking of neocorporatist countries. Sweden, Norway[7] and the Netherlands, followed closely by Denmark, have traditionally been placed at one end of this spectrum, the United States at the other. There is less agreement, however, on why some countries are highly neocorporatist and others are less so.

An obvious starting point would seem to be the availability of suitable interest-group organizations. Neocorporatism at the national level requires the existence of centralized and cohesive economic interest groups. If a three-sided bargain is to be struck between employers, unions and the state, there must be clear agreement on who is entitled to speak for these interests, and the organization that does so must be able to make authoritative commitments on behalf of its members. As we have seen, these conditions pose problems for both the USA and UK. In the United States, there has never been a clear answer as to which organization speaks on behalf of employers; numerous organizations compete for the role. In the UK, there has generally been a fairly clear answer as to who speaks for employers and unions (CBI and

TUC) but the ability of those organizations to make binding commitments on behalf of their members has been very restricted. The CBI could not deliver on agreements for increased investment, and the TUC could not deliver on commitments that affiliated unions would restrict wage claims.[8]

The difficulty comes, however, in determining how an interest group arrives at this dominating position. It is tempting to offer an answer based on 'path-dependency' arguments reaching far back into history. There are important differences in political cultures – themselves the products of history – on how readily representation on the basis of one's occupation or economic interest is accepted. In some countries, such as Germany, the mediaeval guild structure has shaped thinking down to the present day about how economic interests should be organized. Custom, and even law, required firms to join the trade association for their industry, which was in turn affiliated to the 'umbrella' organization for German business, the BDI. People in the Netherlands and Sweden are not shocked by the idea of economic partnership between unions and employers' organizations. The idea that representatives of unions and employers should be involved in developing and administering policies was well-developed in Sweden by the early twentieth century. Social Democrats favoured the practice because they distrusted the bureaucracy while conservatives hoped that it would reduce social conflict. This practice reflected a general approach to governance. At least until recently, the belief has seemed to be that any agreement between employers, unions and government was bound to serve the public interest; these elements taken together constituted the public interest. Swedes have placed a high value on attempting to secure agreement in the legislative process in general. In the 'remiss' procedure, and in the use of Royal Commissions, affected interests are encouraged to try to reach an agreement that can be ratified in legislation. The Netherlands provides another example of a society that places a high value on consensus in governance, influenced by the history of savage religious conflict in the sixteenth century and the need thereafter to achieve a *modus vivendi* between Catholics and Protestants who are almost equal proportions of the population. In Austria, civil war between socialists and anti-socialists preceded the merger of the country with Nazi Germany in the *Anschluss*. In the period after the Second World War, the Austrians experienced occupation by the Soviet Union.

Thus tumultuous history again produced a demand for stable government that found expression in a long period of coalition government, *konkordanzdemokratie* between the Socialist Party and its main rival, the Ostereiche Volks Partei (OVP).

Neocorporatism therefore developed where it was most consistent with the general style of governance. Once established, however, modes of policy-making take on a life of their own. As time passes, the participation of monopolistic, centralized economic interest groups in public policy-making becomes not only tolerated but expected, the normal and appropriate way of making policy.[9] Policy-makers assume that they will work in partnership with economic interest groups and failure to do so is an aberrant, even reprehensibly authoritarian, policy style that shows insufficient sensitivity to society. In contrast, an increase in the degree to which unions (and the employers' organization, the CBI) were involved in developing policy in Britain in the 1970s produced great concern about whether or not unions enjoyed excessive power and a debate over 'Who runs Britain?'. In the United States, there is even less acceptance of close partnership between interest groups, such as unions, and government; such partnerships are almost invariably seen as illegitimate attempts to gain excessive influence by 'special interests'.

An important implication of this 'path dependency' argument is that countries are either neocorporatist or they are not; the appropriate interest group structure is either inherited or it is not. Countries have little choice in the matter. An alternative perspective, however, is that the state can encourage the development and continued existence of an appropriate interest group structure. Businesses in Austria are required to belong to the Economic Chamber (WK). Even in relatively un-neocorporatist Britain there are clear examples of the state nurturing an interest group so that it would be the sole authoritative spokesperson for its interest. The classic example was the National Farmers' Union (NFU) whose monopoly on representing farmers' interests in policy-making was guarded by MAFF (now DEFRA). MAFF followed a deliberate policy of either refusing to talk to rival organizations or, at the very least, of limiting real possibilities to influence policy to the NFU. If strong interest groups with a monopoly on the representation of their interests can be developed with government support, countries that were not considered neocorporatist can become so.

The most interesting example of a country that was never classified as neocorporatist becoming so is the Republic of Ireland.[10] Ireland seemed to lack all the conditions for neocorporatism. Its dominant parties, Fianna Fáil and Fine Gael, were not linked to unions and the stronger party, Fianna Fáil, had a rural rather than an industrial orientation. The unions themselves were strong only in a limited set of industries and were not regarded as key players in national life. In practice dominated by the British economy from independence until the 1990s and possessed of a vision of Ireland that was agrarian and socially conservative, Irish governments had little inclination to try to promote the growth of their industrial economy. In the early 1980s, however, a combination of economic difficulty and industrial unrest produced a major change of attitude. By the late 1980s, public (government) debt was equivalent to 148 per cent of GDP.

Faced with what seemed dire economic and financial problems, the newly elected Fianna Fáil government turned to neocorporatism. Unions were both eager to achieve the higher status in Irish life that neocorporatist arrangements promised and fearful that economic crisis would otherwise reduce their membership and power. Employers were attracted by the promise of reduced wage claims and tax cuts. From 1987 onwards, government, unions and employers entered into what they term a 'social partnership' and developed what they term 'national programmes' or plans. The National Economic and Social Council, itself a neocorporatist body composed of unions, employers, farmers and government, facilitated agreement through the production of an economic strategy document setting out a plan to which all the members agreed. The first of these was known as the Programme for National Recovery and lasted for three years. The same procedures have been followed ever since. During this period, the Irish economy has enjoyed the fastest growth rates in Europe earning the Republic the title of 'the Celtic Tiger'. Considerable inward investment (particularly from the United States) has transformed not only the Irish economy but even Irish society. Unemployment has fallen to around 4.6 per cent. Can neocorporatism be credited with Ireland's success? The stability in industrial relations and reduction in inflationary pressures it provided surely contributed to the country's performance. At the very least, and contrary to what was often said about neocorporatism in the 1980s, it did not seem to inhibit growth and success.

Yet the Irish example should not lead us to conclude that any country is free to adopt neocorporatism whenever it might choose to do so. Ireland, after all, fits the standard expectation for neocorporatism to flourish; it is a relatively small country (in terms of population) heavily dependent on foreign trade. The most fundamental feature of neocorporatist countries is that they are small states in world markets and, in addition, small states with powerful labour movements. Neocorporatist countries are highly dependent on trade; exports and imports constitute a high proportion of GDP. These countries could not survive without some means of reconciling union strength and political pressures for full employment with competitiveness in world markets.

Neocorporatism under Pressure

Ireland's move to neocorporatism would have occasioned little attention in the past. Until the mid 1980s, the tendency had been to portray neocorporatism as a promising path down which those countries would wish to go if they could. Neocorporatism, Schmitter argued, delivered better economic performance, less industrial unrest and greater governability than other countries experienced. Neocorporatist countries were richer, less troubled and more stable economically.[11] By the late 1980s, however, attitudes had changed. Neocorporatism seemed to be in trouble, even in its Scandinavian heartland.

Some of the factors that threatened neocorporatism were domestic in origin.

First, as we have seen, high welfare expenditures were an integral part of neocorporatist systems because increases in welfare state benefits were often the oil that lubricated the machinery of agreements on economic policy. In the last few decades, however, welfare state benefits appear to have reached their limits even in countries such as Sweden renowned for the generosity of their systems. A combination of taxpayer resentment (if not quite revolt) at the costs of the welfare system combined with awareness of abuses of the system (such as the rapid and unbelievable increase in the proportion of the Dutch population classified as disabled) created a limit on the level to which welfare benefits could be raised.

Second, neocorporatist countries, like all advanced industrialized nations, witnessed important social changes. The proportion of the workforce employed in the core industries of union strength (shipbuilding, automobile manufacture, steel, coal-mining and so on) declined while the proportion engaged in white-collar jobs rose. In consequence, the capacity of the traditional union leaders to speak for the workforce as a whole diminished. Moreover, neo-corporatist countries were said by experts such as Streeck[12] to have shared in the phenomenon of class decomposition. In other words, the degree to which manual and skilled workers shared a common identity diminished. In consequence, the workers in successful industrial sectors were less willing to share a common rate of wage increase with workers in troubled sectors whose employers could not afford to pay more. Workers now identified less with workers in other industries and more with the sector or industry in which they worked. These changing class relations were perhaps an underlying reason why the strength of social democratic parties in neocorporatist countries diminished. The Swedish and Austrian social democrats even spent periods out of power, something that had seemed inconceivable in earlier decades.

Third, politics in neocorporatist countries became less dominated by economic and class issues. Such 'post material' progressive concerns as the environment and women's rights became more prominent. So too did less progressive concerns, such as the resentment of immigrants and asylum seekers, resentments that helped to strengthen the far right Freedom Party in Austria.

The most commonly cited pressures on neocorporatism were, however, international. It became the conventional wisdom that neocorporatist arrangements could not withstand globalization. There were several factors that underpinned this belief.

First, neocorporatist systems were said to have inflexible, expensive labour markets. Not only were wages relatively high, but also the employment taxes levied to finance the welfare state further raised the cost of labour. Moreover, the understandable demands of unions for measures to protect the rights of their members increased the inflexibility of the labour market. Employers were not able to 'hire and fire' as the market dictated, but instead had to accommodate the labour laws and regulations that unions had obtained in the course of neocorporatist bargaining. Rights to information and consultation on possible redundancies were supplemented by additional generous requirements on maternity and paternity leave, vacations, sick leave and so on. In brief, in neocorporatist countries, employers found themselves much less able to adapt to changing market forces. As globalization was said to require adaptability and flexibility, neocorporatist countries were considered to be at a real disadvantage. The future, it was thought by many, lay with countries that had relatively ungenerous and therefore cheap welfare states and relatively few restrictions or laws limiting the right of employers to hire and fire. The United States was, of course, the country that came closest to these practices.

Second, globalization was thought to depend on the national character of capital. Business in neocorporatist countries stayed home and bargained with unions and the state rather than simply relocating to a country with more favourable policies and conditions. Wealthy stockholders, such as the Wallenbergs in Sweden, had been content to keep their money in the country even if it meant making compromises through neocorporatist processes with labour. In the new era of globalization, automobile firms such as Volvo and Saab passed into the hands of foreign (American) owners. Capitalists were more likely to take a world view, not a national view, of their investment opportunities. In consequence, with enhanced 'exit' opportunities to shift money around the world, capitalists in neocorporatist countries were expected to see less point in making compromises with their state or unions. If conditions were not right for capital, capital could simply move. Globalization changed the balance of power so much between capital, labour and the state in favour of capital that neocorporatism was no longer an attractive option for capital.

It came as no surprise, therefore, that the most familiar neocorporatist systems seemed to be moving away from their traditional practices in the 1980s and 1990s. National wage bargaining ceased to operate in Sweden in the 1980s, for example. Neocorporatist governments, particularly in Sweden and in Austria, also found it impossible to continue to deliver their part of the bargain, particularly full employment. By the late 1980s, the demise of neocorporatism seemed at hand.

Neocorporatism Fights Back: Competitive Neocorporatism

Reports of the death of neocorporatism turned out to have been greatly exaggerated. As we have seen, neocorporatism gained a new recruit in the Republic of Ireland. The tremendous success of the Irish economy since it adopted neocorporatism made it an example of the success, not the failure, that neocorporatism could bring. Among the long-established examples of neocorporatism, the Netherlands also illustrated how it could be used to achieve the flexibility that the globalized economy required. Drawing on the 'polder' model's (named after the cooperative efforts that had allegedly allowed the Dutch to drain the polders and reclaim land from the sea) emphasis on compromise, consensus and coopera- tion, the Dutch set out in the early 1980s to achieve the flexibility through neocorporatism that Thatcher had attained in Britain through conflict with labour. Abuses in the Dutch welfare system were ended, flexibility in the labour market was achieved partly through encouraging part-time work and, as in Ireland, all the main economic indicators (employment, growth, inflation and balance of payments) were positive.[13] Neocorporatism has long been associ- ated with progressive or left-wing policies – expanding the welfare state, strengthening the rights of workers and so on. Now the Irish and Dutch showed that neocorporatism could work in a different direction. In Ireland, neocorporatist bargaining resulted in tax incentives for employers and wage restrictions for workers; work- ers were compensated not with the promise of an expanded welfare state but with the promise of tax cuts for workers, too. In the Netherlands, neocorporatist bargaining delivered the labour market flexibility.[14] Yet if Irish and Dutch neocorporatism delivered more conservative policy change than had been anticipated, it showed that the system was more resilient and adaptable than had been sup- posed. It began to look as though the decline of neocorporatism in heartland countries such as Sweden was due more to political and social change than to shortcomings in neocorporatism itself.

Why had the resilience of neocorporatism been underestimated? We should note that, as Katzenstein had argued in the 1980s, neo- corporatism is a means by which trade-dependent economies with strong labour movements can adapt to global economic demands.[15] In some respects, neocorporatism could increase, not diminish, the capacity of economies to adapt. For example, when the existence of a single European currency and central bank means that coun- tries can no longer use techniques such as devaluation or changes in interest rates to increase competitiveness and hold down infla- tion, the ability to achieve these goals through neocorporatism is a considerable advantage. If this argument is correct, countries within the European Union, and particularly within the euro zone, that are more neocorporatist are at an advantage, not a disadvantage. This argument has potentially wider significance. The European Union, as the most developed international organization, imposes particularly clear limits on its members' freedom to use economic policy tools such as changing interest rates. It has often been claimed, however, that globalization imposes similar though less tangible constraints on governments in general. In an era of relatively free movement of capital and massive levels of trading on world financial markets, governments must conform to market expectations in their economic policies or pay a severe price for defying them. If this argument is correct, it suggests that neocorporatist countries might be at an advantage in world markets.

Moreover, neocorporatist arrangements deliver benefits to the state and employers as well as to unions. The Netherlands was able to arrange an effective and efficient response to the Kyoto agreement on global warming through neocorporatist means, while the United States rejected it. The Dutch government, relying on the long established habits of cooperation and compromise that the 'polder' model of neocorporatism fosters, was able to arrange with relevant industries a 'Compact' in which industries promised to attain or exceed the highest global standards within five years in return for the government giving them a free choice on how to achieve the goal. Neocorporatism addressed an important problem in ways that were acceptable to both government and business while American pluralism did nothing. It is also noticeable that employers in neocorporatist countries have not complained that neocorporatism placed them at a major competitive disadvantage in world markets. Herrigel[16] and Thelen[17] have argued that employers benefit not only from the absence of wage inflation and stability in labour markets but from the training and other programmes that unions operate in many neocorporatist systems. The cooperation of unions does not carry a cost that employers have to grin and bear but is a positive contribution to systems, such as the German model, that have a long track record of effectiveness.

This is not to argue that neocorporatism will sweep the world. As we have seen, although neocorporatism has been effective, it is found in its clearest forms in a relatively small number of countries.

Moreover, even if the international factors weakening neocorporatism may have been exaggerated, the domestic changes that undermined it, such as class decomposition, the rise of post materialist politics and resistance to high tax regimes, may have been understated. The troubles of neocorporatism in Scandinavia may well relate to the decline of the social democratic state in general rather than neocorporatism itself. Neocorporatism attracted admirers because it seemed to be a progressive alternative to market oriented systems. Neocorporatism has proved the most resilient recently in pursuing, through less confrontational means, the same sorts of changes (greater labour market flexibility, ending abuses of welfare systems, reducing taxation, attracting investment) that were promoted by right-of-centre politicians, such as Thatcher, through other means. Indeed, there is a good argument that the neocorporatist systems that persist today are forms of 'competitive corporatism'[18] that are notably different from neocorporatism in its heyday. Neocorporatism in its prime was part of a 'societal settlement', a bargain between major classes and the state that established their relations across many policy areas. Most observers think that competitive corporatism, even in heartland countries of neocorporatism such as Sweden, has become a more episodic and narrowly-focused form of policy-making, limited to areas such as employment law and wage bargaining. A few observers stress that broad neocorporatist agreements were made in the 1990s in some countries, such as Portugal and Norway.[19] These examples are probably of limited general significance however. Thus, while it is clear that 'competitive corporatism' is valuable in some countries in handling certain policy problems, it appears that neocorporatism in general has suffered a decline. This certainly seems to be implicit in the views of Streeck, who sees a shift in neocorporatism 'from negotiating a secure status for workers and unions, insulating these from economic fluctuations' to 'adjusting the governance of the employment relationship to the imperatives of economic success' such as preserving jobs and, where possible, creating new ones.[20]

The Special Case of Germany

Germany fits uneasily in discussions of neocorporatism. Katzenstein's description – a weak state in a strong society – explains why.[21]

Federal German politics might seem to be a propitious setting for neocorporatist arrangements. The Social Democrats are obviously tolerant of their partners, the unions, playing a major role in policy. The Social Democrats long ago shed their antipathy to capitalism formally accepting in their Bad Godesberg declaration (1959) that they no longer aimed at creating a new socialist order. It is important to note, too, that while the Christian Democrats were seen as the pro-business party, they lacked that antipathy to unions which has been so characteristic of centre-right politicians in the United States and Britain. In common with the other Catholic parties of Western Europe, the Christian Democrats proclaimed themselves to be a party of social solidarity. Christian Democrats sought the support of workers, including organized workers. Catholic social doctrine taught that unrestrained capitalism was wrong. The electoral system made it unlikely until the 1990s that either the Christian Democrats or the Social Democrats could rule without the support of the Free Democrats, a small centrist party that exerted a further moderating effect. The Schröder government, however, has depended on the support of the more radical-sounding Greens, not the Free Democrats. However, the determination of the German Social Democrats, rather as in the case of the British Labour Party, to get and to keep power after a long period in opposition insured that Schröder would not be moved to the left by his new coalition partner.

The consensual world of German federal politics with dominant parties tolerant of both business and labour might have been expected to produce a neocorporatist situation. Yet there is widespread agreement among scholars that the federal government in Germany bears little relation to the role of government that one would expect from the neocorporatist models. Attempts at neocorporatism at the national level, such as the *Konzertierte Aktion* (concerted action) programme between 1967 and 1977, are regarded as having had no real results. There was no history of cross-sector national wage-bargaining coordinated by government, for example, and few institutionalized neocorporatist meetings. The federal government had little responsibility for policy implementation, which was handled by and large by the *länder* (states). For that reason, the federal government was likely to need assistance in policy implementation because policy implementation was more a *länder* responsibility. The economic doctrines that guided West Germany were also likely to minimize the federal government's need for assistance from interest groups. For most of the period after the Second World War – a period in which the West German economy was the first of the celebrated high growth economic 'miracles' – policy rested on the 'social market' approach; the government would allow market forces to operate though operating a generous welfare state. The central bank, the Bundesbank, was one of the most autonomous central banks in the world and steadily pursued a policy of minimizing inflation that helped make the deutschemark the strongest currency in the world. There were of course important historical reasons for this. The hyperinflation of the 1920s had been seen as one of the causes of the fall of the Weimar Republic and the rise of Nazism. The Bundesbank could draw on a huge reservoir of popular support for its emphasis on minimizing inflation. The power of the Bundesbank, however, again served to minimize the strength of the elected national government because the Bundesbank made the decisions it considered correct, not the ones that the government desired.

The weakness of the federal government was however paralleled by an extremely strongly organized society.[22] There is no doubt that Germany's interest-group structure could be used to operate a neocoporatist system. Building on German traditions going back to the Middle Ages, all firms belong to local business organizations, or *kammern*. Firms almost invariably join the appropriate trade associations for the industries in which they are involved. For example, in the 1980s, some 80 per cent of employees in the metal industries were employed in firms that belonged to the relevant trade association, the *Gesamtmetall*.[23]

Trade associations in Germany have a certain measure of authority that their American and British counterparts lack. From the late nineteenth century onwards, German trade associations in manufacturing industry accepted responsibility for the self-regulation of their members. Trade associations appointed inspectors to visit members' factories and make sure that dangerous conditions did not exist. In the modern era, German trade associations have accepted a major responsibility for the self-regulation of their members' environmental standards. In EMAS (Environmental Auditing and Management System), trade associations appoint inspectors from a list approved by the government to examine the environmental standards met by their members and to recommend improvements. EMAS is an unusually strong form of environmental self-management, and the involvement of trade associations, as opposed to merely the firm itself, helps makes it so. German unions represent a relatively modest proportion of the workforce (about one-third) but they are concentrated in strategic industries. Additionally, the proportion of the workforce covered by union agreements is considerably greater than the proportion of union members. Moreover, unions have a highly institutionalized role in German life as we have noted, running the sickness funds and the apprenticeship systems. Although the works councils, established by German law to give workers a voice in the running of their enterprise, are not nominally composed of representatives of unions, in practice the councils give unions an additional opportunity to influence their firms.

The special character of German capitalism extends beyond these relationships, however. German firms are much more likely to be privately-owned than firms in the USA or Britain; a trend, evident in the very late twentieth century, towards more firms being publicly traded (that is, issuing stock that is quoted on the Stock Exchange) has apparently halted since. German corporations are therefore more likely to be anchored to a particular locality and region than American or British firms. Firms are linked closely to banks, which place directors on the boards of their customers and expect to meet their long-term as well as short-term borrowing needs. It has become increasingly common for very large manufacturing firms to place extensive subcontracts in their districts rather than make the entire product themselves. Automobile manufacturers, for example, now outsource the design and manufacture of part of the vehicle. Reliance on local subcontractors again tends to anchor German corporations to a locality. Local ties are enhanced by the fact that in a few cases *länder* governments own part of major corporations in their state. The classic example is the government of Lower Saxony's ownership of about 20 per cent of the stock of Volkswagen. In many cases, *länder* governments have provided loans or other financial aid. Germany's partners in the EU are often troubled by the activities of the banks owned by the *länder*. In conservative Bavaria, as much as in social democratic *länder*, these banks have promoted economic development and sustained troubled firms with low-income loans guaranteed by the *land*. In a sense, therefore, neocorporatism has flourished at the local, or *land*, level even while Germany as a whole is not regarded as neocorporatist.

Yet the winds of change originating in globalization blow even in Germany. The employers' organization, the BDA, has called for a shift from sectoral bargaining to setting wages at the factory or plant level. Similar calls have been made by one of the leading trade associations, *Gesamtmetall*. The number of employers making agreements covering only their own plants (as opposed to participating in sectoral agreements with unions) has risen from 2,550 in 1990 to 6,415 in 2000. Membership of *Gesamtmetall* has declined by about 15 per cent since 1980. Some firms have joined a rival organization, the Association for Metal Sector Employers (*Arbeitvergeband der Metall und Elektroindustrie*), which takes no part in sectoral wage bargaining with unions and confines its role to lobbying government. With perhaps great significance for the future, trade associations and the BDA have not established themselves in former-East Germany. This failure has created a two-track Germany, a highly organized West and a less-organized (and lower-cost) former-East Germany.

Important though these developments may prove to be, they have to change deeply implanted factors which combine to make German capitalism neocorporatist in spirit. There is much more emphasis on agreement between firms, and between firms and unions, than in Britain or the United States. The unrestricted workings of markets are still viewed dubiously. The immediate reaction of Chancellor Schröder to the takeover of the large German firm, Mannesman, by the British firm, Vodafone, was that such activities were not in accordance with the German way of life. The British Prime Minister, Tony Blair, had to remind Schröder forcefully that the laws and spirit of the EU precluded policies aimed at preventing a company from one country (the UK) purchasing a company in another (Germany). Germany, in short, has not developed the fully-fledged institutions of neocorporatism at the national level. It has, however, a powerful spirit of neocorporatism at the local level. To rephrase Katzenstein, we might argue that Germany is a neocorporatist society in a non-neocorporatist state.

6

Transitional Economies

Early in the twenty-first century, the *New York Times* ran a relatively small story on its front page (3 July 2001) that announced that capitalists were now being allowed and encouraged to join the Chinese Communist Party; only two decades earlier, the Party would have been much more likely to call for capitalists to be shot. For most of the last half of the twentieth century, such a story would have been inconceivable. The changes in China are of course part of an even larger and massively important change. Until the 1990s, a huge chunk of the world's population in China, the Soviet Union and various countries allied to them, such as Cuba and Vietnam, lived in socialist economies in which private business was confined to agriculture and relatively small businesses. Capitalism, not socialism, was supposed to be consigned to the dustbin of history. In fact, socialist systems either collapsed dramatically and unexpectedly (as in Eastern Europe after 1989 and Russia after 1991) or were deliberately abandoned by rulers who continued to label themselves as communists (as in China or Vietnam).

Why the socialist systems collapsed is an important, intriguing question that cannot be addressed here. It is important for us to remember, however, as we discuss problems of transitions that socialist economies had failed. Those who administered or who lived in them had decided that socialist economies were incapable of delivering standards of living for people or military equipment for governments that were comparable with capitalism. Whatever difficulties, failings and setbacks have attended the transition to capitalism, we cannot pretend that carrying on as before was an attractive or even viable option for the former socialist countries. A transition from socialism to capitalism seemed to rulers of these states to be unavoidable.

121

Transition Problems

The transition from socialism posed unprecedented problems. Changes of regime, even violent changes of regime, are quite common in history. Democracies have been displaced by dictatorships and, more happily, dictatorships have recently been replaced by democracies, especially in Latin America. In general, however, these changes have been confined to the political arena. Capitalism remained in place in Argentina and Chile when the generals seized power in the 1970s, and also when the generals finally returned to their barracks. Even throughout the massive upheavals that Hitler's rise to power caused in Germany, the basic features of a capitalist order remained in place. In contrast, communist regimes destroyed capitalism. Private enterprise was abolished or restricted to limited economic sectors such as agriculture and small business. Not only were major enterprises taken into state ownership but the infrastructure of capitalism – banks, stock markets and the framework of laws governing privately-owned business – were abolished. In the case of the former communist countries, the political, economic and social orders have had to be rebuilt simultaneously. For some former communist countries, such as China, the challenge has been simplified by retaining a dictatorship inside the shell of the formerly communist regime. China is the major example. For most formerly communist countries, however, the unprecedented challenge has been to accomplish more or less overnight something that took centuries to achieve elsewhere, namely the creation of democracy and capitalism. Moreover, these enormous changes were unleashed unexpectedly and suddenly. No one expected the fall of the Berlin Wall and consequent collapse of East Germany; few expected the sudden unravelling of the Soviet Union. Little or no thought had been given on how to create capitalism. In the west, this process had taken hundreds of years. Now, in the former communist countries, the process had to be radically compressed.

What, more specifically, did the creation of capitalism entail?[1]

In the first place, the state-owned enterprises of the communist era were not set up to function as firms in capitalist systems. Very often, large state-owned enterprises were responsible for running clinics, schools and other functions attached to their factories that are not regarded as part of the responsibility of capitalist firms.

The executives who operated the state-owned enterprises also had little experience of functioning in markets but, rather, were used to producing quantities according to orders from higher up, as set out in the five-year plan. Workers were accustomed neither to the demands for quality production nor the intensity of work common in Europe and North America. The old saying that 'They pretend to pay us and we pretend to work' was often an accurate description of the workplace atmosphere. This is not to say, of course, that individual workers were lazy. It was rather that their energy did not go into their official jobs. A British diplomat posted to East Germany in the 1970s was struck by the degree to which the famed work ethic of Germans was used in the communist system not at people's place of employment but in settings such as gardens and allotments.[2] Capital equipment such as machinery was often old, inefficient and far behind the standards of comparable equipment in the west. Ironically, given the assumption that the socialist system served the public interest better than capitalism, appalling levels of pollution were tolerated; environmental damage was dramatically greater in socialist East Germany, for example, than in capitalist West Germany.

A second and massive problem was the lack of a framework of commercial law. As the state controlled all major enterprises there was little need to set out what would be regarded as the basic framework of capitalism. The law in Russia was silent on the rights of stockholders. There was no effective legal system for asserting the rights of creditors if an enterprise defaulted on its debts. There was no system to force the bankruptcy of failing enterprises; they could continue to trade and avoid paying their debts. Russian enterprises had no effective legal means even for compelling compliance with contracts; if a supplier failed to deliver, or if the company accepting delivery declined to pay, the courts were not likely to enforce the contract. In Chapter 1 we saw that one of the fundamental roles of the state is to set and enforce the market ground rules by which capitalists live. In transition economies, the state did not serve this basic and essential function.

A third problem was that the distribution of goods, as well as their production, had been determined politically. Russian industry sold an important portion of its products to Soviet satellite countries, countries occupied and controlled by Soviet troops. There was no reason to suppose that the satellite countries preferred

Russian products to competing products from, for example, West Germany. Hungary, Poland, Romania and similar countries were simply required to import from the Soviet Union, not the west, whenever possible. Indeed, once the Soviet empire collapsed, Russian industry lost many of its traditional customers. Given the inferior quality of Russian products, they were not likely to find new markets easily.

The fourth problem was the relationship between the transition to democracy and the transition to capitalism. In the 'first world' countries of North America and Europe, capitalism had been established before democracy. Was this a mere historical accident or an important lesson? Democracy, not capitalism, was supposedly the objective of the change from communism. It was hard to see how any regime that did not at least offer the semblance of democracy could have any legitimacy in the post-communist setting. However, it was easy to imagine ways in which democracy could also impede the transition to capitalism. The many workers in inefficient state-owned enterprises, for example, might use the opportunities that democracy provided to insist on subsidies and protection to save their jobs from market forces. These subsidies might be financed by taxes on successful firms, inhibiting their success. In earlier transitions to capitalism, the dispossessed had lacked the political power to inhibit what Schumpeter called the 'creative destruction' of market forces, the tearing down of outmoded industries. The displaced European workers and peasants whose plight in the nineteenth century had impressed Engels had not had the vote or other democratic means to impede the creation of capitalism. In many of the former communist countries they now did.

Transition Strategies

Two sharply contrasting approaches to effecting the transition to socialism and democracy emerged.

The first, associated with the American economist Jeffrey Sachs,[3] argued for a 'sharp shock'. There should be rapid and almost total privatization and the immediate creation of a market economy. Proponents of the sharp shock argued that if democratization preceded the creation of a market economy, workers in unviable industries, that had existed only through government fiat under socialism, would successfully insist on subsidies or protection, thereby thwarting a successful economic transition. The cost of these subsidies would have to be paid out of the resources generated by whatever competitive and successful enterprises did take root, thereby impeding their development. This was a realistic concern. Even after extensive privatization,[4] failing firms in Russia were able to obtain subsidies so extensive that, in 1998, the World Bank estimated that 16 per cent of the country's GDP was spent on subsidies to corporations. It was imperative, therefore, to achieve capitalism through a short sharp shock before democracy facilitated the making of even more claims on the public purse. (This argument was an unconscious reversal of the Leninist argument that socialism could be achieved only through a dictatorial coup!) Proponents of the short sharp shock fully expected that initially output and living standards would decline. It was hoped, however, that the decline would be short-lived, and the graph of national output would take the form of a J-curve; a short decline would be followed by long expansion leading the former communist countries to western standards of living.

By and large, urged on by international bodies such as the IMF or western governments from whom the transitioning countries needed loans, the short sharp shock approach was followed in all the major former communist countries except China. Perhaps it was the only viable approach. It came, however, with significant costs.

First, the approach encouraged the emergence of a form of 'crony capitalism'. In practice, the people best placed to take over a former state-owned enterprise were its managers and local party elites. Even when, as in Russia, shares in former state-owned enterprises were initially widely distributed, the former managers and party officials were able to dominate, partly because, as unemployment and deprivation increased, many ordinary citizens were obliged to sell their shares along with anything else of value. By the late 1990s, a quarter of Russia's population lived below the poverty line. The new managers were not subject to proper market controls. The lack of an adequate framework of company law allowed managers to exploit their companies' bank accounts for their own purposes, often moving ill-gotten gains to safe harbours in Swiss banks or London property. The weakness of commercial law meant that firms were often reduced to bartering with each other, exchanging goods and services rather than selling them for money, because they lacked effective means for enforcing contracts. Although it has since declined, the proportion of barter transactions in the Russian economy reached 54 per cent of GDP in 1998.[5] Foreign investment, essential for growth and development, was lacking because there was no effective system of law to secure its safety from theft or appropriation. Organized crime substituted for the courts in enforcing contracts or agreements. Arguably, the transition from socialism had not been to capitalism but to a hitherto unprecedented form of social organization, a halfway house somewhere between markets and socialism characterized by crime, theft and inefficiency.

Proponents of the short sharp shock had underestimated the task that awaited the new states in creating the structural conditions for capitalism. A certain measure of sympathy with these transitional states may be in order. In most cases, the new states faced predictable problems in securing effective rule. Russia, for example, lacked stable boundaries and soon became embroiled in a most unpleasant war in a would-be secessionist region, Chechnya. Russia also lacked and, strangely, failed to generate effective political parties that could provide stable majorities in its parliament and link its rulers to its people. Czechoslovakia, regarded as one of the more promising former socialist economies, fragmented into the Czech Republic and Slovakia. One of the reasons for the split was that Slovakia was more dependent on heavy industries that seemed unlikely to thrive in the more open market economy Czechs favoured. Only perhaps in Poland and Hungary was there relative political stability. Thus the task of creating the structural framework of a market economy fell on states that were too weak to perform even less demanding responsibilities.

There can be no doubt that, in consequence, the performance of the former communist countries has been disappointing. Russia experienced a severe decline in its gross domestic product that was followed by an even more dramatic and important indicator of severe problems, an actual decline in life expectancy for men from 64 to 57 years between 1989 and 1994.[6] According to official statistics, Russian GDP fell by 44 per cent from 1989 to 1998. While official statistics may exaggerate the decline by overestimating the value of production under communism and excluding tax-avoiding transactions in the 'black economy' today that are not officially recorded, there is little doubt that the decline is substantial. Even in the countries regarded as the most promising – Poland, the Czech Republic and Hungary – it took many years before GDP recovered to its level at the fall of communism. The goal of convergence between their living standards and the west's was remote. Even those former communist countries, such as Poland, that showed economic vigour grew sufficiently slowly that the combination of growth in the western economies and the low starting point of the Polish economy made convergence a remote prospect. Poland, Hungary and the Czech Republic therefore posed a dilemma for the European Union when they applied for membership. It was scarcely possible to deny that they were European countries and part of the continent's cultural core; for example, Mozart's *Don Giovanni* had first been performed in Prague. Yet it was equally obvious that these countries would be a major economic and social burden. Germany, for example, feared a massive wave of immigrants once the European Union policy of free movement of labour among member states was extended to them as a result of EU enlargement.

The former East Germany provided a particularly interesting example of transition to capitalism, partly because the problems caused by the weakness of post-communist states did not arise. East Germany was simply absorbed into a highly successful state, the former West Germany. East Germany's economic statistics had claimed that it was on the same economic level as some western European countries, such as Britain. Many – including a reporter for the British newspaper, *The Guardian*, who published a book on the East German economic miracle – had believed these claims. In reality, the statistics were manufactured. Contrary to the belief that East Germany was the proof that Germans could make any system work, its economy suffered from the same problems as other communist countries; inefficiency, poor equipment and environmental degradation.

The new rulers from West Germany were determined not to allow themselves to be saddled with poorly performing industries. A special agency, the *Treuenhandanstalt* (known generally as the *Treuenhand*) was carefully structured so as to give minimal prospects for political intervention in its decisions.[7] It then proceeded to liquidate the stock of former state-owned enterprises by selling them to whomever would buy them for whatever price could be obtained. The *Treuenhand* therefore carried through one of the most massive privatizations in history. No serious attention seems to have been paid either to the social consequences of its actions or to the possibility that wholly or partially state-owned enterprises could be reformed to compete effectively in market economies, just as Volkswagen or Lufthansa had once done. Cities that had been dependent on a single industry or factory found themselves devastated economically when that factory was bought and large parts of it shut down.

It might have been expected that former East Germany would flourish economically. After all, incorporation of the East into the former West Germany guaranteed some of the factors assumed to be essential for capitalism to flourish, such as a stable political system and the rule of law, including a fully developed body of commercial law. In reality, the East German economy was slow to recover. Some of the reasons for this included legacies of socialism, such as outdated equipment and a poorly motivated workforce. Others included the impact of policy mistakes. Eager to reassure both East and West Germans that unification would be painless, former Chancellor Kohl promised that West German levels of wages and social benefits would apply immediately in East Germany. As East Germany adopted the deutschemark (the West German currency) there was no means by which the hard reality of the lower productivity that prevailed in the east could be translated into sufficiently low wages and prices to attract bargain-hunting employers and investors. Despite being absorbed into a stable state with effective commercial law, a stable political system and an economy that was the powerhouse of Europe, former East Germany languished economically even as, contrary to Chancellor Kohl's promises, the financial burden on West Germans increased.

China provides an interesting and disturbing example of what, so far, has been a successful economic (though not political) transition. In recent years, China, admittedly starting from a low level, has been experiencing double-digit economic growth. In contrast to Russia, China has attracted massive foreign direct investment (FDI). Foreign enterprises account for over 11 per cent of China's GDP. Much of their output is exported, primarily to the USA. In the early years of the twenty-first century, Taiwan, one of the Four Tigers of economic growth previously, began to feel eclipsed by

China itself. Young Taiwanese began to think that the future lay with China and there was discussion in Taiwan of the desirability of some sort of merger with China for economic rather than political reasons. The Taiwanese expected that, even in the electronics and computer industries, they would be overshadowed by China in the foreseeable future. Similarly, Japanese corporations, such as Sony, moved manufacturing facilities to China to take advantage of low labour costs: Chinese workers would accept as pay for two days what Japanese workers would expect for an hour.

Yet, ironically, the Chinese transition has been far slower and less complete than, for example, Russia's. China has, of course, made not the slightest pretence of any transition to democracy. It remained a dictatorship that ruthlessly suppressed dissent, most infamously when troops opened fire on peaceful protesters in Tiananmen Square in Beijing in 1989. China has also not privatized state-owned industries. Nor has it yet established a dependable system of commercial law. The Chinese strategy has been instead to maintain state-owned industries at their current level while allowing private enterprise and foreign-owned firms to expand. Over time, therefore, the proportion of GDP generated by state-owned enterprises declines.[8] The Chinese economy in the early twenty-first century therefore consisted of three very different elements. First, there were the numerous foreign enterprises, such as General Motors, that had moved to establish a presence in China. Second, there were the rapidly-growing indigenous enterprises, often manufacturing goods for western enterprises. A prime example would be the clothing and apparel manufactured in China for labels such as Talbots or Gap. However, high-tech electronic products were also a case in point. Finally, the state-owned sector, including enterprises owned by the armed forces, continued to exist even though their share of GDP diminished as other sectors grew.

Why is the Chinese example disturbing? It is disturbing mainly because it reminds us that the belief in some necessary connection between capitalism and democracy – a belief common in the United States – is clearly false. Just as capitalism flourished under the right-wing dictatorship of General Pinochet in Chile, so capitalism seems to be flourishing (even more ironically) under the dictatorship of the communist party in China. Indeed, it is striking that foreign capitalists have rushed to invest in China in spite of the fact that China suffers from many of the same ills that are seen as inhibiting development in the former communist countries of the Soviet Union and Eastern Europe. Corruption is rife, the infrastructure (especially in transportation) is poor, and commercial law is only partially developed. Li Peng, the Chairman of the Standing Committee of the National People's Congress, recognized the dangers that corruption posed to the stability of the entire system. 'We face the destruction of our party and of our nation if we fail to fight corruption and promote clean government.'[9] China is, of course, a huge market, but Russia is not a small market either. What, then, is so appealing to investors about China? It is hard to resist the conclusion that the maintenance of strong control by the communist party, coupled with its gradualist economic transition, has provided a stable situation which investors find reassuring. Perhaps dictatorship, not democracy, facilitates transitions.

This is not to say that China will necessarily continue to provide stability for investors.[10] The vast economic and social changes unleashed even by gradual transition to capitalism will be significant. As always, there are clear losers in such transitions as well as winners. Farmers in particular are likely to see their relative position worsen as the countryside falls behind the more prosperous cities. In general, income inequality will increase. In spite of attempts by the government to discourage migration, massive movement to the cities is occurring, testing their capacity to absorb large numbers of former peasants. Social unrest has easy and justifiable complaints on which to focus, such as corruption. In short, it is far from clear that over the medium term, as opposed to the short term, the ability of the communists to maintain stability through repression will continue. The examples of successful capitalist developing countries, such as Korea, suggests that, as China grows, it will need to underpin its capitalist structure with a welfare state that will shield workers from the vagaries of the market place.

On a more technical level, the Chinese government will also face ongoing challenges that result from the continued existence of an inefficient state sector in a capitalist economy. Some of these problems are internal; the state sector will continue to control and extract resources that could be used more efficiently elsewhere in the economy. However, there are also external dimensions to this problem. China has been keen to gain membership of international bodies such as the World Trade Organization (WTO) in order to protect its exports from discrimination. China's application was settled in 2001 and membership started in early 2002. Yet these bodies will not tolerate the controls and subsidies that the state-owned enterprises will need for their continued existence. International pressures may therefore add force to the more abstract economic arguments that running a dual economy composed of both an inefficient state sector and flourishing private sector is a bad idea.[11] The obligations that come from belonging to the WTO will certainly add to the domestic strains and pressures that we have noted above. Tariffs on agricultural products, that shielded peasants from foreign competition, were set to be reduced from 22 per cent to 17 per cent and quotas on imports of foreign wheat increased from 2 to 9.3 million tons a year. Similarly, tariffs on imported cars were to be cut from 100 per cent to 25 per cent and quotas abolished. Foreign banks were expected to make giant inroads into the Chinese market. Overall, thirty million jobs were expected to be lost.[12] This would presumably increase social and political tensions.

Transitions to Which Capitalism?

In this chapter so far we have merely talked about transitions to capitalism. Yet a recurring theme throughout this book has been that there is no single thing as capitalism; rather there are varieties of capitalism that differ significantly from each other. An obvious question to ask, therefore, is which model of capitalism will former communist countries adopt?

It might be supposed that history and culture will lead the transitional economies more towards a European, neocorporatist style of business–government relations than to the American model. Decades of socialism might have resulted in poor economic performance, but they may also have habituated people to expect comprehensive healthcare, childcare and other benefits of the welfare state. Although communist regimes discredited government to an important degree, it would be hard to convince people who are accustomed to government control that it is wrong or impossible for government to 'interfere' in markets. The recovery in support for former communists (now pledged to support democracy) in many parts of the former USSR and its satellites is based in part on a wish to maintain the security that government provided under communism. We might have expected, therefore, that continuing demands for security would have produced the combination of welfare state and capitalism that lies at the heart of European systems. However, several factors militate against this.

First, transitions have been happening at a time when faith in the power of markets has been high in intellectual circles and global economic institutions. Urged on by the United States, economists from the OECD, IMF, World Bank and similar organizations have taken the view that best practice in economic policy is to minimize government intervention or regulation and maximize the impact of market forces. International economic advisers probably constitute an epistemic community – a group characterized by common beliefs about how the world works and ought to work. In this worldview, the American model of capitalism is supreme. Apart from the intellectual impact of this advice, complying with it can be the price for obtaining grants and loans, an important consideration for struggling transitional economies. Most transitional economies have been desperate for money and were unable to argue with the 'advice' from the World Bank or IMF that is a condition for loans. Similarly, the understandable desire for swift admission to international organizations, such the EU or WTO, makes it impossible to adopt the policies of promoting exports while protecting the domestic market that characterized Japanese and Korean development. The international environment is far less tolerant of such approaches today.

Second, European models of capitalism are often dependent on a rich 'civil society' of economic interest groups representing business, labour, farmers and so on: groups that share in the tasks of governance with governments. Former communist countries are in general renowned for having weak civil societies. Communist regimes did not tolerate autonomous organizations outside the control of the Party if they could avoid it; the importance of the Catholic Church in Poland was precisely that it was an exception that the Communist Party felt obliged to make to this generalization. Transitional economies have not inherited the network of strong business organizations and unions that countries, such as Germany, have been able to utilize. Former communist countries lack the societal infrastructure to build neocorporatist systems. They also lack the administrative cultures and structures to build developmental states along French or Japanese lines. Communist regimes viewed professional administrators with suspicion and unease. They did not build up cadres of highly regarded, intellectually superior administrators that could guide economic development, as did the top bureaucrats in Japan and France. As we have seen, a major problem for former communist countries has been that they lack a capable and, above all, honest administrative structure to carry out basic regulation and tax collection. In the words of the experts on corruption, Transparency International, 'A decade of post-communist transition brought corrupt privatizations and governments unable to enforce property rights and legal contracts. As a result, societies across the Commonwealth of Independent States (CIS) now have little more than the shadow of a safety net and *corruption is part and parcel of political, economic and social life. From passing university examinations to acquiring passports bribes are the means to get things done*'[13] (emphasis added). In consequence, businesses have turned to organized crime for protection and to enforce contracts.[14]

It is, therefore, unlikely that the former communist countries will evolve into neocorporatist or developmental states. Contrary to the views of conventional economists, however, dependence on market forces alone does not guarantee success. Few states have made a successful transition from relative poverty to prosperity by relying on market forces. If former communist countries do so, they will have made an unusual approach to development work.

There is of course no reason to suppose that all former communist countries will follow the same trajectory. Indeed, it seems unlikely that they will. Several groups of former communist countries can be distinguished. The first, composed of Poland, Hungary and the Czech Republic, may well be regarded as fully marketized countries within the foreseeable future. By 2010, these countries are supposed to be part of the European Union and subject to its constraints on what governments can do to aid enterprises or distort competition. The second group is composed of aspirant countries following the same trajectory but less advanced along it.[15] This group would include countries such as Romania and Bulgaria. A third group is composed of kleptocracies in which former communist leaders allied with cronies to control countries that are travesties of both democracy and capitalism; some of the nations of central Asia may be cases in point. A fourth group includes the most important case, Russia. Signs of successful transition and unsuccessful transition are both evident; the future is all to play for.

Conclusion

As time has passed since the downfall of communism, starting with the fall of the Berlin Wall in 1989, there has been increasing awareness of how difficult it will be to achieve the levels of honesty and regulation (no matter how imperfect they are) common in North America and western Europe. International organizations such as the World Bank have come to realize that a second level of institutional development is necessary. Not only must the basic institutions of capitalism, such as stock markets and company law, be put in place but they need to be operated honestly and efficiently. We know that in the former communist countries and in Latin America, this does not happen; corruption and dishonesty are endemic. The 2002 World Bank *World Development Report* argues that the state plays a vital part in facilitating or preventing development. 'The ability of the state to provide those institutions that support growth and poverty reduction – often referred to as good government – is essential to development.'[16] Institutions, the report argues, have three effects. They either ease or restrict the flow of information on which markets depend, define and enforce property rights and contracts, and increase or decrease competition.[17]

How societies can escape from this situation is unclear. The World Bank offers no blueprint: it suggests that one of the best prospects is to design institutions so that officials have the incentives to provide good governance: 'It is critical to consider the incentives facing public officials.'[18] There are a few examples of once-corrupt countries that have changed. Hong Kong, for example, used to be infamous for corruption but has made the transition to a high level of honesty. This was achieved, however, in large part by the use of almost draconian powers, for example to investigate all transactions in bank accounts and require individuals to establish their probity. Hong Kong was a British colony at the time. Whether this undemocratic form of government was essential for these anti-corruption drives is a troubling question. It is certainly hard to imagine the relatively weak governments in post-communist societies being able to act with such vigour.

In Chapter 1, we stressed how dependent markets are on the state. At one time this might have seemed a controversial claim to make. Orthodox economists liked to think of markets as the antithesis of the state, and indeed only slightly-out-of-favour social scientists talked about the state at all. In recent years, however, as we have seen, such influential and mainstream bodies as the World Bank have come to emphasize the centrality of the state in securing the efficient operation of markets and businesses. There is more or less a consensus around the proposition that the challenge facing transitional economies is not so much securing capital or lagging technology as it is the inadequacy of their states. Unfortunately, state-building is one of the most complex tasks with which people can grapple.

7

Globalization, Internationalization and Governance

Globalization

In the early years of the twenty-first century, *The Economist* noted with amusement that some of its subject matter, that had long been regarded as obscure, dry and dusty, was now the focus of popular argument.[1] Coverage of the World Bank, the International Monetary Fund (IMF) and the World Trade Organization was once confined to relatively advanced university courses. Since the end of the twentieth century, however, these organizations have attracted considerable and often unfriendly attention. Riots in Seattle, Washington DC and Gothenberg established a pattern in which any meeting that involved these organizations or discussion of globalization attracted an international crowd of protesters.[2]

There are doubtless complex reasons why these protests occurred. There is no doubting, however, the intensity of the emotions that they arouse.[3] Why? Several different arguments which we encountered earlier in this book underlie the protests.

First, protesters believe that the entire global economic system is increasingly rigged against developing countries as it moves towards free trade. Free trade, for example, means that poor countries cannot build up their own industries behind high tariff walls, as did Britain, Germany and the United States, for example. Few countries developed without high tariff walls to protect their infant industries. The major examples of rapid economic growth in the late twentieth century were countries such as Japan and Korea whose governments played a major role in fostering and sheltering nascent industries. Neither Japan nor Korea allowed established industries in other countries to threaten the growth of their own firms. Neither country was hindered at this stage of its history by WTO rules; both countries delayed joining the WTO's predecessor, the GATT, until their development was well under way. The developed world in general and the United States in particular tolerated a very imbalanced trading relationship in which Japanese and Korean firms could sell freely into their markets while they remained closed to foreign firms. This willingness to tolerate unbalanced trading relations no longer exists in the developed world.

In principle free movement of capital should help poor countries to attract the resources they need for development. Yet it can also have disadvantages for poorer countries. For example, liberalizing the rules on capital movement helps wealthy elites in poor countries to shift their wealth into safer banks and investments in financial centres such as London, New York and, particularly for rich Latin Americans, Miami. The counter-argument, of course, is that a liberal trading system provides opportunities for poorer nations to raise their living standards by exporting, as Japan, Korea and Taiwan have done. The opportunity to supply low-cost shoes or shirts to American firms, such as Nike, or European companies, such as Adidas and Reebok, has allowed very poor countries, such as Vietnam or Guatemala, to create thousands of jobs that pay very poorly, but better than any alternative employers. Free movement of capital facilitates the flow of investment from wealthy nations into poorer countries, again facilitating their growth. Development in Asian countries such as Thailand would have been much less without Japanese investment.

A second criticism of the global system is that it has created game rules that discriminate against the poor. A good example is the intellectual property system governing patents. The TRIPS agreement, that is part of the WTO regime, obliges all countries to respect each other's patents. American judges have allowed patents to be taken out on an astonishing variety of products such as beans and basmati rice that have been grown for centuries in Mexico and India respectively. Mexicans who wish to grow and export these beans originating in their own country but now patented in the United States find themselves threatened with paying patent royalties to Americans who own the patents to the genetics of them.

A third criticism is that the international organizations take away sovereignty from nation-states. Countries that run into financial problems and need a loan from the IMF or World Bank find that the terms include explicit directions on changes that must be made in their budgets. As these changes often include reductions in social spending that hit the poorest hardest, they may be literally a matter of life or death because expenditure reductions result in lower food subsidies or welfare payments that enable the poor to eat. For more developed countries, the consequences may be less dramatic in terms of policy outcomes but may still result in a loss of sovereignty. The WTO, as we discussed earlier, has ruled against environmental measures adopted by national governments that it deems to be an unacceptable interference with trade. The international regime of open markets and free movement of capital can be seen as enhancing the structural power of business by increasing the ease with which capital can move away from high-tax or strict regulatory environments while doing little to create international regulations and standards.

These arguments are familiar from Chapter 1. We also considered the case that the nation-state has not been incapacitated by globalization and retains its power to a greater degree than might be supposed.[4] However, the question that we tackle here concerns the forms of international governance that affect business. How do government and politics on the international, as opposed to the national, level affect business? We can distinguish several ways.

The first is through the unilateral imposition of standards by a single government or group of governments. We have encountered several American attempts to impose values, such as environmental protection, on other countries by denying them access to the American market if they do not, for example, protect dolphins adequately. The United States has strict laws against price fixing that it argues are applicable to non-American business executives living and working outside the United States as well as to Americans within its territory. The Helms–Burton law attempts to prohibit trade with Cuba by non-American companies. A whole host of lawsuits against foreign companies for deeds committed outside the United States have been launched in American courts. A suit was started in federal court in Brooklyn in 2001 in which French national railways were sued for damages for their part in transporting Jews to Nazi concentration and death camps during the

Second World War. After a long period in which American laws and courts have claimed the right to govern other nations the European Union has followed suit. A striking example of the reach of the European Union into the American economy was its decision to block the merger of two giant companies, GE and Honeywell, in 2001 on the grounds that their merger would create monopolistic conditions in Europe. This rationale is often used by the EU to examine mergers between very large American companies. There is usually close collaboration and agreement on the merits of each case, however, between the EU and the Antitrust Division of the US Department of Commerce. The EU similarly threatened at the turn of the century to prohibit American firms transferring to the United States data they had gathered on EU citizens unless the United States adopted adequate measures to protect privacy. In the end, the EU settled for a weak agreement with the United States for fear of a trade war.[5] The Department of Commerce is supposed to ensure that data gathered on Europeans were used in a way that protected their privacy though it has no resources to do so effectively. Nonetheless the episode illustrated the way in which standards prevalent in one major economic bloc or country could spread around the world. There seems to be an increasing trend, which started in the United States but which may now be spreading, to apply national laws to companies globally, a phenomenon often termed 'extraterritoriality'.[6]

Extraterritoriality suffers from obvious legitimacy problems. People in the rest of the world do not like to be subject to American laws over which they have no control even in pursuit of desirable goals. Americans have been quick to express resentment of decisions by the EU that they see as imposing European policies on American companies and should be able to understand this sentiment. It would seem preferable, therefore, if governments could collaborate to bring international companies under their control. An interesting example of an extraterritorial policy being made international is anti-corruption policy. In the aftermath of Watergate and revelations about misdeeds of US corporations in Chile, the United States adopted a law, the Foreign Corrupt Practices Act, that made it a crime under American law for US companies to bribe officials in other countries. American companies naturally complained that this placed them at a competitive disadvantage in countries where bribery is endemic; American executives could go to prison under US law for paying a bribe whereas the same bribe was a tax-deductible expense for French companies! In response to complaints, the United States pressed other advanced industrialized countries to adopt prohibitions on their corporations paying bribes in foreign countries. The campaign finally bore fruit in an OECD Convention that committed members to outlawing bribery by their nationals and corporations in other countries.[7]

It remains to be seen how much impact the anti-corruption policies will have. We should also note that once the Foreign Corrupt Practices Act had been passed in the USA in 1977, it created a powerful incentive for American corporations and the US government to try to bring other countries into line in case the US lost business to less scrupulous rivals. It might be possible to follow this pathway to reform in other areas, securing reform first in the United States as the most powerful country then spreading the reform to other nations. Attempts to do so face formidable problems, however. While everyone is in theory against corruption, in other policy areas, interests, circumstances and values differ from country to country. Adopting environmental or workplace protection measures to prevent illnesses that take thirty years to develop may seem a luxury for countries that are so poor that few live long enough to suffer from such illnesses and where life expectancy can be increased more effectively by simply providing clean drinking water and proper sanitation. During the Kyoto negotiations on global warming, third world countries argued successfully that they could not be expected to adopt equal reductions in greenhouse gas emissions to advanced countries until they came closer to their economic levels and standards of living. The attempts to launch a new series of negotiations on further liberalizing international trade in Seattle in 1999 were derailed not by the anti-globalization protesters in the streets but by third world countries in the conference hall who feared that the United States (and possibly Europe) was going to try to impose on them first world standards for workplace and environmental conditions. Third world countries believed such a move would impede their attempts to develop economically.

Attempts at international collaboration to govern business are impeded by two further problems.

First, the international system has no established inspectorate or judicial system to impose regulations on companies. To some extent, this problem can be avoided by intercepting complaints from rival companies or public interest groups. Competitors generally know what their rivals are doing and can be expected to complain about breaches of agreements that result in competitive advantage. Public interest groups flourish by attracting publicity, members and contributions when they make dramatic revelations of corporate wrongdoing.

Second, there is a justifiable fear that any attempt to impose regulations on companies through trade policy will be used for protectionist purposes, forcing requirements on overseas suppliers not to serve the public interest but to protect domestic producers from competition. In short, mixing trade policy with the pursuit of important public interest goals may result in disguised protectionism and non-tariff barriers (NTBs).

There are, however, instances where cooperation between governments has materially changed business behaviour. They typically attract little attention from the public, partly because they focus on highly specialized issues and problems. The Montreal Agreement to phase out the use of chlorofluorocarbons (CFCs) that have been linked to holes in the earth's ozone layer is a good example of regulating business by international treaty. If the treaty is implemented fully, it will change business behaviour in a way that protects the global environment, in spite of the difficulties described above. Yet it would be overly optimistic to imagine that this example can be easily replicated on other issues. CFCs are produced in relatively few places and can be tracked more easily than many products. Widespread acceptance of the scientific evidence, the consequences of the danger and the fact that it threatened more or less the entire world's population promoted agreement. Finally, competitors could be expected to report any use of CFCs that placed them at a competitive disadvantage and, in a sense, substituted for a force of government inspectors.

In contrast, attempts to reach agreement on topics such as working conditions or environmental practices face disagreement about the evidence as well as the 'science' of the predicted economic consequences of regulation. There are also obvious conflicts of interest. Workers and employers in the first world who are threatened by cheap imports from the third world naturally favour international agreements to impose minimum standards of pay and working conditions. Third world countries eager for development are likely to take a different view. Dangerous working conditions are evident only to those who have access to the plant, something hostile governments and employers are unlikely to allow. Even pay levels are hard to document and there can be no agreement on what constitutes a 'living wage'. Standards of living deemed unacceptable in even poor European or North American regions may well be regarded as acceptable, even desirable, in Vietnam or Guatemala. There are major differences of opinion even within the European Union about what the rights of workers or unions should be; on a global scale these disagreements are even greater. In consequence, one of the very oldest of the international organizations, the International Labor Organization (ILO), has been able to achieve little.

The very limited ability of the ILO to regulate working conditions has encouraged attempts to link workplace standards to trade agreements. One of the standard fights in the United States Congress at the turn of the century was between Democrats – who insisted that any grant of powers to the president to engage in trade negotiations be accompanied by requirements that resulting agreements should include guarantees of acceptable working conditions – and presidents (of both parties) and Republicans – who argued that trade should be kept separate from labour standards or the environment. Presumably countries that failed to honour the global standards would be punished by loss of trading privileges. Similar arguments took place on whether or not to link environmental standards to trade agreements. It seems somewhat more likely that this might happen. There was more of a history, particularly in the United States, of using trade as a lever to improve other countries' environmental standards. Moreover, it can be argued that poor environmental practices in other countries have a direct impact on the United States (as pollution, for example, knows no boundaries) in a way that inadequate working conditions do not. In the aftermath of GATT and WTO attempts to force the United States to abandon policies aimed at forcing other countries to raise their environmental standards, the WTO signalled an increased willingness to take environmental considerations into account. The WTO, as we have seen, opened a dialogue with environmental groups and accorded them permission to file their own briefs (as opposed to relying on their national government to represent them) in hearings before its panels.

Nonetheless, there is no general agreement that trade issues should be complicated by environmental issues.

The weakness of global government in the face of growing global economic integration has prompted increased interest in whether a global civil society of international non-governmental organizations (NGOs) might emerge to offset the power of business and the weakness of governments.[8] How might this work?

The most obvious way in which NGOs can play a role in constraining the power of business internationally is by operating as pressure groups on international organizations. As we have seen, this has been a controversial issue in the case of the World Trade Organization. Although first world NGOs understandably believe that they are serving the public interest, it can be argued that they inevitably reflect first world values and priorities. Third world countries in particular have resisted the idea of giving NGOs from rich countries a right to participate in WTO deliberations. For example, third world countries fear that first world NGOs will subordinate economic development to the maintenance of a pure environment, a priority that third world countries think a luxury. Nonetheless, the right of NGOs to participate in WTO procedures has been secured. A similar story can be told about the World Bank. The president of the Bank was even accused of being excessively interested in the views of NGOs.[9] NGOs have a prominent and widely-accepted role in international discussions of human rights policies and practices. However, NGOs still face considerable difficulties in dealing with international organizations. First, it is expensive to maintain an office in a city such as Geneva where many international organizations are located. Second, NGOs have no direct leverage over international organizations. International organizations are not elected; their natural constituency is governments, not voters. Governments generally prefer to deal with each other rather than with interest groups and NGOs from other countries.

NGOs often respond to these problems by placing pressure on national governments. International organizations know that their funding, success and even continued existence may depend on, if not popular support, then at least popular acceptance in member countries. Here the special character of the United States in world politics and the special character of American politics comes into play. As David Vogel has noted,[10] the American political system has been unusually welcoming to diverse interests, such as those of consumers and environmentalists that are geographically scattered but widely shared. Environmentalists have been able to exert significant leverage within American politics, and through American policy on international organizations. Trade policy is again a good example. The United States took the lead in the creation of the WTO and, without American leadership, the prospects for further trade liberalization are limited. Environmentalists have been able to exert leverage on the WTO because they have been able, in partnership with labour, to prevent presidents obtaining 'fast track' authority to negotiate an agreement without the threat of Congress amending it. Fast track guarantees that an agreement reached by the President will be accepted or rejected by Congress within a finite period. But Congress must explicitly grant this authority to Presidents and, for most of the 1990s, a coalition of labour and environmental groups denied Clinton this power. The WTO has attempted to break up this coalition by offering concessions to environmental groups. American environmental groups have therefore been able to exert leverage on the WTO by exerting leverage in American politics.

A specific example of American environmental groups exerting international leverage concerned the attempts of Latin American countries to use GATT (the predecessor of the WTO) to prevent the United States imposing dolphin-protection measures on any country exporting tuna to the United States. GATT ruled against the United States, but environmental groups were able to block implementation of the ruling until the Latin American countries negotiated a compromise with environmental groups. Compliance with the GATT ruling required a change to an American law, the Marine Mammal Protection Act. Dolphins are very popular creatures; very few legislators were prepared to vote for 'GATTzilla', as one anti-trade group labelled it, rather than to protect 'Flipper' (the dolphin hero of a popular movie). Interest group or NGO power at the national level was used to exert leverage at the international level to the point of obliging national governments to negotiate with American interest groups.

Interest groups, even in the United States, do not always, or even often, have the opportunity to exert leverage that trade policy provides. For that reason, there has been considerable interest in the ability of NGOs to put pressure directly on corporations.

Most of us think of corporations as hardheaded organizations, motivated by profits alone. Yet one of the striking features of modern corporations is their unwillingness to ignore public opinion. Corporations instead are more likely to worry about their image. Business advisers point to the advantages of being involved in a 'virtuous circle' of a favourable public image with consumers, a reputation that attracts quality personnel and investors. Conversely, a poor image handicaps a corporation in all these areas. Modern marketing sells consumers not only a product but also an image or a lifestyle: buying Nike athletic shoes makes you like Michael Jordan, the right type of bottled water makes you young and glamorous. It is important, therefore, to protect the integrity of the company's brand image.[11] Failure to do so has direct, adverse commercial consequences in terms of recruiting, attracting capital and marketing a product. Presumably, relatively few graduates of prestigious business schools long to work for tobacco companies. Major financial institutions have no wish to be associated with controversial companies by lending to them and investors may be reluctant to lend if there is a suspicion of 'trouble' surrounding an industry. After all, as with the asbestos and possibly tobacco industries, vague talk of 'trouble' with the product may evolve into bankruptcy. As we have noted, the association of a brand with a lifestyle may make consumers unwilling to buy from a company with a 'dirty' environmental record.

Multinational corporations face potential challenges to their reputations, not only in the countries where they are legally accountable, but also wherever they have significant sales or investment. In other words, NGOs such as Greenpeace can challenge corporations' actions not necessarily where there is legal accountability but they are weak but also in countries' where corporations have important operations and the NGOs are strong. The classic example is the Brent Spar saga described in Chapter 1.[12] Shell wished to dispose of a North Sea oil storage facility, the Brent Spar, by sinking it. The legal authority, the British government, agreed that this plan was the least damaging environmentally and the then British prime minister, John Major, held to this position in the face of strong criticism from fellow heads of government in the EU. Shell, however, felt it could not withstand the campaign against it in the Netherlands and Germany. Not only did

Shell surrender on this issue but the episode prompted a considerable re-evaluation of its 'green' credentials.

The *potential* for NGO protests may even promote better environmental practices. A Dutch-owned company, Oserian Development Company, produces 250 million cut flower stems a year, for export to the Netherlands, on the shores of Lake Naivasha in Kenya. Lake Naivasha is a highly vulnerable freshwater lake and the Kenyan government lacks the administrative capacity or the will to protect it adequately. It would be easy to subvert what few environmental restrictions exist. However, Oserian cannot afford to have sales of its luxury product dependent on discretionary expenditures associated with exploitation of the environment or local people. A campaign by Dutch NGOs against it would be devastating. Oserian has therefore implemented state-of-the-art measures to protect the environment and improve the lot of its workers. The use of pesticides is limited to immediate threats, rather than potential threats, to plants, a drip irrigation system minimizes water use, gravel pits have been dug at the edge of fields to reduce run-off, and a corridor has been created for wildlife to reach the lake. In order to protect the lake, Oserian has even worked to reduce pollution from human and cattle waste not resulting from its own operations but from, for example, cattle-grazing by locals. Oserian has similarly provided its workforce with adequate housing and healthcare. The major reasons why the company has been so progressive are that it has needed an effective workforce and that 'customers in the Netherlands demand that products such as flowers and vegetables be produced under conditions that pay adequate wages, provide safe working conditions and support environmental quality.'[13]

The threat of campaigns against corporations has prompted many of them to enter into discussions that come close to negotiations with interest groups. One senior British executive claimed that twenty years ago, it would have inconceivable for CEOs to have discussions with groups such as Friends of the Earth or Greenpeace. Now such discussions are commonplace.[14] These discussions are not merely symbolic. Corporations have been willing to change their mode of operation at significant cost in order to earn a seal of approval from environmental groups. Again, however, we should not exaggerate the ability of NGOs to constrain business behaviour through such negotiations.

NGOs have limited resources and no ability to compel corporations to give them information on their activities. It is difficult to imagine, therefore, that the influence of NGOs could be equivalent to government regulation.

Another form of governance that might substitute for the lack of international governmental authority is self-regulation by industry.[15] At first sight, it would seem even less plausible that business could regulate itself internationally than that governments could do so. In many countries, trade associations lack the authority and institutional capacity to impose standards on their members. It would seem even less likely that international trade associations could manage to do so. In fact, however, there is a surprising amount of international self-regulation. Why does international self-regulation succeed against all the odds?

The first incentive for an industry is to stabilize competition. Firms might agree to certain restrictions on, for example, marketing techniques which they do not wish to use, but would be obliged to implement if their competitors did. A second motive could be to deal with a negative image of the industry. A third important motive could be to forestall government regulation at the national level. Government regulations have the dual disadvantages of being less flexible than self-regulation and, potentially, of differing from country to country, thereby confronting the industry with further problems.

Rongit and Schneider found that all of these factors were at play in several cases of international self-regulation that they studied. The dyes and colourants industry has been very active, for example, in developing an organization, the Ecological and Toxicological Association of Dyes and Organic Pigments (ETAD), that analyzes the safety of industry products and sets guidelines in the ETAD code of ethics for their manufacture and use. An important motive for the industry has been to minimize regulation by governments, with whom, however, ETAD has friendly, trusting relationships.

In the case of the pharmaceutical industry, the International Federation of Pharmaceutical Manufacturers Association (IFPMA) has worked to establish an effective code of conduct on marketing techniques. The IFPMA was eager to avoid international government action through the World Health Organization (WHO) even though the IFPMA has a cordial relationship with it.

Finally, the International Chamber of Commerce (ICC) attempts to operate codes of practice on a variety of topics including advertising, promoting products or services on the basis of their environmental qualities, sales promotion, sponsorship and social research practice. The codes are, however, not enforced; there is no machinery for imposing sanctions on firms that fail to comply. The ICC does maintain an International Court of Arbitration to settle disputes between firms. The Court, established in 1923, now enjoys significant standing. The ICC also has a Commercial Crime Services unit that specializes in fighting fraud, maritime crime and commercial counterfeiting. Finally, the ICC works to reduce transaction costs, for example by trying to promote the use of uniform contract language and terms.

A terminology of self-regulation is emerging based on whichever form of inspection and certification of compliance with standards is involved.

- *First party certification.*   Corporations set their own code of practice and monitor its implementation.

- *Second party certification.*   The industry's trade association sets and monitors standards.

- *Third party certification.*   Standards are set in consultation with NGOs, which then take on responsibility for monitoring them.

- *Fourth party regulation.*   International regulation is undertaken by governmental bodies.

All forms of self-regulation have their advantages.

Self-monitoring by firms avoids problems such as overcoming secrecy or unwillingness to cooperate with people outside the firm for reasons of pride, a wish to maintain trade secrets and fear of legal action. Firms exist because transaction costs within them are lower than between contractors and subcontractors. These lower transaction costs within firms can ease environmental regulation as well as normal commercial practice. Self-monitoring may attract the attention of senior management to problems without generating the instinct for self-justification and protection that government regulation generates. The best known example of self monitoring, ISO 14000, requires firms to monitor their environmental performance, set goals for themselves, assess whether or not they have met those goals and then set new ones for the future. Many large image-conscious corporations, such as Ford, now require their subcontractors to obtain ISO 14000 certification.

Monitoring by trade associations provides greater stringency but maintains flexibility in regulations. Firms know that their trade associations are knowledgeable and unlikely to attempt to impose unreasonable or impractical standards on them; after all, firms could choose to leave trade associations that they perceived to be unnecessarily hostile or critical. Yet the fear of being shamed in front of industry counterparts or competitors may be an important incentive for better performance. The most developed examples at the national level are found in countries such as Germany with strong, entrenched trade associations. The EMAS system (as we saw in Chapter 5) is a highly regarded system of environmental protection in which trade associations set and monitor standards.

The involvement of NGOs is likely to promote stricter standards and also to confer greater credibility and legitimacy on the process. Firms can be expected to incur extra burdens or expenses to 'pay' for NGO approval. Citizens might feel that they have more reason to believe a firm is performing well if it is monitored by a disinterested NGO. A particularly well-developed example of third party certification comes from the forest products industry. The Forest Stewardship Council (FSC) was created by the World Wildlife Fund and Greenpeace in 1993 to tackle the problems of deforestation, clear cutting (i.e. felling every tree in an area rather than harvesting trees selectively), loss of biodiversity and polluting effluent from pulp and paper mills. The FSC accepts no money from the industry and has developed a set of principles by which companies seeking its certificate must abide. The certifiers who inspect companies work for private firms, such as SmartWood, Scientific Certification Systems in the USA and the Silva Forest Foundation in Canada. Products that comply with FSC principles can display its logo.

Yet international self-regulation is not necessarily a substitute for government action. All the forms of self regulation we have discussed suffer from significant disadvantages.

First party certification raises some obvious doubts about how rigorously standards will be set and maintained. Will some compromise be made between environmental protection, for example, and other corporate goals such as profits or maintaining employment? It is notable that ISO 14000 is merely a *procedural* requirement.

Nothing in ISO 14000 prevents firms from setting very low standards for themselves, for example, so long as those standards are consistent with national laws and regulations. Admittedly, ISO 14000 involves a commitment to self-improvement. However, that self-improvement can be from a low baseline.

Second party certification suffers from the fact that the number of countries with strong standards is limited and the number of industries with strong international trade associations is similarly low. Although bodies such as the IFPMA or ICC aspire to cover the globe, in reality there are large areas, such as Africa, in which their membership is thin and their organization weak. Even in the first world, not all industries have well-organized, effective national, let alone international, trade associations.

Third party certification by an NGO assumes that there is a well-developed NGO to take part in effective negotiations, make a meaningful agreement and monitor it. Whether or not there are enough NGOs with adequate resources for these tasks is a matter for empirical investigation but may be doubted. Moreover, corporations may well simply ignore critical assessments. Not all corporations are equally vulnerable to pressure from NGOs or even from organizations to which they belong. Even well-established organizations such as the ICC have limited ability to impose sanctions. The risk of adverse publicity from NGOs may be an important incentive; Rongit and Schneider suggest a parallel between corporations being shamed by business organizations for breaking their codes and the use of the pillory to shame criminals in mediaeval times. As we noted earlier, reputation does seem to matter to corporations to a surprising degree. The growth in the importance of brands (Nike, Coca-Cola and so on), therefore, may strengthen the leverage of public interest groups over corporations that market their goods to the general public. Whether loss of reputation is an adequate deterrent to corporate misconduct, however, is as yet unclear. The corporations that are the most vulnerable to NGO pressure are those such as oil companies that have direct contact with the public at the retail level, particularly if image is important in selling a product (Shell gasoline, Nike sports shoes) that does not differ markedly from its competitors. Other companies sell products that are used by other businesses, not by the general public and so are less vulnerable to pressure. Nor should we assume, even when NGOs are involved in dealings with companies, that the interests of the weak and powerless are necessarily protected. In any case, NGOs cannot be regarded as entirely satisfactory guardians of the international public interest. NGOs primarily represent the viewpoints of relatively affluent people in the first world. They tend to prioritize goals such as preserving endangered species over economic growth and development. While these are entirely defensible priorities, they are not the only possible priorities.

A final problem with self-regulation is its uneven international spread; it is much more prevalent in some countries than in others.[16] Ironically, although intended to be an alternative to traditional governmental regulation, self-regulation is much less likely to be adopted in countries that have had the most trouble with traditional regulation. Self-regulation has encountered much more resistance in the United States where complaints of highly adversarial, legalistic government regulation is greatest than in, for example, Great Britain. This is largely because the shadow of legalistic regulation hangs over attempts to create self-regulation. Firms fear that their efforts to monitor and diagnose their own failings will be, in the words of the old British police caution, 'taken down in evidence and used against [them] in a court of law'. In consequence, even the most flexible and voluntary forms of self-regulation such as ISO 14001 have been much less popular in the USA than in countries in which government regulation has so far caused much less anguish.[17] The excessive legalism of government regulation in the United States ironically also makes it harder to adopt private-sector self-regulation there.

We might conclude, therefore, that, while international self-regulation is better than no regulation at all, it is not equivalent to effective national regulation. Often adopted to ward off national regulations, corporate self-government is effective when carried out in partnership with government and when the threat of government action in the absence of self-regulation is plausible. IFPMA, for example, has a good working relationship with national governments and with the World Health Organization (WHO). Pharmaceutical companies understand that the alternative to self-regulation is not no regulation but government regulation. International self-regulation is an aid to an international order but, again, not comparable to a national system of laws and regulations.

Regional Organizations: The Example of the European Union

We have paid considerable attention to globalization. Another trend that has emerged is the creation of regional economic institutions to promote freer trade and fairer competition in the cause of increasing economic growth. Mercosur in Latin America, NAFTA in North America and ASEAN in Asia are all examples. The degree to which these international organizations amount to anything more than a free trade agreement varies. NAFTA contains some capacity to achieve greater similarity in standards in areas such as environmental protection. Mercosur has been simply a trade agreement. It is widely recognized, however, that the European Union is by far the most developed of the regional international organizations, which has evolved from a trade organization to an embryonic state with the capacity to make and enforce policy on its members.

In the last twenty years, the European Union (EU) has taken on enormous importance for business. The number of areas in which the EU, not national government, makes policy, especially in the regulatory sphere that impinges on business, has increased drastically. The EU is now the largest source of regulations covering the environment, working conditions and competition policy. The EU is also the body that negotiates trade agreements with other countries (such as the United States) and will soon take over responsibility for agreements on international air travel.

The European Union came into existence as the 'Common Market' in 1957 under the Treaty of Rome. Although it always aspired to being 'an ever closer union' of nations, at first it was indeed limited to being a 'common market', a trading bloc of a minority of western European countries. In practice, non-tariff barriers to trade limited the degree to which it achieved even this modest goal in the first few decades of its existence. Since the EU has expanded considerably starting in the early 1970s, not only in the number of members (from six to fifteen) but in the 'depth' of institutions, the degree to which it, rather than national government, controls and constrains policy. The EU now has a population of over 360 million and will soon incorporate not only most of the countries of western Europe but also eastern European, former communist countries such as Poland, Hungary and the Czech Republic. The deepening of its policy reach has been equally impressive.

Much of the deepening of the EU has resulted from a realization in the early 1980s that the 'common market' that existed on paper did not exist in practice. National laws and regulations, often supposedly geared to protecting consumers, safety or the environment, had the effect (intentionally or otherwise) of protecting domestic producers and handicapping producers in other member states. The members of the EU, concerned that they were lagging behind the United States and suffering from 'eurosclerosis', agreed to adopt a Single European Act that would provide the mechanisms through which the EU could sweep aside national regulations that impeded trade.

Many feared at first that European integration would result in a sharp shift away from the European traditions of generous welfare states and comprehensive regulation to protect labour. Streeck, for example, argued that the processes launched by the Single European Act had created a version of the 'race to the bottom' that as we have seen critics of globalization fear on a wider scale.[18] Facilitating the movement of goods and capital within Europe would give an advantage to corporations based in lower-tax, less-regulated settings such as Britain and handicap those based in higher-tax and more strictly-regulated countries such as France. Hoover's highly publicized decision to move production from France to a factory in Scotland seemed to show that business would respond by relocating.

In practice, however, there has been no intra-EU race to the bottom. To a considerable extent, higher tax, stricter regulation countries have promoted the adoption of EU measures comparable to their own standards. The best example of this process occurred in the 1992 Treaty of Maastricht by which EU members agreed to a Social Charter establishing common standards of protection for the rights of workers. Britain obtained an 'opt out' but much of this 'opt out' was abandoned after the election of the Blair government in 1997. In any case, major British companies operating throughout the EU could not escape the reach of the EU's Social Charter.

Two features of the EU continue to make it a dynamic source of business regulation. First, the policy-making process within the EU is dominated by its 'bureaucracy', the European Commission. In contrast to the bureaucracies of many democracies, the European Commission provides an institutional setting that rewards bureaucratic innovation and policy leadership. Senior bureaucrats are not

rigidly controlled by politicians but are expected to initiate policies and promote them politically. Bureaucratic success is meas-
ured in large part by success in policy innovation. Second, the EU
itself is largely a regulatory state; its ability to raise taxes is very
constrained and therefore its ability to spend money is also
severely limited. In terms of government expenditures, the EU is
puny compared to the national governments. The authority of the
EU and the goal of 'ever closer union' are promoted by expanding
regulations.[19]

The vitality of the EU as a source of regulations has prompted
a reappraisal of its potential by many on the left. There has been
a tendency for the EU to be seen, not as the danger to the welfare
state and strong regulation that Streeck suggested in the early
1980s, but as a bulwark against globalization. If nation-states are
too small to withstand the pressures of globalization, regional
organizations such as the EU may provide the institutional means
to shelter nation-states and their citizens from the pressures of
global markets. A particularly interesting example of this is the
adoption of the euro as the common currency for nearly all members of the EU (Britain being the largest and most obvious exception) from January 2002. Again, many on the left had criticized the
creation of the euro, in part because of the stability agreements that
committed participating countries to limit their budget deficits and
generally to behave in a prudent, traditionally conservative manner
in managing their finances. However, the left was acutely aware
that foreign currency crises had often obliged left-wing governments to adopt conservative policies. It seemed possible, even to
Britain's Labour Party and unions, that the euro could help shelter
left-of-centre governments from the sort of exchange-rate pressures that had driven the French Socialist government off course
in the early 1980s. Surrendering sovereignty to the EU, therefore,
became the preferable alternative to being controlled by market
pressures.

The increased importance of the EU has naturally brought it
greater attention from business groups. The evolution of business
representation in the European Union provides a fascinating
example of how corporations adapt to changing circumstances.
For many years, firms relied on their own contacts with their own
national governments, either directly or through national employers' associations, to influence EU policy.[20] Not only was this the

easy option but it was also effective. The EU made little policy of direct relevance to business until the moves to create the Single European Market from 1985 onwards. Until the use of Qualified Majority Voting (QMV) became common in the aftermath of the Treaty of Maastricht, firms could also rely on their national government to veto any policy proposal that was seriously damaging to them. The flood of EU legislation affecting business as the Single Market was created combined with the diminished ability of national governments to protect the interests of their firms under QMV made it urgent for business to increase its representation in Brussels.

Ironically, American firms were among the first to recognize the forms of business representation that exerting influence in the European Union would require.[21] Continental European firms, as we have seen, are used to highly institutionalized forms of representation through trade and peak associations. The style of policymaking in Brussels was more reminiscent of Washington, DC than, say, London. Policy entrepreneurs in the Commission went out and built support for their favourite policy without as much regard for procedures and collective responsibility as would be required in Whitehall. In consequence, in a manner again reminiscent of Washington, DC, individual firms felt that they needed their own representation in Brussels. By the end of the twentieth century, over 200 corporations had offices in Brussels to represent their interests. This did not mean that firms ignored trade and peak associations but it did reflect corporations' beliefs that these organizations lacked sufficient standing and credibility in Brussels to exert real influence. For its part, the Commission welcomed the growth of business representation. This was partly because the Commission always likes to strengthen ties between itself and groups in the member countries as a means of increasing loyalty to the EU itself. It was also in part because the Commission was desperately short of technical advice as it grappled with the numerous issues the creation of the Single Market raised.

Some have thought that increased reliance by corporations on their own offices to represent them has created a thoroughly pluralist interest group system in the EU. The reality is more complicated.[22] On the one hand, corporations do rely primarily on their own efforts to influence public policy rather than, as in neo-corporatist countries for example, on trade and peak associations.

On the other hand, there are strong pressures on businesses in Brussels to develop alliances and coalitions. Groups of businesses crossing national boundaries have more credibility with the European Commission than individual firms from a single country. The Commission encourages the formation of such alliances and coalitions, in part for practical reasons. While it needs technical advice, the mushrooming of business representation in Brussels threatened to swamp it with more conflicting advice than it could process. Coalitions and alliances help resolve differences between firms that might otherwise fall to the Commission to resolve. The drive for alliances and coalitions extends beyond the world of business, however. The continental European traditions of working with other 'social partners' such as labour has also carried over to interest group style in the EU. Corporations in Brussels commonly seek partnerships and understandings with groups such as environmentalists with whom conflict would be the norm in Washington. In short, a distinctive style of business representation has emerged in Brussels reflecting both the strategic incentives that European institutions create and the traditions that firms bring with them from the national level.

Conclusion

The international commercial order is not a state of nature in which firm fights firm without ground rules. Yet however interesting one finds the protean world of international business regulation, in none of its forms does it compare with national regulation for thoroughness, effectiveness or comprehensiveness. Whether, as international business increases in importance, international business regulation will also increase will be an important question in the future. It is intriguing to see that the European Union offers a realistic, more immediate alternative to the triumph of market forces. The EU provides at least qualified support for the argument that regional economic organizations may facilitate a degree of 'interference' with market forces that cannot be achieved by the medium-sized and small European nation-states acting individually. It remains to be seen whether similar developments may occur in other regional trading blocs such as NAFTA or Mercosur.

8

Business, Governments and Governance in a New Century

States and societies are constantly changing, although the speed of change varies. The late twentieth century was generally felt to be a period of unusually rapid change. The popularity of the term 'globalization' and the speed with which it entered popular political debate was itself a sign of how an academic debate resonated with a wider public. As we have seen, some academics dispute whether globalization is as great a change as is often supposed. Trade as a proportion of GDP was as high prior to the First World War for many countries (including the United States) as it is today.[1] Under the Gold Standard, financial markets were integrated to a degree that they have not yet attained in our own era. Huge financial flows from London to North and South America as well as to the British Empire financed a globally integrated economy.[2]

Although the historical examples of prior eras of globalization are important, they do not detract from the importance of the change that globalization has occasioned in the modern era. There is general agreement that the state showed unprecedented strength through most of the twentieth century. States waged war on an unprecedented scale between 1914 and 1918 and again between 1939 and 1945, but they then accepted responsibilities once thought to be inappropriate or impossible for them to meet. States moved to educate populations to a level once reserved for elites, to manage their economies to avoid unemployment and inflation while promoting growth, to provide healthcare and other welfare-state services and to improve the environment. Even amongst the

157

most advanced countries, the range and extent of these responsibilities was novel. States created bureaucracies on a scale that had
never been previously attempted, committed an unprecedentedly
large proportion of GDP to government control and expanded dramatically (even in the United States) the legal powers of the state.
The modern large-scale state emerged as the protector of the individual against market forces, a guarantor of economic and social
as well as physical security and the means through which greater
social justice could be attained. We must always be aware that the
arguments that globalization has diminished the capacity of the
state have to be placed in the context of a period in which the state
had attained unprecedented size and power.[3]

Modern globalization has made such an impact partly because
it has allegedly reined in the power of states that had been increasing so markedly. But we should also be aware that the increase in
the power and scope of the state had also generated problems that
are unrelated to globalization. The difficulty of controlling very
large bureaucracies, increasing resistance to the high levels of taxation required to fund the state and unintended consequences of
policies (for example, welfare) had created a reaction against the
expansive state that was purely domestic. Politicians such as
Reagan and Thatcher rode this wave of discontent to power; the
wave even reached the shores of the largest and most generous
welfare states such as Sweden.[4]

Globalization can be understood as a set of forces that have
affected all countries. But the impact of globalization on each
country is not necessarily the same, just as a storm passing over
a forest has a different impact on different trees. The emotional
power of globalization is that it is perceived to shift the power balance between contending domestic interests in favour of business
and also reduce the capacity of the state to control business.[5]
Business gains, according the classic argument about globalization, because it can 'get up and leave', by shifting capital overseas
or by outsourcing part or all of the production process. Wise
unions are careful not to bargain hard enough to prompt this shift
to occur. Similarly, governments are careful not to tax or regulate
corporations too vigorously in case they prompt them to relocate
to a country with a more favourable business climate. In the first
edition of this book (published 1985), I argued that, even in countries where business had seemed most secure (such as the United

States), the balance of power between it and other groups had shifted against business. This shift resulted from the rise of groups, such as environmentalists and consumer activists, with resources that were limited but still sufficient to hold significant influence. The days when business had not needed to make an effort to defend its interests had ended; businesses could still win politically but they had to do so through engaging more vigorously in conventional pluralist interest-group politics. Those who warned of the dangers of globalization[6] suggested that interest groups, such as environmentalists, unions and so on, and national governments had both lost power because globalization had increased the 'privileged position' of business through which it could demand favourable treatment as the price of not relocating.[7] As we discussed in Chapter 1, and several times thereafter, the simple argument that globalization has changed everything is not adequate. We must remember that business has more varied needs than minimizing taxes and regulations; we must also remember that the ability to relocate varies considerably between businesses. In this section, we are concerned not so much with differences between industries, however, as with differences among the states in which they operate. The impact of globalization has been felt by and mediated through significantly different states. Every state is different, but it is possible to group them for discussion into some very broad categories. It is worth taking a moment to revisit and distinguish these categories.

Failing States

The end of the European (British, French, Dutch, Belgian) empires in the second half of the twentieth century increased the number of states to record levels. Yet while all states claimed much the same set of formal rights, including sovereignty, in reality many of the new states had a minimal existence. It was said of many, perhaps the majority, of new African states that the state extended only a limited distance, perhaps fifty miles, beyond the state capital. Further than that, the ability of the state to assert its will, collect taxes or even – to use Max Weber's definition of the state – maintain a monopoly on the legitimate use of force was non-existent. In some cases, such as the former Belgian Congo,

colonialism left behind little in the form of a functioning bureaucracy or an effective education system. Indeed, colonialism in
these countries left behind not a benign legacy but problems, not
the least of which was the lack of correspondence between ethnic and national boundaries. Civil wars, rebellions and unrest
resulted. Even where the legacy of colonialism was more substantial, as in former British colonies such as Uganda and Nigeria,
coups, civil wars and corruption rapidly reduced the capacity of
the state. Uganda at independence had a functioning bureaucracy
and even a good university (Makerere). Not long thereafter it fell
under the brutal, despotic rule of Idi Amin and lost both of these
institutions. Throughout much of Africa, to the extent that state
capacity remained, it was often used to enrich the rulers of what
became known as predatory states. In one of the most notorious
cases, President Mobutu of the Congo transferred billions of dollars of his nation's resources into his personal bank accounts in
Switzerland.

What has been the impact of globalization on these countries?
Many former colonies had of course been made part of the global
economy by their colonial rulers. The production of tropical
goods such as cocoa from the Gold Coast (now Ghana) was a typ-
ical example. Such tropical production was usually controlled by
large corporations based in the imperial country. Colonies were
also the site of much extractive industry; diamonds, oil, precious
minerals and other valuable resources were explored and
exploited by firms from the imperial country. Decolonization
ended the privileged position of the imperial nations' corporations. Belgium's Union Minière could no longer expect the state
to exclude competing companies from the Congo, although it may
have hoped that this special position could be maintained if the
province in which its operations were chiefly located (Katanga)
broke away and became independent. Shell was no longer assured
by the British government that it could continue to monopolize
the development of oil fields in Nigeria. Perhaps more importantly, the end of colonialism meant that firms could no longer
expect that the state would provide them with an effective, stable
legal system within which to operate. The British liked to boast
that they had brought a framework of laws and justice to their
colonies. While such a framework is desirable for ordinary citizens, it is essential for businesses to carry on their work.
Conversely, the shift after the colonial era to arbitrary exploitative

rule had terrible consequences for citizens. It also created problems for foreign corporations. Not only were they faced with the practical problems of dealing with a possibly corrupt regime but they had to be concerned about the prospect that their investments could be expropriated either by the current rulers or, at some future date, by the leaders of the coup or revolution that displaced them.

Corporations have followed a variety of responses to this situation, none of them very edifying. Some have complied with the demands of the predatory state, paying vast sums to a dictator personally rather than to the country's treasury. Mobutu's private bank accounts benefited considerably in this way.[8] Similarly, leading multinational oil companies have been the object of intense criticism by activists in the developed world for acquiescence in the rule of brutal military dictators in Nigeria. Until it became the object of intense criticism from activists in the developed world, Shell acquiesced in the rule of brutal military dictators in Nigeria. Doubtless these and similar corporations felt that they had little choice if they wished to continue to operate in those countries. There can even be legitimate disagreement on the degree to which corporations *ought* to try to impose the standards of the first world country from which they come on a third world country in which they operate.

Problems of the ineffective state have also been handled by the corporations themselves providing what are normally state services such as security. We encountered a particularly benign example of this in the previous chapter with Oserian's provision of education, training, healthcare and sewerage not only for its own workers but for people in the surrounding community. This strategy is not without its risks. The area around a corporation's paternalistic community with unusually high quality services may become a magnet for people from the surrounding region who lack adequate services. Paternalism is also expensive. Perhaps not surprisingly, more often corporations have simply hired private armies as did Shell in Nigeria. This tactic too is not cheap and the corporation runs the risk of attracting intense criticism from first world NGOs. Shell did not want to lose its brand's reputation by sinking the Brent Spar. It also did not wish to lose its reputation by appearing to be the brutal oppressor of Africans.

Yet corporations need their plant and equipment to be safe in order to operate. If neither the government nor the corporation could provide this security, another option was to leave. The attractiveness of this option depends in part on whether or not alternative sources of the product in question are readily available. It is noticeable that, in spite of the desperately low levels of wages in failing or minimal states, little or no production of basic goods, such as T-shirts, has been moved to them. Corporations have been able to manufacture T-shirts more safely in slightly more expensive, but somewhat more secure, settings. One option in countries on the margin is to arrange for local entrepreneurs to produce under contract. Reebok, Nike and clothing companies shift responsibility for many of the problems of operating in undesirable states onto local entrepreneurs. Athletic shoes and clothing can be produced in South East Asian or Central American factories – some would say sweat shops – that are not actually owned by the corporations that put their labels on the goods produced; these corporations have attempted (with varying degrees of success) to argue that they are not responsible for working conditions and practices of these plants. However, in the truly weak countries such as those in most of Africa, it is unlikely that local entrepreneurs could be found to take on such manufacturing by contract.

In some cases, such as diamonds and oil, alternative production sites are simply not available; the commodities exist in only a limited number of places. A further possibility in such instances is for corporations to seek validation by an NGO for their practices, seeking to show that they are doing the best they can to be responsible corporate citizens in difficult circumstances. One corporate response in failing states is the unlikelihood of increased investment. Corporations that do not have a compelling need to be involved in such countries are unlikely to invest there. The danger that confronts these countries is that they will be ignored by most of the global economy, linked to it, as under colonialism, largely by supplying scarce commodities.

More Effective but Non-Developmental States

Other third world countries have been more effective states in terms of their reach, but not necessarily in terms of economic development. There is no doubt that, even if corruption is a significant problem, these states have effective control of their territory and the ability to implement a range of policies within it. On the other hand, their economic performance has been poor or modest.

For much of the modern era, Argentina and India, though at very different levels of development, have fallen in this category. In both cases, prevailing economic doctrines, domestic political alliances and nationalism combined to foster the adoption of import substituting policies. Excluding imports or taxing them heavily encouraged domestic industries. Workers, as well as domestic entrepreneurs, benefited from higher incomes in the short term than they would otherwise have received. In India, the policy could be cloaked in Ghandian rhetoric of self-sufficiency, in Argentina in the political alliances of Peronism. Peron and the party he built provided a higher level of wages and government services for workers by taxing imports. Local entrepreneurs also benefited from import taxes, of course, through the protection from competition. In India, Ghandi's promotion of self-sufficiency was applied to the national economy in the form of protection for such apparently un-Ghandian industries as steel and automobiles. Any exporting sector (such as agriculture in Argentina) was a loser; it paid higher than world prices for products or materials it used while receiving world prices for its own output.

Both Argentina and India paid a significant price for their economic policies. Argentina declined comparatively from one of the world's richest countries in terms in GDP per capita to the ranks of third world countries. India experienced what was sometimes called the 'Hindu rate of growth', an intractably modest rate that contrasted with the dynamism of other Asian economies. In 1960, India and South Korea were in much the same position in terms of GDP per capita. By the end of the century, South Korea had climbed into the ranks of the OECD while India remained poor. In both India and Argentina, inefficient local industries were sheltered from competition, decreasing the likelihood of innovation. The lack of emphasis on exports meant that domestic industries were not motivated to reach international standards in price and quality.

Globalization raised the stakes for countries that cut themselves off from full integration into the global economy. India did not explicitly discourage foreign investment, but its regulations and laws made India an unattractive place in which to locate. Apart from the loss of investment that resulted, discouraging foreign investment reduced the flow of new techniques and technology into the country. The increased economic dynamism associated with globalization raised the costs of rejecting integration. The costs of Ghandian doctrines of self-sufficiency for the Indian economy, for example, were highlighted by the successes of the Tigers. While India grew modestly with growth rates of less than 5 per cent per annum, the Tigers enjoyed massive development and growth.

We may make a special subset of these categories for the former communist countries. These were extremely effective states in terms of their ability to control their populations. Yet, alongside their political and moral bankruptcy, these were also extremely ineffective states economically. Prisoners of their ideologies, these states were locked into lower standards of living and technology. They could escape only by ending the socialist system.

Faced with the increasing costs of their policies, most of these effective but non-developmental states have adopted new approaches. Communism has disappeared from large parts of the globe and where it survives nominally (as in China), has in practice been abandoned. Even India has claimed to be repealing regulations that inhibited foreign investment and trade, although the extent to which regulation has happened is uncertain. How far these changes have been taken is a matter of debate, but there is no doubting the shift in approach. This group of countries has been substantially affected, therefore, by globalization. Under its impact, although very reluctantly, these countries have shifted away from long-standing approaches to economics, which were often deeply rooted in national politics. It is also questionable whether or not the new liberal economic policies could be sustained. Argentina, celebrated as an exemplar of adopting liberal economic approaches, suffered a drastic economic crisis as the new century began. The collapse of Argentina threatened not only the future of liberal economic policies in that country but also a reappraisal throughout Latin America. One Latin American critic of liberal policies voiced what seemed to be a common sentiment: 'We privatized and we do not have less poverty, less unemployment. On the contrary, we have more poverty and unemployment. We are not debating theoretically here. We are looking at reality.'[9]

The Developmental States

There has been substantial discussion of the impact of globalization on developmental states earlier in this book. It suffices here to summarize that discussion. The early stages of globalization facilitated the rise of the developmental states. Increasingly easy access to export markets gave first Japan, then the Tigers, the opportunity to grow through exporting. Later, however, the growth of those economies in an increasingly globalized world economic system undermined the developmental state itself. Governments could not intervene effectively to promote industries because the rules of international organizations such as GATT and the WTO prohibited the techniques they had long employed to boost their favoured industries. Liberalization of rules on capital movements made it harder for developmental states to control investment funds, so large corporations established major overseas operations beyond the influence of their national governments. In short, globalization first fostered then ended the developmental state.

Neocorporatist and Other Forms of More Organized Capitalism

As we have seen, there has been considerable debate about the impact of globalization on necorporatist states and, more generally, on countries in which market forces are constrained by strong welfare states and highly-organized economic interests. The initial expectation was that globalization would erode rapidly either the ability of these countries to compete or the distinctive features of their socio-economic systems. It was said that globalization demanded flexible, low-cost workforces and economies in which market forces could operate untrammelled. Neocorporatist systems could not possibly provide such flexibility, it was argued. Welfare states inevitably had higher tax rates than less generous countries, making it more costly to employ people and often difficult to fire them if the economy turned down. In consequence, economic integration at the regional level (through the EU) and more generally through globalization was said to endanger both the European welfare state and neocorporatism.

Yet as we have seen, reality has been more complicated. There has not been any evidence of a general retreat from the welfare state in the face of globalization. A number of countries such as Sweden and the Netherlands have reformed their welfare systems to prevent obvious abuses such as people falsely claiming to be disabled so as to avoid work. Yet the fact that these reforms have been made, sometimes, as in the Netherlands, through neocorporatist policy-making processes, has shown also that these systems have a greater adaptability than their opponents suggested. Neocorporatism has been an answer to some countries' problems in grappling with globalization (as in the Netherlands) and has even been adopted for the first time by one of Europe's most successful economies, Ireland, as part of its development strategy. While unemployment remains high in Germany, it also remains Europe's strongest economy, providing a high standard of living for its citizens. France has achieved significant growth rates in recent years in spite of high unemployment, a generous welfare system and entrenched rights for employees that make economic liberals despair.

We may conclude, then, that for these countries the jury is still out on the impact of globalization. Abstract reasoning suggests that globalization should be a major problem for them. Experience seems to suggest that these countries may fare better than conventional economists would have predicted.

Conformers to Globalization

These are countries that for a variety of reasons have found it easy to conform to the policy adaptation required by globalization. The United States is a country in which a restricted role for the government, a very imperfect welfare state and limited rights for employees are mandated by the prevailing ideology; to the degree that they are also required by globalization, the United States was already on the right track. Britain is a more complex case. Support for a more extensive role for government has been widespread; Britain was once a leader in the development of the welfare state. Thatcherism did embody some principles of economic liberalism and conventional economics. Yet Thatcherism might not have been adopted had it not been for the bankruptcy of other approaches such as attempts to establish neocorporatism in the 1960s and 1970s. Thatcher used to be fond of saying that 'There is no alternative' to her approach. Many in Britain at the time believed she was right. Most of Thatcher's policies have been continued or accepted by the Blair government. Blair believed that the British economy was most likely to prosper by minimizing regulation, lowering tax rates to increase incentives and generally embracing market principles.

Although the demands of globalization are, therefore, not in principle unwelcome to policy-makers in the United States and Britain, challenges remain. For the United States, the obvious challenge is how to ensure that the enormously high productivity of American workers continues to provide the world's highest standard of living. Globalization enables technological improvements to be transferred to lower-cost countries with unprecedented speed and their products imported into the USA without duties or restrictions. Staying ahead is more difficult than ever. For Britain, the challenges come from having an unusually large percentage of its workforce unskilled and poorly trained by European standards. Combined with the excellence of its financial sector in investing worldwide, this makes maintaining the competitiveness of manufacturing industry problematic. Ironically, while Britain has enormous success in attracting overseas investment, it has continuing problems in securing adequate investment in British-owned industries. This old problem is harder than ever to address in the era of globalization, which facilitates the movement of capital and eases importing.

Trends and Prospects

The first edition of this book set out a series of examples of different forms of capitalism. It argued that there was no relationship between the success of these forms of capitalism and the degree to which they conformed to the principles of conventional economics. Since then, globalization has given a boost to those who have argued that government regulations, welfare states and the involvement of economic interests, such as labour, in policy-making are incompatible with economic success. Yet our survey at the start of a new century suggests that differences persist, and that there is no clear evidence that there is only one path to success. Different models of capitalism persist and prosper.

The process of writing a drastically revised third edition of this book has made several points abundantly clear, however.

The first is that the literature of business and government has increased and improved almost out of all recognition. The study of business and government was once the Cinderella of the political science discipline; the literature was comparatively small and of limited quality. This is no longer the case.

The second clear point is that there is a great deal of variation in the relationship between business and government. As we have noted earlier, there are persistent differences between nations in terms of how government and business interact. Although globalization has proved a challenge to neocorporatism, for example, those systems remain noticeably different from the business–government relationship in Britain or the United States. Yet, while national systems remain tethered to their starting points, it also seems that there are international trends that have pulled business–government systems in the same direction. We may compare the patterns of business–government relations to boats in a harbour. The tide comes in and the boats move towards the shore. Unless there is a catastrophe, however, they remain anchored or tethered. They are not, for example, swept into a tangle of boats on the shore.

What tides have been obvious in recent years? The period from the late 1960s until the late 1970s witnessed an upsurge of interest in more organized relationships between business and government. In some countries, the relationship was already highly organized and little change was possible. To return to our analogy, some boats were already pulled up on the beach and could not be moved further towards the land by the incoming tide. In France, indicative planning had resulted in a relatively organized form of capitalism; in Japan the developmental state rested on a close and highly organized partnership between business and government. The neocorporatist countries such as Sweden and Norway had somewhat different, tripartite modes of relations between business and government, but clearly they were highly organized.

More interesting were the trends towards more organized forms of capitalism in countries in which it had appeared to be absent. In Britain, for example, both Labour and Conservative governments experimented with innovations borrowed from overseas such as indicative planning and tripartite bargaining between the state, labour and business. The creation of the employers' organization, the CBI, during a Labour government, the creation of the tripartite National Economic Development Council (NEDC) by a Conservative government and the 'social contract' between government, labour and business in the 1970s were all evidence of this trend. Even in the United States, the experiment with a prices and incomes policy by President Nixon and attempts to create a more impressive or unified business umbrella organization in the 1970s, as evidenced in the creation of the Business Roundtable and efforts to merge the Chamber of Commerce and National Association of Manufacturers, were part of this movement.

The tide turned with the election of Margaret Thatcher in Britain in 1979 followed by the victory of Ronald Reagan in 1980. But the tide was more powerful than might have been supposed simply by the victory of a few right-of-centre politicians. Soon Labour governments in countries such as Australia and New Zealand were implementing policies similar to, or more radical than, those of Thatcher and Reagan. This tide was the tide of market-based, less-organized capitalism. It carried in policies to privatize state-owned industries, deregulate, cut back on the welfare state and reduce taxes on business and the wealthy in the name of economic efficiency. The boat already furthest out towards sea was the United States, which moved toward even more of a market-based form of capitalism. Tax cuts, welfare reform, deregulation and measures to weaken labour unions were part of the process. In terms of the political organization of business, the growth of PACs and of the Washington offices of individual corporations reaffirmed that they, not trade associations or business umbrella groups, were the core of business political activity. More dramatic changes occurred in Britain where the commitment to market capitalism was seriously in question. The privatization of government-owned industries, measures to weaken labour unions and the abolition of the vestiges of neocorporatism, such as the NEDC, were evidence of the power of the tide. Even those boats apparently immune to the tide because they were pulled up on the beach of organized capitalism felt its power. Noecorporatist countries such as Sweden experienced a real crisis of confidence; as we have seen, the question of whether neocorporatism could survive was debated vigorously in the 1980s and 1990s. Neocorporatism adapted. Developmental states also felt the pull of the market tide. In some cases, arguably France, they were pulled away from their moorings of organized capitalism; in other countries, notably Japan, they were unable to change even in the face of deepening crisis. This, then, was the tide that made many wonder whether the forces of globalization would move everyone into an American mode of business–government relations.

The recession that began before the terrorist attacks on the United States in September 2001, but was perhaps deepened by them, marked the end of the era of extreme confidence in market capitalism. The aftermath of the terrorist attacks provided a nice example; contrary to the wishes of President George W. Bush, the Senate voted almost unanimously to place the security inspections of baggage and passengers in the hands of federal government workers rather than those of private-sector contractors whose inadequate performance was revealed by the September 11th attacks. Even before the attacks, the American economy was clearly entering a recession and the Stock Market had tumbled. The argument that the flexible, market-based American economy had entered a period of permanent prosperity was undermined. The American model – as well as the American economy – suffered another blow in 2002 when the wave of financial scandals described in Chapter 2 undermined investors' confidence and prompted a crash on the Stock Market. The misdeeds of Enron, Arthur Anderson, Worldcom etcetera showed that laws and regulations were not as effective in controlling capitalism as enthusiasts for the American model had suggested. It was unlikely that any laws would be adopted, however, that would prevent similar crises in the future. Congress refused to close all the loopholes in corporate law that had made the crisis possible. Democratic as well as Republican friends of business worked to dilute some of the legal reforms proposed after the crash that executives disliked. Senator Joe Lieberman (D. Connecticut), his party's Vice Presidential candidate in 2000, succeeded in blocking a requirement that companies acknowledge in their accounts the cost of stock options, the opportunity companies give favoured executives to pay today's prices for its stock if prices rise tomorrow. Stock options are given overwhelmingly to the very highest paid business executives, and had been a major factor in tempting them to issue misleading accounts. They reinforced the tendencies towards a short term preoccupation with the Stock Market rather than long term investment that has been seen as a recurring weakness in American capitalism.

Yet even if there has been greater resolve among American politicians, perhaps less dependent than in the past on political contributions from business, there are always limits to what can be achieved through law and regulation. Regulators and law enforcement authorities always have limited resources. Laws and regulations cannot be written tightly enough to cover every possible underhand scheme. There are nearly always major financial rewards for those who can discover a loophole in current laws or regulations. Ultimately, therefore, even market capitalism needs its practitioners to show some restraint, to refrain from actions that may make them money in the short term but damage the economy and society in the long term. The consequences of the absence of such restraint in the United States in the 1990s suggested, it seemed, that there was something to be said after all for forms of capitalism that blended concern for market forces with a sense of social responsibility.

Moreover, more organized capitalist countries had shown that they had the capacity to adapt rather than abandon their systems. The Netherlands, for example, met the challenge of globalization through its neocorporatist system rather than despite it. The Republic of Ireland enjoyed an unprecedented level of prosperity achieved through a neocorporatist approach. The Asian economic crisis of the late 1990s convinced many that totally unrestricted capital markets could exacerbate financial crises and panics. In Britain, the Labour government began to explore the possibility of inviting the private sector to enter into a partnership with it to promote superior environmental performance – a partnership that was reminiscent of neocorporatism.

The changes that take place in business–government relations should caution against any triumphalist conclusion that any one model is about to achieve a permanent victory. There have been periods in which it has seemed blindingly obvious that more organized forms of neocorporatism are superior and, more recently, a period in which market capitalism seemed to be sweeping the world. Doubtless the tides will continue to flow in and out, changing the location of the boats somewhat though not their relative positions. The United States will doubtless always be a more market-based type of capitalism, the Netherlands a more organized, neocorporatist form. Yet the degree to which the United States is a more purely market-based form of capitalism, or Germany a more organized form of capitalism will change somewhat over the years. The business–government relationship will continue to be highly important yet subject to change.

The Power of Business: Pluralism, Privilege and Democracy

The classic question in the study of business and politics has been whether the power of business is compatible with democracy. Critiques of capitalist democracy made by Marxist and other radical scholars argued that, whatever the claims of the formal constitution, real power was exercised by business, not the people. This normative concern remains evident in criticisms of such obvious forms of attempted influence as the contributions of corporate PACs in the United States. It finds echoes in the scepticism often expressed by the citizens of advanced democracies about the degree to which their views or interests are taken into account by their rulers.

At first sight, the shift towards discussions of different forms of capitalism reflects a move away from this long-established normative concern. The focus appears to be more on whether the developmental states, the neocorporatist states or the more market-oriented states are best able to achieve growth and prosperity. In part this shift does reflect the anxieties about basic economic goals such as employment and growth that afflicted advanced democracies from the first of the oil shocks in 1973 until the boom of the 1990s. In part, however, the shift in the nature of the debate reflected an awareness that there was not one answer to the question of how powerful business is in advanced democracies. The nature of the compromises or settlements made between business, other interests such as labour or environmentalists and government differed from country to country. Part of the appeal of neocorporatism, for example, was that it forced business to sit down and bargain with unions; the implication was that business was better able to dominate in non-neocorporatist countries. However, neocorporatism also facilitates business influence by giving it a very privileged role in policy-making. In this respect, neocorporatism may not be so very different from pluralism which offers business opportunities (for example, to lobby and to make campaign contributions) and also provides the constraint of working against other interest groups such as consumer groups, environmentalists and labour.

At times it seems as though disputes about the power of business continue because there is no metric for assessing the power of an interest group. Some see setbacks for business, such as tougher environmental standards, as proof that it is no longer pre-eminent. Others look at the same evidence and see a marginal reduction in what they believe to be the overwhelming power of business. Yet although this stalemate continues, arguments about the power of business have changed in several respects in recent decades.

First, it has become hard to make the once popular argument that business hoodwinks us into accepting its dominance through a 'third face' of power.[10] Of course business uses its vast resources – as do all interest groups that can afford to do so – in attempts to project a favourable image among both the mass public through commercials and intellectuals through the judicious distribution of grants. But to suggest, as radical scholars once did, that the public is incapable of thinking anti-business thoughts is both insulting and unsustainable.

The second change in arguments about the power of business is the recognition that business is not just an ordinary interest group but also enjoys a degree of power or influence that results from its structural position in society, controlling investment and the location of growth. Note that the argument is not that this power is total; it is a degree of power, not absolute power. Just as large campaign contributions do not always produce total political victory, so the structural power of business is not always decisive. Both campaign contributions and structural power are, however, advantages that it is better to have than to lack. Recognition that business enjoys a degree of power from its structural position had long been expressed in Marxist circles. It moved into the political science mainstream in 1977 with the publication of *Politics and Markets* by the establishment scholar, Charles Lindblom. Since then the argument has appeared extensively – often expressed in such an extreme form that it cannot be sustained – in discussions of 'the race to the bottom', in which governments compete for investment by lowering taxes and easing regulations either within trading blocs such as the European Union, or, in this era of globalization, world-wide. It is doubtful if anyone today thinks that policy affecting business is the result merely of normal interest group politics.

The third change is that, in contrast to the preceding argument, few would now think that business can rely solely on what Lindblom called its 'privileged position'. At one time Marxists argued that the state was but the executive committee of the bourgeoisie that could be trusted to serve the interests of business. One problem in sustaining this argument is that it convinces very few business executives. The last third of the twentieth century showed a dramatic mobilization by business in countries such as the United States in which mobilization had previously seemed unnecessary. The billions of dollars that business spends on lobbying, campaign contributions and so on – about which critics of business complain so understandably – are proof that business itself does not feel free to ignore practical politics and rely on its privileged position. The existence of PACs, trade associations, business umbrella groups and so on are all proof that, whatever Lindblom might argue, business executives think that political activity by business is necessary.

Perhaps, then, we have reached a conclusion that the power of business is indeterminate. We cannot say that any one structure of business–government relations results in business dominance or that business is, or is not, more powerful than governments or interest groups. Circumstances not only differ between countries but also within them. We cannot say that business is bound to win or that its opponents are doomed to lose. Critics of business need not despair that in an era of globalization, they are bound to lose. Business executives should not suppose that even after the retreat of socialism, that they are immune from challenge.

Appendix Tables

Table 1   *General government total outlays as percentage of GDP*

France	51.0
Germany	43.3
Japan	36.6
South Korea	23.1
Sweden	52.7
United Kingdom	37.0
United States	29.9

Source: Compiled by the author from OECD statistics.

Table 2   *Union density (union membership as a percentage of wage and salary earners)*

	1985	1995
France	14.5	9.1
Germany	35.0	28.9
Japan	28.8	24.0
South Korea	12.4	12.7
Sweden	83.8	91.1
United Kingdom	45.5	32.9
United States	18.0	14.2

Source: Compiled by the author from ILO, *World Labour Report*, 1997–1998.

Table 3   *Trade exposure*

	Imports as percentage of GDP (2000)	Exports as percentage of GDP (2000)	FDI into country as percentage of GDP (1999)
France	27.2	28.7	2.6
Germany	33.0	33.4	2.5
Japan	8.4	10.0	0.3
South Korea	42.2	45.0	2.1
Sweden	42.1	47.4	25.0
United Kingdom	29.1	27.2	5.8
United States	13.5	10.7	3.1

Sources: Compiled by the author from OECD, 'Main Economic Indicators', November 2001.

Table 4   *Economic success*

	Unemployment as a percentage of workforce (2000)	GDP per capita, PPP adjusted (2000)	Average annual GDP growth (1990–2000) (%)
France	9.5	23,276	1.7
Germany	7.9	24,931	1.5
Japan	4.7	26,484	1.3
South Korea	4.3	17,636	5.7
Sweden	5.9	24,309	1.8
United Kingdom	6.6	22,882	2.5
United States	4.0	35,724	3.4

Sources: Compiled by the author from OECD, 'Main Economic Indicators', November 2001; World Bank, *Countries at a Glance*, September 2001.

Notes and References

Preface

1. Andrew S. Shonfield, *Modern Capitalism: The Changing Balance of Public and Private Power* (Oxford and New York: Oxford University Press, 1969).
2. Graham K. Wilson, *Only in America?* (Chatham, NJ: Chatham House, 1997).

1   Introduction

1. See Morton J. Horwitz, *The Transformation of American Law 1770–1860* (Cambridge, Mass.: Harvard University Press, 1973) for an interesting example of the importance of legal change in creating American capitalism.
2. Peter Hall, *Governing the Economy: The Politics of State Intervention in Britain and France* (Oxford: Oxford University Press, 1986); Fred Block, 'The Roles of the State in the Economy', Ch. 28 in *The Handbook of Economic Sociology* (Princeton, NJ: Princeton University Press, 1994); Herman Schwartz, *States Versus Markets: History, Geography and the Development of the International Political Economy* (New York: St. Martin's Press, 1994).
3. Gosta Esping Andersen, *The Three Worlds of Welfare Capitalism* (Princeton, NJ: Princeton University Press, 1990).
4. Marc Allen Eisner, Jeff Worsham and Evan J. Rehnquist, *Contemporary Regulatory Policy* (Boulder, Col.: Lynne Reiner, 2000).
5. US Department of Commerce, *Statistical Abstract of the United States* (Washington, DC: Government Printing Office, 2000), Table 1375.
6. Cathie Jo Martin, *Shifting the Burden: The Struggle Over Growth and Corporate Taxation* (Chicago: University of Chicago Press, 1991). See also Sandra Suarez, *Does Business Learn? Tax Breaks, Uncertainty and Political Strategies* (Ann Arbor: University of Michigan Press, 2000).
7. Theodore Lowi, 'American Business, Public Policy and Case Studies and Political Theory', *World Politics*, 16 (1964), pp. 677–715.
8. The great work that first drew attention to differences between national variants of modern capitalism was Andrew Shonfield, *Modern Capitalism: The Changing Balance of Public and Private Power* (Oxford: Oxford University Press, 1969). For a more recent, though now outdated, study see Jeffrey Hart, *Rival Capitalists: International Competitiveness in the US, Japan and Western Europe* (Ithaca: Cornell University Press, 1992). See also J. Rodgers Hollingsworth, Philippe Schmitter and Wolfgang Streeck,

Governing Capitalist Economies: Performance and Control of Economic Sectors (New York: Oxford University Press, 1994).

9. Wolfgang Streeck and Philippe Schmitter (eds), *Private Interest Government: Beyond Market and State* (London and Beverly Hills: Sage, 1985).

10. For the classic statement of the importance of MITI see Chalmers Johnson, *MITI and the Japanese Economic Miracle; The Growth of Industrial Policy 1925–75* (Stanford: Stanford University Press, 1982).

11. For a good description of orthodox pluralism and its critics see Frank R. Baumgartner and Beth L. Leech, *Basic Interests: The Importance of Groups in Politics and Political Science* (Princeton: Princeton University Press, 1998).

12. Perhaps the best example of a revisionist pluralist is David Vogel, *Fluctuating Fortunes: The Political Power of Business in America* (New York: Basic Books, 1989).

13. Mancur Olson, *The Logic of Collective Action: Public Goods and the Theory of Groups* (Cambridge, Mass.: Harvard University Press, 1967).

14. For a statement of this argument in the Ameircan context, but extended to other organizations as well as business, see Robert H. Salisbury, *Interests and Institutions: Substance and Structure in American Politics* (Pittsburgh: Pittsburgh University Press, 1992).

15. See Neil J. Mitchell, *The Conspicuous Corporation* (Ann Arbor: University of Michigan Press, 1997) and Mark A. Smith, *American Business and Political Power: Public Opinion Elections and Democracy* (Chicago: University of Chicago Press, 2000).

16. Charles E. Lindblom, *Politics and Markets: The World's Political Economic Systems* (New York: Basic Books, 1977).

17. Vogel, *Fluctuating Fortunes*. See also David Vogel, 'The Power of Business in the United States: A Re-Appraisal', *British Journal of Political Science*, 17 (1987) pp. 385–408.

18. Terrence Guay, *The United States and the European Union: The Political Economy of a Relationship* (Sheffield: Sheffield Academic Press, 1999) and www.eurunion.org/profile/EUUSStats.htm.

19. Suzanne Berger and Ronald Dore, *National Diversity and Global Capitalism* (Ithaca: Cornell University Press, 1996); Robert Boyer and Daniel Drasche (eds), *States Against Markets: The Limits of Global Capitalism* (London: Routledge, 1996); William Greider, *One World, Ready or Not: The Manic Logic of Global Capitalism* (New York: Simon & Schuster, 1998); Thomas Friedman, *The Lexus and the Olive Tree* (New York: Farrar, Strauss & Giroux, 1999); Herman Schwartz, *States versus Markets: History, Geography and the Development of the International Political Economy* (New York: St. Martin's Press, 1994).

20. William Greider, *One World Ready or Not: The Manic Logic of Global Capitalism* (New York: Simon & Schuster, 1997).

21. Geoffrey Garrett, *Partisan Politics in the Global Economy* (Cambridge: Cambridge University Press, 1998); Robert Wade, 'Globalization and its Limits' in Suzanne Berger and Robert Dore (eds), *National Diversity and Global Capitalism* (Ithaca: Cornell University Press, 1996); Linda Weiss, *The Myth of the Powerless State* (Ithaca: Cornell University Press, 1998).

22. David Vogel, *Trading Up: Consumer and Environmental Regulation in a Global Economy* (Cambridge, Mass.: Harvard University Press, 1995).

23. For the Brent Spar story see Grant Jordan, *Shell, Greenpeace and the Brent Spar* (Basingstoke: Palgrave, 2001).

24. See Richard Freedman, 'Single Peaked versus Diversified Capitalism: The Relationship Between Economic Institutions and Outcomes', National Bureau of Economic Research working paper 7526 (Washington DC: NBER, 2000). See also 'One True Model?', *The Economist*, 8 April 2000, p. 86.

25. Philippe Schmitter, 'Still the Century of Corporatism?', *Review of Politics*, 36 (1974), pp. 85–131; Schmitter, 'Regime Stability and Systems of Interest Intermediation in Western Europe and North America', in Suzanne Berger (ed.), *Organizing Interests in Western Europe* (Cambridge: Cambridge University Press, 1984); Schmitter, 'Interest Intermediation and Regime Governability in Western Europe and North America', in Suzanne Berger, *Organizing Interests in Western Europe*. See also Peter Katzenstein, *Small States in World Markets: Industrial Policies in Europe* (Ithaca: Cornell University Press, 1985).

2   Business and Politics in the United States

1. Anthony King, 'Ideas, Institutions and the Policies of Government', *British Journal of Political Science*, 3 (July 1973), pp. 291–313. See also Andrew Shonfield, *Modern Capitalism: The Changing Balance of Public and Private Power* (Oxford: Oxford University Press, 1969).

2. *Public Opinion*, June–July 1980.

3. For a discussion of the extent and causes of American exceptionalism, see Graham K. Wilson, *Only In America?* (Chatham, NJ: Chatham House, 1997).

4. For an excellent discussion of the failure of socialism in the United States, see Seymour Martin Lipset, 'Why No Socialism in the United States?', in Seweryn Bialer and Sophia Sluzar (eds), *Sources of Contemporary Radicalism*, Vol. 1, pp. 291–313 (Boulder, Col.: Westview Press, 1977).

5. Werner Sombart, *Why is There No Socialism in the United States?*, trans. by Patricia M. Hocking and C. T. Husbands; ed. by C. T. Husbands (White Plains, NY: International Arts and Sciences Press, 1976).

6. Louis Hartz, *The Liberal Tradition in America* (New York: Harcourt Brace & World, 1955). For powerful critiques of Hartz's ideas, see Rogers M. Smith, *Civic Ideals: Conflicting Visions of Citizenship in U.S. History* (New Haven, Conn.: Yale University Press, 1997).

7. Rogers Smith, *Civic Ideals*. See also Elizabeth Sanders, *Roots of Reform: Farmers, Workers, and the American State, 1877–1917* (Chicago: University of Chicago Press, 1999), for examples of the diversity of popular political economic thinking in late-nineteenth-century America.

8. It is also interesting to note that the price increases in the 1970s prompted the United States to adopt a far more elaborate attempt at price control than any of the other advanced industrialized democracies at that time; perhaps

Americans' love of driving overcame their love of free markets in this instance.

9. Martha Derthick, *Up In Smoke: From Legislation to Litigation In Tobacco Politics* (Washington, DC: CQ Press, 2002).

10. For an argument that the United States is afflicted and hurt competitively by unnecessarily intrusive and antagonistic regulation, see Pietro Nivola (ed.), *Comparative Disadvantages? Social Regulations and the Global Economy* (Washington, DC: Brookings Institution Press, 1997).

11. Sven Steinmo, *Taxation and Democracy: American, British and Swedish Approaches to Financing the State* (New Haven: Yale University Press, 1993); John F. Witte, *The Politics and Development of the Federal Income Tax* (Madison: University of Wisconsin Press, 1985).

12. Sandra L. Suarez, *Does Business Learn? Tax Breaks, Uncertainty and Political Strategies* (Ann Arbor: Michigan University Press, 2000).

13. Cathie J. Martin, *Shifting the Burden: The Struggle over Growth and Corporate Taxation* (Chicago: University of Chicago Press, 1991). See also Jeffrey H. Birnbaum and Alan S. Murray, *Showdown at Gucci Gulch: Lobbyists and the Unlikely Triumph of Tax Reform* (New York: Random House, 1987).

14. Sven Steinmo, 'Why is Government So Small in the United States?', *Governance*, 8, no. 3 (1995), pp. 303–34. See also Graham K. Wilson, *Only in America? The Politics of the United States in Comparative Perspective* (Chatham, N.J.: Chatham House, 1998).

15. David Vogel, 'Why American Businessmen Distrust Their State', *British Journal of Political Science*, 11 (1981).

16. Alfred D. Chandler, *The Visible Hand: The Managerial Revolution in American Business* (Cambridge, Mass.: Belknap Press, 1977).

17. Stephen Skowronek, *Building a New American State: The Expansion of National Administrative Capacities, 1877–1920* (Cambridge and New York: Cambridge University Press, 1982).

18. Judith Goldstein, *Ideas, Interests, and American Trade Policy* (Ithaca: Cornell University Press, 1993).

19. Michael Goldfield, *The Decline of Organized Labour in the United States* (Chicago: University of Chicago Press, 1987). See also Thomas Ferguson and Joel Rogers, *Right Turn: The Decline of the Democrats and the Future of American Politics* (New York: Hill & Wang, 1986).

20. I.M. Destler, *American Trade Politics*, 3rd edn (Washington, DC: Institute for International Economics; New York: Twentieth Century Fund, 1995).

21. Donald F. Kettl, *Leadership at the Fed* (New Haven: Yale University Press, 1986). See also John Woolley, *Monetary Politics: The Federal Reserve and the Politics of Monetary Policy* (Cambridge and New York: Cambridge University Press, 1984).

22. Bob Woodward, *Maestro: Greenspan's Fed and the American Boom* (New York: Simon & Schuster, 2000).

23. Kenneth R. Mayer, *The Political Economy of Defence Contracting* (New Haven: Yale University Press, 1991); Nick Kotz, *Wide Blue Yonder Money, Politics and the B1 Bomber* (New York: Pantheon Book, 1988).

24. Kenneth R. Mayer, *The Political Economy of Defence Contracting* (New Haven: Yale University Press, 1991).

25. For excellent studies of business tactics, see Mark A. Smith, *American Business and Political Power: Public Opinion, Elections and Democracy* (Chicago: University of Chicago Press, 2000) and Neil J. Mitchell, *The Conspicuous Corporation: Business, Public Policy and Representative Democracy* (Ann Arbor: University of Michigan Press, 1997).

26. Graham K. Wilson, 'Corporate Political Strategies', *British Journal of Political Science*, 20 (1990), pp. 281–7. See also Suarez, *Does Business Learn?*

27. For a good summary of research on PACs, campaign contributions and Congress, see John Wright, *Interest Groups and Congress: Lobbying, Contributions, and Influence* (Boston: Allyn & Bacon, 1996).

28. For surveys of lobbying in Washington, see Kay Lehman Schlozman and John Tierney, *Organized Interests and American Democracy* (New York: Harper & Row, 1986); John P. Heinz, Edward O. Laumann, Robert L. Nelson and Robert H. Salisbury, *The Hollow Core: Private Interests in National Policy Making* (Cambridge, Mass.: Harvard University Press, 1993).

29. Ronald C. Fisher, *State and Local Government Finance*, 2nd edn (Chicago: Irwin, 1996), pp. 637–8.

30. Fisher, *State and Local Government Finance*, p. 605. For a more positive view of state policies, see Peter K. Eisinger, *The Rise of the Entrepreneurial State: State and Local Economic Development Policy in the United States* (Madison: University of Wisconsin Press, 1988).

31. 'Restating the '90s', *Business Week*, 1 April 2002, p. 70.

32. Taylor Dark, *The Unions and the Democrats: An Enduring Alliance* (Ithaca: Cornell University Press, 1999).

33. Ronald Inglehart, *Culture Shift in Advanced Industrialized Society* (Princeton, NJ: Princeton University Press, 1990).

34. On the rise – and success – of public-interest groups, see Jeffrey Berry, *The New Liberalism: The Rising Power of Citizen Groups* (Washington, DC: Brookings Institution, 1999).

35. Mancur Olson, *The Logic of Collective Action: Public Goods and the Theory of Groups* (New York: Schocken Books, 1968).

36. David J. Vogel, *National Styles of Regulation* (Ithaca: Cornell University Press, 1986).

37. Terry Moe, 'An Assessment of the Positive Theory of Congressional Dominance', *Legislative Studies Quarterly*, 12 (1987), pp. 475–500.

38. David Vogel, *Fluctuating Fortunes: The Political Power of Business in the United States* (New York: Basic Books, 1989).

39. This was the term used by the chairman of the Federal Reserve, Alan Greenspan to describe the causes of corporate misdeals.

40. *Proverbs* (16:18) (King James version).

41. Kevin Philips, *Wealth and Democracy* (New York: Broadway Books, 2002), p. 129, Chart 3.9b.

3   Government and Politics in Britain

1. There is a huge body of literature on Thatcherism, its causes and its consequences. See Peter Jenkins, *Mrs Thatcher's Revolution: The Ending of*

the Socialist Era (London: Jonathan Cape, 1987); Andrew Gamble, *The Free Economy and the Strong State: The Politics of Thatcherism*, 2nd edn (London: Macmillan, 1994); Peter Riddell, *The Thatcher Era and Its Legacy* (Oxford: Basil Blackwell, 1991); Hugo Young, *One of Us: A Biography of Margaret Thatcher* (London: Macmillan, 1991): Margaret Thatcher, *The Downing Street Years* (London: HarperCollins, 1993).

2.   Martin J. Weiner, *English Culture and the Decline of the Industrial Spirit* (Cambridge: Cambridge University Press, 1981).

3.   Anthony King (ed.), *Why Is Britain Becoming Harder To Govern?* (London: BBC, 1976); Michel Crozier, Samuel Huntington and Joji Watanuki, *The Crisis of Democracy: Report to the Trilateral Commission* (New York: New York University Press, 1975).

4.   For a history of Britain's shifts towards and away from neocorporatism, see Keith Middlemas, *Politics in Industrial Society* (London: Deutsch, 1979).

5.   For a most useful survey, see Wyn Grant, *Business and Politics in Britain*, 2nd edn (London: Macmillan, 1993).

6.   Frank Longstreth, 'The City, Industry and the State', in Colin Crouch (ed.), *State and Economy in Contemporary Capitalism* (London: Croom Helm, 1979). For structural constraints on British policy, see also Peter Hall, *Governing the Economy: The Politics of State Intervention in Britain and France* (Cambridge, Mass.: Polity Press, 1988).

7.   Giandomenico Majone, *Understanding Regulatory Growth in the European Community* (Fiesole: European University Institute, 1994).

8.   Wolfgang Streeck, *From National Corporatism to Transitional Pluralism* (Notre Dame, Ind.: Kellogg Institute, 1991).

9.   Samuel Edward Finer, *Anonymous Empire: A Study of the the Lobby in Britain* (London: Pall Mall Press, 1958); Peter Self and Herbert J. Storing, *The State and the Farmer: Agricultural Politics and Policy in Britain* (Berkeley: University of California Press, 1963); A.G. Jordan and J.J. Richardson, *Government and Pressure Groups in Britain* (Oxford: Clarendon Press, 1987); Wyn Grant, *Pressure Groups and British Politics* (Basingstoke: Macmillan, 2000).

10.   See Graham K. Wilson, *Special Interests and Policymaking* (Chichester and New York: John Wiley, 1977).

11.   Wyn Grant and David Marsh, *The Confederation of British Industry* (London: Hodder & Stoughton, 1977).

12.   Neil J. Mitchell, *The Conspicuous Corporation: Business, Public Policy and Representative Democracy* (Ann Arbor: University of Michigan Press, 1997).

13.   Ibid, p. 106.

14.   Ibid, p. 130.

15.   Ibid, p. 109.

16.   Anthony Seldon (ed.), *The Blair Effect* (London: Little Brown, 2001).

17.   Richard Rose, 'Two and One Half Cheers for Capitalism', *Public Opinion*, June–July 1983.

18.   David Vogel, *Fluctuating Fortunes: The Political Power of Business in America* (New York: Basic Books, 1989).

4   The Decline of the Developmental State

1.   On France, see Vivien Schmidt, 'The Decline of Traditional State Dirigisme in France: The Transformation of Political Economic Policies and Policy Making Processes', *Governance*, 9 (1996), pp. 375–406; Vivien Schmidt, *From State to Market: The Transformation of French Business and Government* (New York: Cambridge University Press, 1996); Jack Hayward, *The State and the Market: Industrial Patriotism and Economic Intervention in France* (New York: New York University Press, 1986). For enthusiastic assessments of the Asian developmental state, see Chalmers Johnson, *MITI and the Japanese Economic Miracle: The Growth of Industrial Policy 1925–75* (Stanford: Stanford University Press, 1982); Robert Wade, *Governing the Market: The Role of the State in East Asian Industrialization* (Princeton: Princeton University Press, 1990). For a debate on the applicability of industrial policy to the United States, see Chalmers A. Johnson (ed.), *The Industrial Policy Debate* (San Francisco: ICS Press, 1984). For a discussion of the decline of the develpmental state in Latin America, see Kurt Weyland 'From Leviathan to Gulliver? The Decline of the Developmental State in Brazil', *Governance*, 11 (1998), pp. 51–76.
2.   Philip Maynard Williams, *Crisis and Compromise: Politics in the Fourth Republic* (Hamden Connecticut: Archon Books, 1964).
3.   Laurence Wylie, *Village in the Vaucluse* (Cambridge, Mass.: Harvard University Press, 1957).
4.   Agriculture provides an excellent example. See John Keeler, *The Politics of Neocorporatism in France: Farmers, the State and Agricultural Policymaking in the Fifth Republic* (New York: Oxford University Press, 1987). See also Steven J. Warnecke and Ezra Suleiman (eds), *Industrial Policy in Western Europe* (New York: Praeger, 1975).
5.   For a discussion of planning in its later years, see Saul Estrin and Peter Holmes, *French Planning in Theory and Practice* (London: George Allen & Unwin, 1983) and Peter Hall, *Governing the Economy* (New York: Oxford University Press, 1986).
6.   See Ezra Suleiman, *Elites in French Society: The Politics of Survival* (Princeton: Princeton University Press, 1978).
7.   John Zysman, *Governments, Markets and Growth: Financial Systems and the Politics of Industrial Change* (Ithaca: Cornell University Press, 1983).
8.   Ezra Suleiman, *Politics, Power and Bureaucracy in France: The Administrative Elite* (Princeton: Princeton University Press, 1979).
9.   Philip Maynard Williams and Martin Harrison, *Politics and Society in de Gaulle's Republic* (London: Longman, 1971).
10. Peter Hall, 'Socialism in One Country: Mitterand and the Struggle to Define a New Economic Policy for France', in Philip Cerny and Martin Shain (eds), *Socialism, the State and Public Policy in France* (London: Frances Pinter, 1985).
11. Schmidt, 'The Decline of Traditional State Dirigisme in France', p. 399.
12. Chalmers Johnson, *Japan, Who Governs? The Rise of the Developmental State in East Asia* (New York: Norton, 1995); Peter Hall, 'The Japanese

Civil Service and Economic Development in Comparative Perspective', in Hyung-Ki Kim *et al.* (eds), *The Japanese Civil Service and Economic Development* (Oxford: Clarendon Press, 1995).

13. Rowan Callick, 'East Asia and the Pacific' in Transparency International *Global Corruption Report* (www.globalcorruptionreport.org), p. 13.

14. T.J. Pempel, *Regime Shift*. For more information on the corruption and logrolling of the LDP see Karel von Wolferon, *The Enigma of Japanese Power: People and Politics in a Stateless Nation* (New York: Alfred Knopf, 1989).

15. For a useful summary of the debate, see Jeffrey Bernstein, 'Japanese Capitalism', in Thomas K. McCraw (ed.), *Creating Modern Capitalism* (Cambridge, Mass.: Harvard University Press, 1997).

16. Richard J. Samuels, *The Business of the Japanese State: Energy Markets in Comparative and Historical Perspective* (Ithaca: Cornell University Press, 1987).

17. Karel van Wolferen, *The Enigma of Japanese Power: People and Politics in a Stateless Nation* (New York: Knopf, 1989).

18. For the early stages of Korean industrial policy, see Stephan Haggard, *Pathways from the Periphery: The Politics of Growth in the Newly Industrializing Countries* (Ithaca: Cornell University Press, 1990); Alice Amsden, *Asia's Next Giant: South Korea and Late Industrialization* (New York: Oxford University Press, 1989). For later stages, see Mark L. Clifford, *Troubled Tiger: Businessmen, Bureaucrats and Generals in South Korea*, rev. edn (London: M.E. Sharpe, 1998).

19. Donald Clark (ed.), *The Kwangju Uprisings: Shadows Over the Regime in South Korea* (Boulder, Col.: Westivew Press, 1988).

20. Tun-Jen Cheng and Eun-Mee Kim, 'Making Democracy: Generalizing the South Korean Case', in Edward Friedman (ed.), *The Politics of Democratization: Generalizing East Asian Experiences* (Boulder, Col.: Westview Press, 1994).

21. Tun-Jen Cheng and Stephan Haggard (eds), *Political Change in Taiwan* (Boulder, Col.: Lynne Reiner, 1992).

22. Danny Lam and Cal Clark, 'Beyond the Developmental State: The Cultural Roots of "Guerilla Capitalism" in Taiwan', *Governance*, 7 (1994), pp. 412–30.

23. Victor Mallett, *The Trouble With Tigers* (London: HarperCollins, 2000).

5   The Past, Present and Future of Neocorporatism

1. For classic discussions of neocorporatism, see Gerhard Lehmbruch and Philippe C. Schmitter (eds), *Patterns of Corporatist Policymaking* (Beverly Hills: Sage, 1982); Colin Crouch and Ronal Dore (eds), *Corporatism and Accountability: Organized Interests in British Public Life* (Oxford: Oxford University Press, 1990); Peter J. Katzenstein, *Corporatism and Change: Austria, Switzerland and the Politics of Industry* (Ithaca: Cornell University Press, 1984); Peter J. Katzenstein, *Small States in World Markets* (Ithaca: Cornell University Press, 1985); Jonas Pontusson, *The Limits of Social*

Democracy: Investment Politics in Sweden (Ithaca: Cornell University Press, 1992).

2. For evidence supporting this view see Jan Erik Lane, 'The Twilight of the Scandinavian Model', *Political Studies*, 41 (1993), pp. 315–24.

3. For this process in its heartland of Scandinavia, see Jan Erik Lane, 'The Twilight of the Scandinavian Model'.

4. For a discussion of the reasons for Ireland's economic success, see Paul Sweeney, *The Celtic Tiger: Ireland's Economic Miracle Explained* (Dublin: Oak Tree, 1985); Robert MacSharry and Paul White, *The Making of the Celtic Tiger: The Inside Story of Ireland's Boom Economy* (Cork: Mercier Press, 2000).

5. John L. Campbell, J. Rogers Hollingsworth and Leon N. Lindberg, *The Governance of the American Economy* (Cambridge: Cambridge University Press, 1991); J. Rogers Hollingsworth, Philippe C. Schmitter and Wolfgang Streeck (eds), *Governing Capitalist Economies: Performance and Control of Economic Sectors* (New York: Oxford University Press, 1994).

6. Philippe Schmitter, 'Regime Stability and Systems of Interest Intermediation in Western Europe and North America', in Suzanne Berger (ed.), *Organized Interests in Western Europe* (Cambridge: Cambridge University Press, 1981).

7. Johan P. Olsen, *Organized Democracy: Political Institutions in a Welfare State, The Case of Norway* (New York: Columbia University Press, 1983).

8. For arguments that different forms of capitalism are deeply rooted in different countries, see *Unions, Employers and Central Banks: Macroeconomic Coordination and Institutional Change in Social Market Economies*. Torben Iversen, Jonas Pontusson and David Soskice (eds) (New York: Cambridge University Press, 2000).

9. James G. March and Johan P. Olsen, *Rediscovering Institutions: The Organizational Basis of Politics* (New York: Free Press, 1989).

10. For a discussion placing the Irish case in a wider context, see Martin Rhodes, 'Globalization, Labour Markets and Welfare States: A Future of Competitive Corporatism?', in Martin Rhodes and Yves Meny, *The Future of European Welfare: A New Social Contract?* (London: Macmillan, 1998).

11. Philippe C. Schmitter in Suzanne Berger and Ronald Dore (eds), *National Diversity and Global Capitalism* (Ithaca: Cornell University Press, 1996); John H. Goldthorpe (ed.), *Order and Conflict in Contemporary Capitalism* (New York: Oxford University Press, 1984).

12. Wolfgang Streeck, *From National Corporatism to Transnational Pluralism* (Notre Dame: Kellog Institute, 1991). See also, for discussion of challenges to neocorporatism, Jonas Pontusson, 'At the End of the Third Road: Swedish Social Democracy in Crisis', *Politics and Society*, 20 (1991), pp. 302–32.

13. For the success of neocorporatist adjustment in the Netherlands, see Jelle Visser and Anton Henijck, *A Dutch Miracle: Job Growth, Welfare Reform and Corporatism in the Netherlands* (Amsterdam: University of Amsterdam Press, 1997) and Romke van der Veen and Willend Trommel, 'Managed Liberalization of the Dutch Welfare State', *Governance*, 12 (1999), No. 3, pp. 289–310.

14. See Rhodes, 'Globalization, Labour Markets and Welfare States'; Robert Henry Cox, 'From Safety Net To Trampoline; Labor Market Activation in the Netherlands and Denmark', *Governance*, 11 (1998), pp. 397–414.
15. Peter J. Katzenstein, *Small States in World Markets* (Ithaca: Cornell University Press, 1985).
16. Garry Herrigel, *Industrial Constructions: The Sources of German Industrial Power* (New York: Cambridge University Press, 1996).
17. Kathleen A. Thelen, *Union of Parts; Labor Politics in Postwar Germany* (Ithaca: Cornell University Press, 1991).
18. Martin Rhodes, 'Globalization, Labour Markets and Welfare States: A Future of "Competitive Corporatism"?', Working Paper No. 97/36 (Fiesole: European University Institute, 1997).
19. Stefan Berger and Hugh Compston (eds), *Policy Concertation and Social Partnership in Western Europe: Lessons for the 21st Century* (Oxford: Berghahn, 2001).
20. Wolfgang Streeck, 'The Internationalization of Industrial Relations in Europe: Prospects and Problems', MPIfG Discussion Paper 98/2 (Cologne: MPIfG, 1998).
21. Peter J. Katzenstein, *Small States in World Markets*.
22. For discussions of German capitalism, see Peter J. Katzenstein, *Industry in Government in West Germany* (Ithaca: Cornell University Press, 1989); Jeffrey Fear, 'German Capitalism', in Thomas McCraw (ed.), *Creating Modern Capitalism* (Cambridge, Mass.: Harvard University Press, 1997); Wolfgang Streeck, 'German Capitalism: Does It Exist? Can It Survive?', in Colin Crouch and Wolfgang Streeck (eds), *Modern Capitalism or Modern Capitalisms?* (London: Frances Pinter, 1999).
23. Anke Hassell, 'The Erosion of the German System of Industrial Relations', *British Journal of Industrial Relations*, 37 (1999), pp. 65–94.

6   Transitional Economies

1. For transitions to capitalism, see Chrystia Feeland, *Sale of the Century: Russia's Wild Ride from Communism to Capitalism* (New York: Crown, 2000); Rose Brady, *Kapitalizm: Russia's Struggle to Free Its Economy* (New Haven: Yale University Press, 1999); Timothy Frye, *Brokers and Bureaucrats: Building Market Institutions in Russia* (Ann Arbor: University of Michigan Press, 2000); Anders Aslund, Peter Boone and Simon Johnson, 'How to Stabilize: Lessons for Post Communist Countries', *Brookings Papers on Economic Activity*, 1 (1996), pp. 217–91; Anders Aslund, *How Russia Became a Market Economy* (Washington, DC: Brookings Institution, 1995).
2. Interview with the author.
3. For a discussion of his approach, see Jeffrey D. Sachs and Katherinea Pistor, *The Rule of Law and Economic Reform in Russia* (Boulder, Col.: Westview, 1997).
4. On the Russian privatization programme, see Maxim Boycko, Adrei Shleifer and Robert W. Vishny, *Privatizing Russia* (Cambridge, Mass.: MIT Press, 1995).

5. Anders Aslund, 'Russia', *Foreign Policy*, July/August 2001, p. 20.

6. Anders Aslund, 'Russia', p. 23.

7. Mark Cassell, *How Governments Privatize: The Politics of Divestment in the United States and Germany* (Washington, DC: Georgetown University Press, 2001); Mark Cassell, 'Privatization and the Courts: How Judicial Structures Shaped German Privatization', *Governance*, 14 (2001), pp. 429–55.

8. On issues in the Chinese transition, see Barry Naughton, 'China's Emergence and Prospects as Trading Nation', *Brookings Papers on Economic Activity*, 2, 273337, pp. 341–4; Barry Naughton, 'Chinese Institutional Innovation and Privatization from Below', *American Economic Review*, 8 (1994), pp. 266–70; Barry Naughton, *Growing Out of the Plan* (Cambridge: Cambridge University Press, 1996).

9. Quoted by Rowan Callick, 'East Asia and the Pacific', in Transparency International, *Global Corruption Report 2001* (www.globalcorruptionreport.org).

10. For a discussion of poltical problems of transitions, see Barrett L. McCormick, 'Political Change in China and Vietnam: Coping with the Consequences of Economic Reform', in Anita Chan, Benedict J. Tria Kerkvliet and Jonathan Unger (eds), *Transforming Asian Socialism: China and Vietnam Compared* (Lanham, Md: Rowan & Littlefield, 1999).

11. William R. Freeney, 'China and the Multilateral Economic Institutions', in Samuel Kim (ed.), *China and The World: Chinese Foreign Policy Faces the New Millennium* (Boulder: Westview Press, 1998).

12. Craig S. Smith, 'Multinationals at the Gate', *New York Times*, 18 October 2001, W1.

13. Luke Allnutt, Jeremy Druker and Jen Tracey with Dima Bit-Suleiman, Alisha Khamidov, Sophia Kermiencka and Alex Znakevich, 'The CIS' Transparency International, *Global Corruption Report 2001* (www.globalcorruptionreport.org).

14. Federico Varese, *The Russian Mafia: Private Protection in a New Market Economy* (Oxford: Oxford University Press, 2001).

15. Wade Jacoby, 'Tutors and Pupils: International Organizations, Central European Elites and Western Models', *Governance,* 14 (2001), pp. 169–200.

16. World Bank, *World Development Report 2002* (Washington, DC: World Bank, 2001), p. 115.

17. World Bank, *World Development Report 2002*, p. 115.

18. World Bank, *World Development Report 2002*, p. 116.

7 Globalization, Internationalization and Governance

1. 'Summit Protesters and Economic Excitement', *The Economist*, 21 June 2001.

2. For a description of the different types of protesters, see *Financial Times*, 18 July 2001, p. 18.

3. For the case against globalization, see William Greider, *One World Ready or Not: The Manic Logic of Global Capitalism* (New York: Simon & Schuster, 1998).

4. Laura Weiss, *The Myth of the Powerless State* (Ithaca: Cornell University Press, 1998). See also Robert Wade, 'Globalization and Its Limits: Reports of the Death of the National Economy Are Greatly Exaggerated', in Suzanne Berger and Ronald Dore (eds), *National Diversity and Global Capitalism* (Ithaca: Cornell University Press, 1996); Robert Boyer and Daniel Drache (eds), *States Against Markets: The Limits of Globalization* (London: Routledge, 1996); Robert Boyer, 'The Convergence Hypothesis Revisited: Globalization But Still the Century of Nations?', in Suzanne Berger and Robert Dore (eds), *National Diversity and Global Capitalism*; Geoffrey Garrett, *Partisan Politics in the Global Economy* (New York: Cambridge University Press, 1998).

5. For a useful article on this subject, see Gregory Shaffer, 'Globalization and Social Protection: The Impact of EU Rules in the Ratcheting Up of US Privacy Standards', *Yale Journal of International Law*, 25 (2000). Also see Mark A. Pollack and Gregory Shaffer, *Transatlantic Governance in the Global Economy* (Lanham, Md: Rowman & Littlefield, 2001).

6. For a useful framework for thinking about the state and globalization, see Edward S. Cohen, 'Globalization and the Boundaries of the State: A Framework For Analyzing the Changing Practices of Sovereignty', *Governance*, 14 (2001), No. 1, pp. 75–97.

7. OECD Convention on Combating Bribery of Foreign Public Officials in International Business Transactions (http://www.oecd.org/daf/nocorruption/20novel.htm).

8. For stimulating discussions of NGOs and international business, see Marina Ottoway, 'Reluctant Missionaries', *Foreign Policy*, July/August 2001, pp. 44–55 and Gary Gereffi, Ronie Garcia-Johnson and Erika Sasser, 'The NGO-Industrial Complex', *Foreign Policy*, July/August 2001, pp. 56–65. For more extensive discussion, see Ronie Garcia-Johnson, *Exporting Environmentalism: U.S. Multinational Chemical Companies in Brazil and Mexico* (Cambridge, Mass.: MIT Press, 2000); Kathryn Sikkink, *Activists Without Borders: Advocacy Coalitions in International Politics* (Ithaca: Cornell University Press, 1998).

9. Stephen Fidler, 'Who's Minding the Bank', *Foreign Policy*, September/October 2001, pp. 40–50. See also, for a critical account by a prominent economist who worked in the World Bank, Joseph Stiglitz, 'The Insider', *The New Republic*, 17–24 April 2000.

10. David Vogel, 'The Representation of Diffuse Interests', in Kent Weaver and Bert A. Rockman (eds), *Do Institutions Matter? Government Capabilities in the United States and Abroad* (Washington, DC: Brookings Institution)

11. Ans Kolk, Rob van Tulder and Calijn Welters, 'International Codes of Conduct and Corporate Social Responsibility: Can Transnational Corporations Regulate Themselves?', *Transnational Corporations*, 8, No. 1, 1999; Naomi Klein, *No Longer Taking Aim at the Brand Bullies* (New York: Picador, 2000).

12. Grant Jordan, *Shell, Greenpeace and the Brent Spar* (Basingstoke: Palgrave, 2001).

13. William R. Moonaw, 'Expanding the Concept of Environmental Management Systems to Meet Multiple Social Goals', in Cary Coglianese

and Jennifer Nash (eds), *Regulating from the Inside: Can Environmental Management Systems Achieve Policy Goals?* (Washington, DC: Resources for the Future, 2001), p. 136.

14. Interview with the author, June 2001.
15. Karsten Rongit and Volker Schneider, 'Global Governance Through Private Organizations', *Governance*, 12 (1999), No. 3, pp. 243–66.
16. For a valuable study of the reasons for the differing willingness of firms to adopt environmental policies overseas, see Aseem Prakash, *Greening The Firm: The Politics of Corporate Environmentalism* (Cambridge: Cambridge University Press, 2000).
17. Kelly Kollman and Aseem Prakash, 'Green By Choice: Cross National Variation in Firms, Openness to EMS Based in Environmental Regimes', *World Politics*, 53 (April 2001), pp. 399–430.
18. William Greider, *One World Ready or Not. The Manic Logic of Global Capitalism* (New York: Simon & Schuster, 1998).
19. Giandomenico Majone, *Understanding Regulatory Growth in the European Community* (Fiesole, It.: European University Institute, 1994).
20. Wyn Grant, 'Pressure Groups and the European Community: An Overview' in Stephen Mazey and Jeremy Richardson (eds), *Lobbying in the European Community* (Oxford: Oxford University Press, 1993).
21. Maria Green Cowles, 'The EU Committee of AmCham: The Powerful Voice of American Firms in Brussels', *Journal of European Public Policy*, 3 (1996), pp. 339–58.
22. For invaluable information and insight into the representation of business in Brussels see David Coen, 'The European Business Interest and the Nation State: Large-firm Lobbying in the European Union and Member States', *Journal of Public Policy*, 18 (1998), pp. 75–100; David Coen, 'The Evolution of the Large Firm as a Political Actor in the European Union', *Journal of European Public Policy*, 4 (1997), pp. 91–108.

8 Business, Governments and Governance in a New Century

1. Robert Boyer, 'The Convergence Hypothesis Revisited: Globalization but Still the Century of Nations?', in Suzanne Berger and Ronald Dore (eds), *National Diversity and Global Capitalism* (Ithaca: Cornell University Press, 1996); Robert Wade, 'Globalization and Its Limits: Reports of the Death of the National Economy are Greatly Exaggerated', in Suzanne Berger and Ronald Dore (eds), *National Diversity and Global Capitalism*.
2. Barry Eichengreen, *Globalizing Capital: A History of the International Monetary System* (Princeton: Princeton University Press, 1996); Ethan Kapstein, *Governing the Global Economy: International Capital and the State* (Cambridge, Mass.: Harvard University Press, 1994).
3. Alberta Sbragia, 'Government, the State and the Market: What is Going On?', *Governance*, 13 (2000), pp. 243–7; Graham K. Wilson, 'In a State?', *Governance*, 13 (2000), pp. 235–40.
4. For discussions of the crisis of the extensive state, see Anthony King, 'Overload: Problems of Governing in the 1970s', *Political Studies*, 23

(1975), pp. 284–96; B. Guy Peters and Jon Pierre, *Governance, Politics and the State* (New York: St. Martin's Press, 2000).

5. But see Laura Weiss, *The Myth of the Powerless State* (Cambridge: Cambridge University Press, 1998), for a counter view.

6. William Greider, *One World Ready or Not: The Manic Logic of Global Capitalism* (New York: Simon & Schuster, 1998).

7. Charles E. Lindblom, *Politics and Markets* (New York: Basic Books, 1977).

8. Crawford M. Young and Thomas Turner, *The Decline of the Zairian State*, (Madison, WI: University of Wisconsin Press, 1985) pp. 175–84 on Mobuto's ill-gotten fortune; Michela Wrong, *In the footsteps of Mr Kurtz: Living on the brink of disaster in Mobuto's Congo* (New York: HarperCollins, 2001).

9. Juan Forero, 'Still Poor, Latin Americans Protest Push for Open Markets', *New York Times*, 19 July 2002, Al, A7.

10. Stephen Lukes, *Power: A Radical View* (London: Macmillan, 1974).

Bibliography

Amsden, Alice, *Asia's Next Giant: South Korea and Late Industrialization* (New York: Oxford University Press, 1989).

Aslund, Anders, *How Russia Became a Market Economy* (Washington, DC: Brookings Institution, 1995).

Aslund, Anders, 'Russia', *Foreign Policy*, July/August 2001, p. 20.

Aslund, Anders, Boone, Peter and Johnson, Simon, 'How to Stabilize: Lessons for Post Communist Countries', *Brookings Papers on Economic Activity*, 1 (1996), pp. 217–91.

Andersen, Gosta Esping, *The Three Worlds of Welfare Capitalism* (Princeton: Princeton University Press, 1990).

Baumgartner, Frank R. and Leech, Beth L., *Basic Interests: The Importance of Groups in Politics and Political Science* (Princeton: Princeton University Press, 1998).

Berger, Stefan and Compston, Hugh (eds), *Policy Concertation and Social Partnership in Western Europe: Lessons for the 21st Century* (Oxford: Berghahn, 2001).

Berger, Suzanne and Dore, Ronald (eds), *National Diversity and Global Capitalism* (Ithaca: Cornell University Press, 1996).

Bernstein, Jeffrey, 'Japanese Capitalism', in Thomas K. McCraw (ed.), *Creating Modern Capitalism* (Cambridge, Mass.: Harvard University Press, 1997).

Berry, Jeffrey, *The New Liberalism: The Rising Power of Citizen Groups* (Washington, DC: Brookings Institution, 1999).

Birnbaum, Jeffrey H. and Murray, Alan S., *Showdown at Gucci Gulch: Lobbyists and the Unlikely Triumph of Tax Reform* (New York: Random House, 1987).

Boycko, Maxim, Shleifer, Adrei and Vishny, Robert W., *Privatizing Russia* (Cambridge, Mass.: MIT Press, 1995).

Boyer, Robert, 'The Convergence Hypothesis Revisited: Globalization But Still the Century of Nations?', in Suzanne Berger and Robert Dore (eds), *National Diversity and Global Capitalism*.

Boyer, Robert and Drasche, Daniel (eds), *States Against Markets: The Limits of Global Capitalism* (London: Routledge, 1996).

Brady, Rose, *Kapitalizm: Russia's Struggle to Free Its Economy* (New Haven: Yale University Press, 1999).

Campbell, John L., Hollingsworth, J. Rogers and Lindberg, Leon N., *The Governance of the American Economy* (Cambridge: Cambridge University Press, 1991).

Cassell, Mark, *How Governments Privatize: The Politics of Divestment in the United States and Germany* (Washington, DC: Georgetown University Press, 2001).

Cassell, Mark, 'Privatization and the Courts: How Judicial Structures Shaped German Privatization', *Governance*, 14 (2001), pp. 429–55.

Cerny, Philip and Shain, Martin (eds), *Socialism, the State and Public Policy in France* (London: Frances Pinter, 1985).

Chandler, Alfred D., *The Visible Hand: The Managerial Revolution in American Business* (Cambridge, Mass.: Belknap Press, 1977).

Cheng, Tun-Jen and Kim, Eun-Mee, 'Making Democracy: Generalizing the South Korean Case', in Edward Friedman (ed.), *The Politics of Democratization: Generalizing East Asian Experiences* (Boulder, Col.: Westview Press, 1994).

Clark, Donald (ed.), *The Kwangju Uprisings: Shadows Over the Regime in South Korea* (Boulder, Col.: Westivew Press, 1988).

Clifford, Mark L., *Troubled Tiger: Businessmen, Bureaucrats and Generals in South Korea*, rev. edn (London: M.E. Sharpe, 1998).

Coen, David, 'The Evolution of the Large Firm as a Political Actor in the European Union', *Journal of European Public Policy*, 3 (1996), pp. 339–58.

Coen, David, 'The European Business Interest and the Nation State: Large Firm Lobbying in the European Union and Member States', *Journal of Public Policy*, 18 (1998), pp. 75–100.

Cohen, Edward S., 'Globalization and the Boundaries of the State: A Framework For Analyzing the Changing Practices of Sovereignty', *Governance*, 14 (2001), No. 1, pp. 75–97.

Cohen, Edward S., *The Politics of Globalization in the United States* (Washington, DC: Georgetown University Press, 2001).

Cowles, Maria Green, 'The EU Committee of Am Cham: The Powerful Voice of American Firms in Brussels' *Journal of European Public Policy,* 3 (1996), pp. 339–58.

Cox, Robert Henry, 'From Safety Net to Trampoline; Labor Market Activation in the Netherlands and Denmark', *Governance*, 11 (1998), pp. 397–414.

Crouch, Colin and Dore, Ronald (eds), *Corporatism and Accountability: Organized Interests in British Public Life* (Oxford: Oxford University Press, 1990).

Crozier, Michel, Huntington, Samuel and Watanuki, Joji, *The Crisis of Democracy: Report to the Trilateral Commission* (New York: New York University Press, 1975).

Dark, Taylor, *The Unions and the Democrats: An Enduring Alliance* (Ithaca: Cornell University Press, 1999).

Destler, I.M., *American Trade Politics*, 3rd edn (Washington, DC: Institute for International Economics; New York: Twentieth Century Fund, 1995).

Eichengreen, Barry, *Globalizing Capital: A History of the International Monetary System* (Princeton: Princeton University Press, 1996).

Eisinger, Peter K., *The Rise of the Entrepreneurial State: State and Local Economic Development Policy in the United States* (Madison: University of Wisconsin Press, 1988).

Eisner, Marc Allen, Worsham, Jeff and Rehnquist, Evan J., *Contemporary Regulatory Policy* (Boulder, Col.: Lynne Rienner, 2000).

Estrin, Saul and Holmes, Peter, *French Planning in Theory and Practice* (London: George Allen & Unwin, 1983).

Fear, Jeffrey, 'German Capitalism', in Thomas McCraw (ed.), *Creating Modern Capitalism* (Cambridge, Mass.: Harvard University Press, 1997).

Feeland, Chrystia, *Sale of the Century: Russia's Wild Ride from Communism to Capitalism* (New York: Crown, 2000).

Ferguson, Thomas and Rogers, Joel, *Right Turn: The Decline of the Democrats and the Future of American Politics* (New York: Hill & Wang, 1986).

Fidler, Stephen, 'Who's Minding the Bank', *Foreign Policy*, September/October 2001, pp. 40–50.

Finer, Samuel Edward, *Annonymous Empire: A Study of the the Lobby in Britain* (London: Pall Mall Press, 1958).

Fisher, Ronald C., *State and Local Government Finance*, 2nd edn (Chicago: Irwin, 1996).

Friedman, Thomas L., *The Lexus and the Olive Tree* (New York: Farrar, Strauss & Giroux, 1999).

Freeney, William R., 'China and the Multilateral Economic Institutions', in Samuel Kim (ed.), *China and The World: Chinese Foreign Policy Faces the New Millennium* (Boulder, Col.: Westview Press, 1998).

Frye, Timothy, *Brokers and Bureaucrats: Building Market Institutions in Russia* (Ann Arbor: University of Michigan Press, 2000).

Garcia-Johnson, Ronie, *Exporting Environmentalism: U.S. Multinational Chemical Companies in Brazil and Mexico* (Cambridge Mass.: MIT Press, 2000).

Garrett, Geoffrey, *Partisan Politics in the Global Economy* (New York: Cambridge University Press, 1998).

Gereffi, Gary, Garcia-Johnson, Ronie and Sasser, Erika, 'The NGO-Industrial Complex', *Foreign Policy*, July/August 2001, pp. 56–60.

Goldfield, Michael, *The Decline of Organized Labor in the United States* (Chicago: University of Chicago Press, 1987).

Goldstein, Judith, *Ideas, Interests, and American Trade Policy* (Ithaca: Cornell University Press, 1993).

Goldthorpe, John H. (ed.), *Order and Conflict in Contemporary Capitalism* (New York: Oxford University Press, 1984).

Grant, Wyn, *Business and Politics in Britain*, 2nd edn (London: Macmillan, 1993).

Grant, Wyn, *Pressure Groups and British Politics* (London: Macmillan, 2000).

Grant, Wyn and Marsh, David, *The Confederation of British Industry* (London: Hodder & Stoughton, 1977).

Wyn, Grant, 'Pressure Groups and the European Community: An overview', in Mazey, Stephen and Jeremy Richardson (eds), *Lobbying in the European Community* (Oxford: Oxford University Press, 1993).

Greider, William, *One World Ready or Not: The Manic Logic of Global Capitalism* (New York: Simon & Schuster 1998).

Haggard, Stephan, *Pathways from the Periphery: The Politics of Growth in the Newly Industrializing Countries* (Ithaca: Cornell University Press, 1990).

Hall, Peter, *Governing the Economy: The Politics of State Intervention in Britain and France* (Oxford: Oxford University Press, 1986).

Hall, Peter, 'The Japanese Civil Service and Economic Development in Comparative Perspective', in Hyung-Ki Kim *et al.* (eds), *The Japanese Civil Service and Economic Development* (Oxford: Clarendon Press, 1995).

Hartz, Louis, *The Liberal Tradition in America* (New York: Harcourt Brace & World, 1955).

Hassell, Anke, 'The Erosion of The German System of Industrial Relations', *British Journal of Industrial Relations*, 37 (1999), pp. 65–94.

Hayward, Jack, *The State and the Market: Industrial Patriotism and Economic Intervention in France* (New York: New York University Press, 1986).

Heinz, John P., Laumann, Edward O., Nelson, Robert L. and Salisbury, Robert H., *The Hollow Core: Private Interests in National Policy Making* (Cambridge, Mass.: Harvard University Press, 1993).

Herrigel, Garry, *Industrial Constructions: The Sources of German Industrial Power* (New York: Cambridge University Press, 1996).

Hollingsworth, J. Rogers, Schmitter, Philippe C. and Streeck, Wolfgang (eds), *Governing Capitalist Economies: Performance and Control of Economic Sectors* (New York: Oxford University Press, 1994).

Horwitz, Morton J., *The Transformation of American Law 1770–1860* (Cambridge, Mass.: Harvard University Press, 1973).

Jacoby, Wade, 'Tutors and Pupils: International Organizations, Central European Elites and Western Models', *Governance*, 14 (2001), pp. 169–200.

Johnson, Chalmers, *MITI and the Japanese Economic Miracle: The Growth of Industrial Policy 1925–75* (Stanford: Stanford University Press, 1982).

Johnson, Chalmers A. (ed.), *The Industrial Policy Debate* (San Francisco: ICS Press, 1984).

Johnson, Chalmers, *Japan, Who Governs? The Rise of the Developmental State in East Asia* (New York: Norton, 1995).

Jordan, A.G. and Richardson, J.J., *Government and Pressure Groups in Britain* (Oxford: Clarendon Press, 1987).

Jordan, Grant, 'Indirect Causes and Effects in Policy Change: Shell, Greenpeace and the Brent Spar', paper prepared for delivery at the 1998 Annual Meeting of the APSA, Boston, Mass., 1998.

Jordan, Grant, *Shell, Greenpeace and the Brent Spar* (Basingstoke: Palgrave, 2001).

Kapstein, Ethan, *Governing the Global Economy: International Capital and the State* (Cambridge, Mass.: Harvard University Press, 1994).

Kapstein, Ethan, *Governing the Global Economy: International Capital and the State* (Cambridge, Mass.: Harvard University Press, 1994).

Katzenstein, Peter J., *Corporatism and Change: Austria, Switzerland and the Politics of Industry* (Ithaca: Cornell University Press, 1984).

Katzenstein, Peter J., *Small States in World Markets* (Ithaca: Cornell University Press, 1985).

Katzenstein, Peter J., *Industry in Government in West Germany* (Ithaca: Cornell University Press, 1989).

Keeler, John, *The Politics of Neocorporatism in France: Farmers, the State and Agricultural Policymaking in the Fifth Republic* (New York: Oxford University Press, 1987).

King, Anthony, 'Ideas, Institutions and the Policies of Government', *British Journal of Political Science*, 3 (1973), pp. 291–313.

King, Anthony, 'Overload: Problems of Governing in the 1970s', *Political Studies*, 23 (1975), pp. 284–96.

Klein, Naomi, *No Longer Taking Aim at the Brand Bullies* (New York: Picador, 2000).

Kolk, Ans, van Tulder, Rob and Welters, Calijn, 'International Codes of Conduct and Corporate Social Responsibility: Can Transnational Corporations Regulate Themselves?', *Transnational Corporations*, 8, No. 1, 1999.

Kotz, Nick, *Wide Blue Yonder: Money, Politics and the B1 Bomber* (New York: Pantheon Books, 1988).

Kollman, Kelly and Prakash, Aseem, 'Green By Choice: Cross National Variation in Firms' Openness to EMS Based in Environmental Regimes', *World Politics*, 53 (April 2001), pp. 399–430.

Lam, Danny and Clark, Cal, 'Beyond the Developmental State: The Cultural Roots of "Guerilla Capitalism" in Taiwan', *Governance*, 7 (1994), pp. 412–30.

Lane, Jan Erik, 'The Twilight of the Scandinavian Model', *Political Studies*, 41 (1993), pp. 315–24.

Lehmbruch, Gerhard and Schmitter, Philippe C. (eds), *Patterns of Corporatist Policymaking* (Beverly Hills: Sage, 1982).

Lindblom, Charles E., *Politics and Markets: The World's Political Economic Systems* (New York: Basic Books, 1977).

Lipset, Seymour Martin, 'Why No Socialism in the United States?', in Seweryn Bialer and Sophia Sluzar (eds), *Sources of Contemporary Radicalism, Vol. 1* (Boulder, Col.: Westview Press, 1977), pp. 291–313.

Longstreth, Frank, 'The City, Industry and the State', in Colin Crouch (ed.), *State and Economy in Contemporary Capitalism* (London: Croom Helm, 1979).

Lowi, Theodore, 'American Business, Public Policy and Case Studies and Political Theory', *World Politics*, 16 (1964), pp. 677–715.

MacSharry, Robert and White, Paul, *The Making of the Celtic Tiger: The Inside Story of Ireland's Boom Economy* (Cork: Mercier Press, 2000).

Majone, Giandomenico, *Understanding Regulatory Growth in the European Community* (Fiesole, It.: European University Institute, 1994).

Mallett, Victor, *The Trouble With Tigers* (London: HarperCollins, 2000).

March, James G. and Olsen, Johan P., *Rediscovering Institutions: The Organizational Basis of Politics* (New York: Free Press, 1989).

Martin, Cathie Jo, *Shifting the Burden: The Struggle Over Growth and Corporate Taxation* (Chicago: University of Chicago Press, 1991).

Mayer, Kenneth R., *The Political Economy of Defense Contracting* (New Haven: York University Press, 1991).

McCormick, Barrett L., 'Political Change in China and Vietnam: Coping with the Consequences of Economic Reform', in Anita Chan, Benedict J. Tria Kerkvliet and Jonathan Unger (eds), *Transforming Asian Socialism: China and Vietnam Compared* (Lanham, Md: Rowan & Littlefield, 1999).

Middlemas, Keith, *Politics in Industrial Society* (London: Deutsch, 1979).

Mitchell, Neil J., *The Conspicuous Corporation: Business, Public Policy and Representative Democracy* (Ann Arbor: University of Michigan Press, 1997).

Moonaw, William R., 'Expanding the Concept of Environmental Management Systems to Meet Multiple Social Goals', in Cary Coglianese and Jennifer Nash (eds), *Regulating from the Inside: Can Environmental Management Systems Achieve Policy Goals?* (Washington, DC: Resources for the Future, 2001).

Naughton, Barry, 'China's Emergence and Prospects as Trading Nation', *Brookings Papers on Economic Activity*, no. 2 (1996), pp. 273–337.

Naughton, Barry, 'Chinese Institutional innovation and Privatization from Below', *American Economic Review*, 8 (1994), pp. 266–70.

Naughton, Barry, *Growing Out of the Plan* (Cambridge: Cambridge University Press, 1996).

Nivola, Pietro (ed.), *Comparative Disadvantage? Social Regulations and the Global Economy* (Washington, DC: Brookings Institution Press, 1997).

Olsen, Johan P., *Organized Democracy: Political Institutions in a Welfare State, The Case of Norway* (New York: Columbia University Press, 1983).

Olson, Mancur, *The Logic of Collective Action: Public Goods and the Theory of Groups* (Cambridge, Mass.: Harvard University Press, 1967).

Ottoway, Marina, 'Reluctant Missionaries', *Foreign Policy*, July/August 2001, pp. 44–55.

Pempel, T.J., *Regime Shift* (Ithaca: Cornell University Press, 1998).

Peters, B. Guy and Pierre, Jon, *Governance, Politics and the State* (New York: St. Martin's Press, 2000).

Phillips, Kevin, *Wealth and Democracy: A Political History of the American Rich* (New York: Broadway Books, 2002).

Pollack, Mark A. and Shaffer, Gregory, *Transatlantic Governance in the Global Economy* (Lanham, Md: Rowman & Littlefield, 2001).

Pontusson, Jonas, 'At the End of the Third Road: Swedish Social Democracy in Crisis', *Politics and Society*, 20 (1991), pp. 302–32.

Pontusson, Jonas, *The Limits of Social Democracy: Investment Politics in Sweden* (Ithaca: Cornell University Press, 1992).

Rhodes, Martin, 'Globalization, Labour Markets and Welfare States: A Future of Competitive Corporatism?', in Martin Rhodes and Yves Meny, *The Future of European Welfare: A New Social Contract?* (London: Macmillan, 1998).

Rongit, Karsten and Schneider, Volker, 'Global Governance Through Private Organizations', *Governance*, 12 (1999), No. 3 pp. 243–66.

Rose, Richard, 'Two and One Half Cheers for Capitalism', *Public Opinion*, June–July 1983.

Sachs, Jeffrey D. and Pistor, Katherinea, *The Rule of Law and Economic Reform in Russia* (Boulder, Col.: Westview, 1997).

Salisbury, Robert H., *Interests and Institutions: Substance and Structure in American Politics* (Pittsburgh: Pittsburgh University Press, 1992).

Samuels, Richard J., *The Business of the Japanese State: Energy Markets in Comparative and Historical Perspective* (Ithaca: Cornell University Press, 1987).

Sanders, Elizabeth, *Roots of Reform: Farmers, Workers, and the American State, 1877–1917* (Chicago: University of Chicago Press, 1999).

Sbragia, Alberta, 'Government, the State and the Market: What is Going On?', *Governance*, 13 (2000), pp. 243–7.

Schlozman, Kay Lehman and Tierney, John, *Organized Interests and American Democracy* (New York: Harper & Row, 1986).

Schmidt, Vivien, 'The Decline of Traditional State Dirigisme in France: The Transformation of Political Economic Policies and Policy Making Processes', *Governance*, 9 (1996), pp. 375–406.

Schmidt, Vivien, *From State to Market: The Transformation of French Business and Government* (New York: Cambridge University Press, 1996).

Schmitter, Philippe, 'Still the Century of Corporatism?', *Review of Politics*, 36 (1974), pp. 85–131.

Schmitter, Philippe, 'Regime Stability and Systems of Interest Intermediation in Western Europe and North America', in Suzanne Berger (ed.), *Organizing Interests in Western Europe* (Cambridge: Cambridge University Press, 1984).

Schmitter, Philippe, 'Interest Intermediation and Regime Governability in Western Europe and North America', in Suzanne Berger (ed.), *Organizing Interests in Western Europe.*

Schmitter, Philippe and Streeck, Wolfgang, *Governing Capitalist Economies: Performance and Control of Economic Sectors* (New York: Oxford University Press, 1994).

Schwartz, Herman, *States Versus Markets: History, Geography and the Development of the International Political Economy* (New York: St Martin's Press, 1994).

Seldon, Anthony (ed.), *The Blair Effect* (London: Little, Brown, 2001).

Self, Peter and Storing, Herbert J., *The State and the Farmer: Agricultural Politics and Policy in Britain* (Berkeley: University of California Press, 1963).

Shaffer, Gregory, 'Globalization and Social Protection: The Impact of EU Rules in the Ratcheting Up of US Privacy Standards', *Yale Journal of International Law*, 25 (2000).

Shonfield, Andrew, *Modern Capitalism: The Changing Balance of Public and Private Power* (Oxford: Oxford University Press, 1967).

Sikkink, Kathryn, *Activists Without Borders: Advocacy Coalitions in International Politics* (Ithaca: Cornell University Press, 1998).

Skowronek, Stephen, *Building a New American State: The Expansion of National Administrative Capacities, 1877–1920* (Cambridge and New York: Cambridge University Press, 1982).

Smith, Craig S., 'Multinationals At The Gate', *New York Times*, 18 October 2001.

Smith, Mark A., *American Business and Political Power: Public Opinion, Elections and Democracy* (Chicago: University of Chicago Press, 2000).

Smith, Rogers M., *Civic Ideals: Conflicting Visions of Citizenship in U.S. History* (New Haven, Conn.: Yale University Press, 1997).

Sombart, Werner, *Why is there no Socialism in the United States?*, trans. by Patricia M. Hocking and C. T. Husbands; edited and with an introductory essay by C. T. Husbands, and with a foreword by Michael Harrington (White Plains, NY: International Arts and Sciences Press, 1976).

Soskice, David, 'Macroeconomic Analysis and the Political Economy of Unemployment', in Torben Iversen, Jonas Pontusson and David Soskice (eds), *Unions, Employers and Central Banks: Macroeconomic Coordination and Institutional Change in Social Market Economies* (New York: Cambridge University Press, 2000).

Steinmo, Sven, 'Why is Government So Small in the United States?', *Governance*, 8, No. 3 (1995), pp. 303–34.

Steinmo, Sven, *Taxation and Democracy: American, British and Swedish Approaches to Financing the State* (New Haven: Yale University Press, 1993).

Stiglitz, Joseph, 'The Insider', *The New Republic*, 17–24 April 2000.

Streeck, Wolfgang, *From National Corporatism to Transitional Pluralism* (Notre Dame, Ind.: Kellogg Institute, 1991).

Streeck, Wolfgang, 'German Capitalism: Does It Exist? Can It Survive?,' in Colin Crouch and Wolfgang Streeck (eds), *Modern Capitalism or Modern Capitalisms?* (London: Frances Pinter, 1999).

Streeck, Wolfgang and Schmitter, Philippe (eds), *Private Interest Government: Beyond Market and State* (London and Beverly Hills: Sage, 1982).

Suarez, Sandra, *Does Business Learn? Tax Breaks, Uncertainty and Political Strategies* (Ann Arbor: University of Michigan Press, 2000).

Suleiman, Ezra, *Elites in French Society: The Politics of Survival* (Princeton: Princeton University Press, 1978).

Sweeney, Paul, *The Celtic Tiger: Ireland's Economic Miracle Explained* (Dublin: Oak Tree, 1985).

Thelen, Kathleen A., *Union of Parts; Labor Politics in Postwar Germany* (Ithaca: Cornell University Press, 1991).

U.S. Department of Commerce, *Statistical Abstract of the United States* (Washington, DC: Government Printing Office, 2000).

van der Veen, Romke and Trommel, Willend, 'Managed Liberalization of the Dutch Welfare State', *Governance*, 12 (1999) No. 3, pp. 289–310.

Varese, Federico, *'The Russian Mafia: Private Protection in a New Market Economy* (Oxford: Oxford University Press, 2001).

Visser, Jelle and Henijck, Anton, *A Dutch Miracle: Job Growth, Welfare Reform and Corporatism in the Netherlands* (Amsterdam: University of Amsterdam Press, 1997).

Vogel, David J., *National Styles of Regulation* (Ithaca: Cornell University Press, 1986).

Vogel, David, 'The Power of Business in the United States: A Re-Appraisal', *British Journal of Political Science*, 17 (1987) pp. 385–408.

Vogel, David, *Fluctuating Fortunes: The Political Power of Business in America* (New York: Basic Books, 1989).

Wade, Robert, *Governing the Market: The Role of the State in East Asian Industrialization* (Princeton: Princeton University Press, 1990).

Warnecke, Steven J. and Suleiman, Ezra (eds), *Industrial Policy in Western Europe* (Praeger: New York, 1975).

Weiner, Martin J., *English Culture and the Decline of the Industrial Spirit* (Cambridge: Cambridge University Press, 1981).

Weiss, Laura, *The Myth of the Powerless State* (Ithaca: Cornell University Press, 1998).

Weyland, Kurt, 'From Leviathan to Gulliver? The Decline of the Developmental State in Brazil', *Governance*, 11 (1998), pp. 51–76.

Williams, Philip Maynard, *Crisis and Compromise: Politics in the Fourth Republic* (Hamden, Conn.: 1964).

Williams, Philip Maynard and Martin Harrison, *Politics and Society in de Gaulle's Republic* (London: Longman, 1971).

Wilson, Graham K., *Special Interests and Policymaking* (Chichester and New York: John Wiley, 1977).

Wilson, Graham K., 'Corporate Political Strategies', *British Journal of Political Science*, 20 (1990), pp. 281–7.

Wilson, Graham K., *Only in America? The Politics of the United States in Comparative Perpective* (Chatham NJ: Chatham House, 1998).

Witte, John F., *The Politics and Development of the Federal Income Tax* (Madison: University of Wisconsin Press, 1985).

Wolferen, Karel van, *The Enigma of Japanese Power: People and Politics in a Stateless Nation* (New York: Knopf, 1989).

Woodward, Bob, *Maestro: Greenspan's Fed and the American Boom* (New York: Simon & Schuster, 2000).

Woolley, John, *Monetary Politics: The Federal Reserve and the Politics of Monetary Policy* (Cambridge and New York: Cambridge University Press, 1984).

World Bank, *World Development Report 2002* (Washington, DC: World Bank, 2001) p. 115.

Wright, John, *Interest Groups and Congress: Lobbying, Contributions, and Influence* (Boston: Allyn & Bacon, 1996).

Wrong, Michela, *In the footsteps of Mr Kurtz: Living on the brink of disaster in Mobuto's Congo* (New York: HarperCollins, 2001).

Young, Crawford M. and Turner, Thomas, *The Decline of the Zairian State*, (Madison, WI: University of Wisconsin Press, 1985) pp. 175–84.

Zysman, John, *Governments, Markets and Growth: Financial Systems and the Politics of Industrial Change* (Ithaca: Cornell University Press, 1983).

Index